# Managing Human Assets

*Michael Beer*

*Bert Spector*

*Paul R. Lawrence*

*D. Quinn Mills*

*Richard E. Walton*

THE FREE PRESS
*A Division of Macmillan, Inc.*
NEW YORK

Collier Macmillan Publishers
LONDON

The Free Press
A Division of Macmillan, Inc.
866 Third Avenue, New York, N.Y. 10022

Collier Macmillan Canada, Inc.

Printed in the United States of America

printing number

9  10

*Library of Congress Cataloging in Publication Data*

Main entry under title:

Managing human assets.

   Includes bibliography and index.
   1. Personnel management—Addresses, essays,
lectures.   I. Beer, Michael.
HF5549.M31347   1984      658.3       84-14996
ISBN 0-02-902390-4

# Contents

# Preface

THIS IS a book for managers. It is particularly relevant to general managers, who want to learn about the critical issues and the strategic questions they will have to consider in managing large aggregates of employees in the 1980s and beyond. In the last several years American business has begun to place more emphasis on the management of human resources. Buffeted by recession, deregulation in some industries, and international competition in others, business executives have been looking for ways to improve productivity and quality. They began to realize these goals could not be achieved without a dramatic change in the relationship between management and workers and between union and management. Simultaneously, improvements in the development of managers would be needed. When they looked to Japan, our chief competitor, they saw a different yet successful management model. Within the context of their own society and culture, the Japanese had developed a collaborative relationship between management and labor and between unions and management. Improved productivity and quality were the results.

It has become quite clear to many large American enterprises such as General Motors, Cummins Engine, Ford Motor, Bethlehem Steel, Honeywell Corporation, People Express, and Goodyear Tire and Rubber, to name a few, that they must manage their human resources quite differently if they are to compete successfully. American corporations have learned to manage their financial and other resources effectively. Enormous time, care, and effort goes into ensuring that money is employed most effectively; the most current ideas and methods are applied to obtain the greatest return on invested capital; strategic alternatives are carefully developed and weighed using strategic planning models and processes. Yet implementation of any of these plans requires committed, concerned, and competent employees.

The evidence seems to indicate, however, that in many corporations, human resources are underutilized and underemployed. Adversarial union-management relations, low employee motivation and trust of management, excessive layers of management, restrictive work practices, and employee resistance to changes required by competitive forces are examples of the problems. Just as instructive in assessing the extent to which human resources are underutilized are the human commitment, productivity, and quality that are obtained not only by Japanese companies but by American corporations that have invested in developing more effective human resource management policies and practices. When such significant improvements in productivity, quality, and union-management relations are demonstrated with a relatively low financial investment, the potential for effective human resource management becomes quite clear. Given the relative sophistication in the management of financial and other resources, human resources may offer the best opportunity for management to improve competitiveness.

The corporation's survival in the marketplace is not the only force that has led to a greater emphasis on human resource management. Just as competitive pressures have raised questions about the obligations of employees, so the past decade has seen increasing questions in American society about employee rights. A more highly educated work force has challenged management to find ways of increasing employee involvement, responsibility, and participation in the enterprise. The traditional authority relationship between managers and employees is less acceptable to these employees, just as it is costly in terms of underutilization and lowered commitment. Changing demographics, particularly the entry of more women and minorities into the work force, has raised many questions about fair employment practices. Concern about the rights of employees is reflected in a number of societal trends as well. There has been significant legislation governing fair employment practices in the last two decades, particularly equal employment opportunity legislation and legislation governing age discrimination. Similarly, a number of states have proposed legislation governing plant closings, suggesting concern in society about the obligation of the corporation to the well-being of employees and the community. That concern was long ago translated by Europeans into restrictive legislation concerning layoffs and into legislation imposing workers councils and codetermination on employers. Similarly, in the United States there is increasing involvement of the courts in questions of fair employment practices. The increasing number of legal suits about the right of corporations to hire and fire employees makes it clear that corporations must be concerned about employee rights.

In response to changes in society and the competitive environment, a consensus developed among the alumni and faculty of the Harvard Business School that a new required course in Human Resource Management (HRM) was needed. That course was launched in 1981. The last new required course, Managerial Economics, was introduced into the curriculum nearly 20 years ago. The introduction of a new course into the core curriculum reflects important changes in the knowledge and skills that the school believes general managers will require in the future. There have been new developments in the fields of organizational behavior and development, personnel administration, and labor relations. These are the disciplines that underlie the management of people in organizations and are typically represented in the personnel or human resource function of large corporations. Whereas historically these professional fields of practice have operated independently, the changes described above are now causing a need to integrate these perspectives into a human resource strategy.

As a result of its emphasis on interpersonal relations, leadership, group management, organizational design, and the management of change, the Harvard Business School has long been a leader in the field of organizational behavior. However, the question of how managers might translate their understanding about effective management of people into policies and practices that govern large aggregates of employees had not been fully developed in our required curriculum or thinking. Nor were the institutional constraints of unions and government legislation or the realities of personnel practice adequately integrated with these ideas. What we hope to present here is a synthesis of these perspectives, a synthesis which we believe must also occur within corporations.

This book is an outgrowth of our efforts to develop a new course in human resource management. The synthesis of the organizational behavior/development, labor relations, and personnel administration perspectives came in large part from the varied perspectives the original teaching group brought to the course. In a very real sense our need to work as a team to develop a core course required us to confront our different perspectives and to fit them together in a way that would help general managers manage human resources more effectively. Moreover, our contact with companies and executives as we developed course materials shaped our thinking about human resource management in a particularly relevant way.

The general management perspective places HRM in the context of business strategy and society. It places emphasis on asking important strategic questions rather than emphasizing personnel techniques and practices. Much of personnel management has been narrowly focused on methods and techniques, performance appraisal, salary surveys, or grievance management, without raising important questions about what the relationship of employees to the organization should be or could be. We came to develop a way of thinking about this important question that can provide a strategic perspective useful to general managers. Our experiences as teachers, researchers, and consultants put us in contact with corporations that were also thinking differently about human resource problems and were translating this new thinking into fundamentally different approaches to managing human resources. We have incorporated these innovative approaches in our discussion of various topics in HRM.

In sum we believe that this book presents a framework for thinking and managing human resources that general managers will find useful. We raise questions about how much influence and participation employees should have in the corporation, about the potential for union-management collaboration, about the role and value of a lifelong employment policy, about how employee effectiveness might be assessed. We also raise questions about how that information might be incorporated into succession planning and better personnel planning, about the role of compensation in motivation, and about the potential for design of work systems and organizations to increase dramatically employee commitment and competence.

For readers who may want to pursue the ideas in this book further, we recommend a companion book published by The Free Press: *Readings in Human Resource Management*. It contains articles and excerpts from other books that elaborate on our own ideas. For the reader who might like access to cases that illustrate problems in HRM or examples of innovative practice, we recommend the case textbook *Human Resource Management: A General Manager's Perspective*, also published by The Free Press. That book contains cases on the Air Controllers strike, on Nippon Steel's handling of employment security in a recessionary environment, on efforts of People Express to institute participative management, on the collaborative efforts of General Motors and the United Auto Workers to institute a quality of work life program, on Dana Corporation's use of a gains-sharing plan to develop cooperation between union, management, and workers, and on Hewlett-Packard's efforts to develop high levels of commitment through longstanding human resource policies, among others.

The development of a new course and book based on that course requires the help and cooperation of many people. We wish to acknowledge some of them here. The course required the approval of the whole Harvard Business School faculty which took risks in doing so. We thank them for their confidence in us. John McArthur, Dean of the Harvard Graduate School of Business, supported the idea of a new required Human Resource Management course. He was instrumental in bringing two separate groups, Production and Operations Management as well as Organizational Behavior, together to undertake the development of the new course. Wick Skinner was a member of the original teaching group that planned and taught this course for the first time. We appreciate his support and contributions. Richard von Werssowetz was a research associate assigned to help in the development of new cases. His insights and suggestions helped shape our thinking. Our thanks also go to Rita McSweeney who typed some of the chapters. And special thanks should go to the dedicated people of the Harvard Business School's Word Processing Center who typed the final versions of all chapters and proofread the manuscript. Finally, we wish to acknowledge the support of the Division of Research and its director, Raymond E. Corey. The division made it possible for Michael Beer and Bert Spector to dedicate a year to course development.

# Chapter 1

# Introduction

IN ORDER FOR A CORPORATION to meet effectively its obligations to shareholders, employees, and society, its top managers must develop a relationship between the organization and employees that will fulfill the continually changing needs of both parties. At a minimum, the organization expects employees to perform reliably the tasks assigned to them and at the standards set for them, and to follow the rules that have been established to govern the workplace. Management often expects much more: that employees take initiative, supervise themselves, continue to learn new skills, and be responsive to business needs. At a minimum, employees expect the organization to provide fair pay, safe working conditions, and fair treatment. Like management, employees often expect more, depending on the strength of their needs for security, status, involvement, challenge, power, and responsibility. Just how ambitious the expectations of each party are will vary from organization to organization.

Human resource management (HRM) involves all management decisions and actions that affect the nature of the relationship between the organization and employees—its human resources. General managers make important decisions daily that affect this relationship, but that are not immediately thought of as HRM decisions: introducing new technology into the office place in a particular way, or approving a new plant with a certain arrangement of production operations, each involves important HRM decisions. In the long run, both the decisions

1

themselves and the manner in which those decisions are implemented have a profound impact on employees: how involved they will be in their work, how much they trust management, and how much they will grow and develop new competencies on the job. Deciding how fast a company should grow in response to market demand is another significant HRM decision made by general managers. A decision on growth affects the stress employees will experience as circumstances change, as well as the probabilities that employees will be able to avoid obsolescence and that the organization will have employees with the required talents and skills for the future. Deciding on whether investments are to be financed through internally generated funds or through debt or equity is yet another general management HRM decision. Such financing decisions can make the firm more or less dependent on external stockholders, bankers, and the investment community, thereby influencing a number of HRM policies, most notably, decisions of employment security and investments in employee development. Similarly, general management decisions concerning geographic location of facilities, diversification through acquisition, and business strategy all have, in our view, important implications for the human resources of the firm. Finally, the manner in which supervisors deal with their subordinates, particularly in the expectations they create, the feedback they provide, the trust they generate, and the responsibility they delegate, can do more than any personnel policy or system to shape and reshape the employee-organization relationship. Their actions can reinforce the effective utilization of human resources by the organization; they can also undermine that effectiveness.

None of the above decisions and actions reside in the personnel or labor relations function. Indeed, functional specialists are often not even involved in these or other decisions which affect in a profound way the relationship between the organization and its employees. Just as important, personnel and labor relations departments are sometimes engaged in the administration of policies and systems that have little relationship to the needs of line managers or to the central strategic thrust of the corporation or division. Furthermore, many of these personnel and labor relations activities and systems seem to have a life of their own, isolated from and independent of other personnel and labor relations activities and systems.

The general isolation of personnel decisions has taken place because general managers have counted upon the personnel department and its specialists to play a key role in the management of human resources. Our approach emphasizes two features which are appropriate to HRM. First, the general manager accepts more responsibility for ensuring the alignment of competitive strategy, personnel policies, and other policies impacting on people. Second, the personnel staff has the mission of setting policies which govern how personnel activities are developed and implemented in ways that make them more mutually reinforcing. This is what we mean by a general manager's perspective. The reasons for this are best understood by reviewing the past development of personnel activities.

Ask managers what their personnel departments do or what their own personnel responsibilities are and they will list a series of seemingly disjointed activities such as labor relations, compensation, staffing (recruitment, placement, and promotion), performance appraisal, training, organization development, equal employment opportunity, and health and safety. Indeed, personnel or labor relations functions are generally composed of many separate departments each performing one or more of these activities. Historically, at least, each of these departments has developed a set of policies and systems which provide guidelines for personnel decisions by line managers. These personnel departments also provide a diverse set of services to line management that often bear little relationship to each other and sometimes conflict with each other. The policies, systems, and services developed by each personnel activity or department are generally determined by the tradition of that practice field. For example, compensation departments develop bonus pay plans, organization development departments engage in team building, and labor relations departments deal with grievances and union negotiations.

The disunity of the personnel and labor relations approaches is not surprising, given that personnel activities in corporations have been added in reaction to specific problems and needs rather than as a response to a stated purpose. Personnel departments originally emerged because as corporations grew in size and complexity, there was a need for a central administrative department to hire and pay people. Labor relations departments were added later to negotiate and administer increasingly complex contracts in those corporations organized by unions. Organization development departments were added to solve problems of conflict, motivation, communication, and coordination which emerged as corporations grew even larger, more diverse, and more complex. And equal employment opportunity departments were added to ensure corporate compliance with government legislation and policy in this area. As a result, HRM often emerged as a set of staff activities lacking a coherent structure or central purpose imprinted by general managers. It is also not surprising that, lacking a coherent structure for policy decisions, HRM tends to be reactive rather than proactive in shaping a relationship between the organization and its employees that is suitable to its long-term needs.

Such coherent structure and central purpose will be added only when HRM is seen as more than just the responsibility of a specific functional department. This will occur only when general managers develop a viewpoint of how they wish to see employees involved in and developed by the enterprise, and of what HRM policies and practices might achieve these goals. Without either a central philosophy or a strategic view—whch can be provided *only* by general managers— HRM is likely to remain a set of independent activities, each guided by its own practice tradition.

In our opinion, the ability to develop a coherent HRM policy that contributes to corporate performance, employee needs, and societal well-being does not require general managers to be experts in personnel and labor relations. Therefore, much of the theory and methodology of those two fields has not been included in this book. Developing an HRM strategy does require that general managers be able to ask the right quesitons when confronted with HRM problems, questions that will allow them to link alternative HRM approaches to business strategy, to assumptions about employee needs and values, to societal expectations and government regulations, and to their own management style and values. With the help of HRM specialists, general managers must then create the HRM policies and systems that will make it possible for managers at all levels of the organization to attract, select, promote, reward, motivate, utilize, develop, and keep and/or terminate employees consistent with business requirements, employee needs, and standards of fairness. In short, *HRM is the development of all aspects of an organizational context* so that they will encourage and even direct managerial behavior with regard to people.

## THE EMERGENCE OF HUMAN RESOURCE MANAGEMENT AS A CONCERN OF GENERAL MANAGEMENT

In the past, general managers were content to delegate rather narrowly defined personnel responsibilities to functional specialists. Today, however, a great many pressures are demanding a broader, more comprehensive and more strategic perspective with regard to the organizations' human resources. A list of such pressures would include the following:

1. *Increasing international competition* is creating the need for dramatic improvements in human productivity. The competitive crises in the automobile and steel industries are two such examples. American executives look overseas, especially to Japan, and see employment and management practices that appear to

increase employee commitment while ensuring companies a long-term supply of people with necessary competencies and skills.

2. *Increasing complexity and size* of organizations has resulted in multiple layers of bureaucracy. Some companies are concerned with the high costs of such layers. Others see over-bureaucratization as serving to isolate employees from both the organization and the competitive environment in which that organization must operate. By reducing levels, these organizations hope to put employees in closer touch with their environment, thereby increasing their commitment to the organization as well as their ability and competence to work more effectively. Geographical spread, particularly the emergence of multinational firms, presents new challenges in managing human resources in diverse societies where laws and prevailing social values may be quite different.

3. *Slower growth* and in some cases declining markets have dramatically affected an organization's ability to offer advancement opportunities to high potential employees and employment security to long-service employees.

4. *Greater government involvement* in human resource practices such as employment security (particularly in Europe) and fair employment practices (in the United States) are causing corporations to reexamine their HRM policies and practices and to develop new ones. In the United States, individual employee suits and class action suits for large employee groups have raised the possibility of costly settlements, thereby increasing the importance of HRM in the eyes of general managers.

5. *Increasing education of the work force* is causing corporations to reexamine their assumptions about the capacity of employees to contribute and therefore the amount of responsibility they can be given.

6. *Changing values of the work force*, particularly relative to authority, are causing corporations to reexamine how much involvement and influence employees should be given and what mechanisms for employee voice and due process need to be provided.

7. *More concern with career and life satisfaction* is causing corporations to reexamine traditional assumptions about career paths, to provide more alternative career paths and to take into account employee lifestyle needs in transferring employees and scheduling work.

8. *Changes in work force demography*, particularly the infusion of women and minorities into organizations, are causing corpora-

tions to reexamine all policies, practices, and managerial values that affect the responsibilities, treatment, and advancement of these employee groups.

It is not surprising that such pressures have created the need for more institutional attention to people, a longer time perspective in managing people, and consideration of people as a potential asset rather than merely a variable cost. But why has the potential for greater effectiveness inherent in better management of human resources eluded many managers until now? In part there has been a tendency in the education, development, and training of managers to emphasize the analytical and technical aspects of work, leaving some companies with managers who have wide variance in terms of their skills in managing people fairly and effectively. So why are companies now turning more to the human side of the enterprise in order to solve business problems? In part that answer lies in societal pressures. Just as concern over the condition of blue-collar workers found its way into labor legislation during the 1930s, concern over equitable and fair treatment found its way into civil rights and equal opportunity legislation in the 1960s and 1970s. Such legislation called attention to and helped shape companies' HRM practices, as did social values concerning individual satisfaction and well-being. In part, the reason lies in the failure of other approaches to live up to their expectations of improving organizational effectiveness. Administrative systems, marketing, technology, operations management, industrial engineering, diversification, portfolio management, and more recently computerization have all solved some problems. But they have created new ones; often human problems.

Many managers who eagerly adopted new technology or new approaches to portfolio management, for instance, face redesign of HRM with far greater reluctance. Technology or portfolio management seem easier to implement because such approaches do not *seem* to require managers to confront basic values and assumptions about human nature. They do not *seem* to raise questions about personal style and individual power. Of course, such perceptions are not entirely correct. The introduction of new technology, for instance, *does* affect people and power relationships. Indeed, it is often the failure to recognize the intricate relationships between ''impersonal'' systems and people that causes such approaches either to fail or to fall short of their promise. HRM issues, on the other hand, require that fundamental and sometimes threatening questions about our personal values and assumptions be addressed. Nevertheless, competitive pressures and changes in employees have highlighted fundamental HRM questions about how to unleash people's energies and creativity. In fact, a number of major American corporations have begun to address these HRM issues and are leading a trend that will fundamentally alter the practice of human resource management.

Experience has shown that severe external pressures may be required for a firm to reexamine and dramatically change HRM policies. Indeed both research and experience suggest that fundamental changes are rarely addressed until dissatisfaction with the status quo is high and models for new behavior exist. The factors listed earlier have led to such dissatisfaction, while new HRM models, such as Japanese employment and management systems and union-management quality of work life projects, to name only two of the more prominent ones, are also emerging. Unfortunately, companies that undertake fundamental changes in the relationship between management and employees while they are under competitive pressure have little slack in time, money, and good will of employees to engineer such changes. To avoid the difficulties of trying to change longstanding approaches to HRM virtually "overnight" in response to competitive pressures, it can be suggested that companies continually reexamine HRM policies. That way they might evolve a relationship with employees that will stand the rigorous test of constantly shifting competitive pressures.

Unfortunately, companies with a good deal of growth and profitability seldom see a reason to innovate in HRM practices in order to build a relationship between the organization and its employees that will pass the tests of greater competition and the shrinking economic pie. There are exceptions, however. Companies like Hewlett-Packard, Lincoln Electric, and IBM, whose founders had a strong set of values concerning what the relationship between employees and their employing organization ought to be, have devoted a good deal of attention to developing and maintaining consistent and effective HRM policies, even in the absence of strong competitive pressures. Other companies not yet under competitive pressures can, if they so choose, make a conscious decision to examine systematically and continuously the effectiveness of their HRM policies and practices. New rapid-growth companies can develop HRM policies with long-term perspective because it is generally more difficult to change a culture than to develop one from the beginning. This book can help managers grapple with some of the major human resource issues that corporations should examine.

## FOUR MAJOR HRM POLICY AREAS

We propose that many diverse personnel and labor relations activities may be subsumed under four human resource policy areas. Each of the following policy areas defines a major HRM task that general managers must attend to whether or not the firm is unionized, whether blue-collar or managerial employees are involved, and whether the firm is growing or declining.

### Employee Influence

A corporation has a variety of stakeholders, among them shareholders, unions, various groups of employees, government, and the community. This policy area has to do with a key question that all managers must ask: How much responsibility, authority, and power should the organization voluntarily delegate and to whom? If required by government legislation to bargain with unions or consult with worker councils, how should management enter into these institutional relationships? Will they seek to minimize the power and influence of these legislated mechanisms? Or will they share influence and work to create greater congruence of interests between management and the employee groups represented through these mechanisms? The managerial task here is to develop the organization's policy regarding the amount of influence employee stakeholders have with respect to such diverse matters as business goals, pay, working conditions, career progression, employment security, or the task itself; and to attempt to implement these policies. Inevitably, decisions about employee influence affect traditional management prerogatives and can reshape the very purpose of the firm. Employee influence decisions are therefore critical general management decisions whether they are made explicitly, or as is often the case, implicitly.

In many situations managers are the only ones who can initiate a decision-making process about how much participation and due process employees are to have and what mechanisms to develop for their voice to be heard and their influence to be felt. Unless challenged by employees through unions, turnover, government legislation, or lawsuits, managers possess much of the decision-making power in the organization, so a lack of action in regard to employee influence amounts to a decision not to share and delegate much of that power and influence. Self-management groups in Japan, task forces or group decision making at the management level, membership on quality of work life committees at the working level, open-door policies, and ombudsmen are examples of mechanisms managers can select. It is our assumption that choices about employee influence, in the long run, are inevitable. Democratic societies have tended to legislate influence mechanisms whenever employees have felt aggrieved or underrepresented in decisions governing their welfare.

## Human Resource Flow

This policy area has to do with the responsibility shared by all managers in an organization for managing the flow of people (at all levels) into, through, and out the organization. Traditional personnel practice areas such as recruitment, internal staffing, performance appraisal, and outplacement are all subsumed in this area. But the task goes further. Personnel specialists and general managers must work in concert to ensure that personnel flow meets the corporation's long-term strategic requirement for the "right" number of people and mix of competencies. Selection, promotion, and termination decisions must also meet the needs of employees for job security, career development, advancement, and fair treatment, and they must meet legislated standards of society. General managers must ask themselves how much employment security employees should be granted and how much the corporation should invest in employee development. Inevitably, decisions in this area will affect and be affected by fundamental business decisions about profit goals, growth rates, and dividend policy, to name only a few. When characterized as a whole the pattern of practices in this area constitutes the organization's flow policies. Such policies affect the very capacity of the organization to achieve its strategic objectives and obligations to employees and society. Human resource flow policy decisions must be made and reviewed by general managers.

## Reward Systems

Rewards, both financial and otherwise, send a powerful message to employees of an organization as to what kind of organization management seeks to create and maintain, and what kind of behavior and attitudes management seeks from its employeees. It is up to all managers of an organization, and not just pay specialists, to attend to certain questions under this HRM managerial task: Do we want an organization that rewards individual or group behavior? How shall we use money: as an incentive to stimulate desired behavior, or as equitable recognition of effective performance? Do we wish to share economic gains (profits or improvements in costs, for example) with various employees or employee groups? The answers to these questions lead to the task of designing and administering equitable and fair reward systems to attract, motivate, and retain (satisfy) employees at all levels. Management may have complete control over the design and administering of the organization's reward system, or they may have to negotiate these policies and systems with a union. There are choices to be made by managers concerning rewards for nonunion workers, as managers consider the extent to which they want to involve those workers in design and administration. Decisions about participation and the mix of rewards offered need to be consistent with business strategy, management philosophy, employee needs, and other HRM policies. The extent to which compensation should be used as an incentive, the mix between extrinsic and intrinsic rewards, and the extent to which rewards should be tied to individual versus organizational performance are some of the questions that only general managers can decide. Such decisions have a fundamental and pervasive effect on the nature of the organization-employee relationship, and the extent to which that relationship is based on an individual calculation of personal gains or on identification with the firm's tasks and goals.

## Work Systems

At all levels of an organization, managers must face the task of arranging people, information, activities, and technology. In other words, they must define and design work. Management choices about these arrangements affect the quality of the decisions people make, coordination between functions and tasks, the extent to which people's competencies are utilized, the extent to which people are committed to organizational goals, and the extent to which people's needs for development and quality of work life are met. Decisions by managers about manufacturing processes at the plant level (extent of divisions of labor and application of technology, for example), about new information technology in the office (such as computerized information systems), about organization design, and about planning and goal-setting systems at the management level are examples of policy decisions in the work systems area. General managers, not personnel or labor relations specialists, make conscious or unconscious choices about the quality of decisions and commitment of employees when they make decisions in the work system area or when they allow such decisions to be made by others.

The four-policy framework can stimulate managers to plan how to accomplish the four major HRM tasks in a unified, coherent manner rather than in a disjointed approach based on some combination of past practice, accident, and ad hoc response to outside pressures. An HRM policy involves a choice by managers about how employees will be managed; a choice that ultimately influences the nature of the relationship between the organization and its employees. For such a choice to be effective it must be put into operation through the development of HRM policies and practices. Conscious choices about policies then can lead to the development of HRM systems and practices consistent with them.

# THE HRM PERSPECTIVES GUIDING THIS BOOK

The preceding discussion of the HRM policy areas reflects a number of the choices we made about how to view the HRM task. These choices can be made more explicit.

The first central theme cuts across all four policy areas and is the conceptual framework we will propose in Chapter 2: *stakeholder interests*. We view the role of top management as balancing and, where possible, integrating the interests of the many stakeholders of the enterprise: shareholders, employees, customers, suppliers, host communities, labor unions, trade associations, governments, and so on. This view of employees as important stakeholders in the enterprise underscores the need of top managers to consider how the interests of various stakeholders differ, how much weight those distinct interests should be given, and the mechanisms by which those various stakeholders can exercise influence over the enterprise. Because this book is about human resource management, the tensions between the interests of employees or institutions that represent them (unions and government) and the interests of management and shareholders receive most of our attention.

If employees are major stakeholders in the enterprise, then it is critical that managers design and administer various mechanisms for *employee influence*, a second major theme of this book. This policy area will be discussed in depth in Chapter 3. For now, we wish to make the point that employee influence in its broadest sense is a central perspective in the formulation of all human resource management policies (see Figure 1–1). All policies, the design and implementation of technology and work systems, the design and administration of compensation, and the design and administration of systems for hiring, promoting, placing, and terminating employees should be examined from the perspective of how much influence employees are given over decisions in these areas. Thus, the employee influence policy area goes well beyond the traditional activities of union-management relations or employee relations or even participative management initiatives that some companies have undertaken. The policy area poses a question much broader than that typically associated with these personnel practices: how to develop a process of mutual influence between two sets of stakeholders—management and employees. Stating the task this way allows the inclusion of worker councils, grievance systems, sensing groups, open-door policies, attitude surveys, ombudsmen, and other due process mechanisms as alternatives or additions to the mix of practices that may be applied in the interest of achieving a mutual influence process appropriate to the strategy of the firm, the values of top management, and

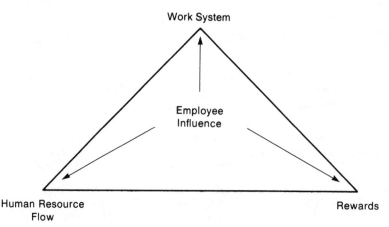

**FIGURE 1-1     Human Resource System**

the expectations of employees and society. The task of designing and managing a process of mutual influence is primary; the means or the activity is secondary, and is to be judged on the basis of its contribution to this basic HRM task.

After the stakeholder and employee influence perspectives, a third perspective of the book involves an emphasis on the need for a reasonable amount of consistency, or *fit*, between each of the four policy areas. For example, efforts to increase commitment to the goals of the enterprise through increasing the responsibility of workers and their participation in work decisions will probably have to be supported eventually by flow policies that provide some job security, and by compensation systems that encourage the acquisition of skills and provide some form of sharing with employees of cost or profit improvement. Internal consistency between policies is needed to provide clear signals to people about the behavior that is expected and that will be rewarded.

Fourth, we view human resources as *social capital*. The implication is that the development of work-force capabilities, attitudes, and internal relations must be thought of within an investment paradigm. People can seldom be thought of mainly as budgeted expenses. Rather they constitute the firm's social capital, which results from front-end investments and which yields a stream of benefits over time. Broad employee competencies, for example, can lead to flexible assignment practices, while a relationship of trust between management and workers can increase employee commitment to reassignments that respond to shifting business conditions. This capital can also be degraded by neglect or poor maintenance and can become obsolete unless retrained in line with changing requirements. As with other investments, there are risks associated with the estimates of future stream of benefits—for example, whether an investment in developing employee attitudes and skills will, in fact, lead to enhanced product quality or some other key success factor. As with other investment decisions, a long-term perspective, sometimes well beyond the current accounting period, is required.

Fifth, we view the management of human resources from a *strategic* perspective. An enterprise has an external strategy—a chosen way of competing in the marketplace. It also needs an internal strategy to determine how its human resources are to be developed, deployed, motivated, and controlled. There are several implications of this perspective. One implication is that the internal and external strategies must be *linked*. Each provides goals and constraints for the other. A competitive strategy based on becoming the low-cost producer may indicate different approaches to compensation and employment security than a competitive strategy that depends on product innovation. The very idea of an internal strategy implies there is consistency among all of the specific tactics or activities which affect human resources. Hence, the need for practices to be guided by conscious policies—to increase the likelihood that practices will reinforce each other and will be consistent over time.

The analytical framework we advance in Chapter 2 requires the analysis of fit: fit between competitive strategy and internal HRM strategy and fit among the elements of the HRM strategy.

Sixth, we emphasize the need for *multiple levels of social evaluation* in assessing the outcomes of HRM policies and practices. It is not enough to ask how well the management of human resources serves the interests of the *enterprise*. One should ask how well the enterprise's HRM policies serve the well-being of the *individual employee*. At a higher level of analysis, one should ask how well the company's HRM policies and practices serve the interests of *society*. Of course, other stakeholders may be relevant in particular cases. Moreover, the relative weighting that management will give to these three evaluative considerations will vary from management to management and from case to case. Our view is that the weighting should be more explicit in the future than it has been in the past. This perspective serves to raise the following question: Are there HRM policies that increase the likelihood that they will *simultaneously* serve the interests of the enterprise, the individual, and society?

Our seventh perspective derives from all of the above. It is that *HRM is a part of the general management function*. If the HRM strategy must fit the competitive strategy, if human resource development involves investment decisions with long-term implications, and if employees are viewed as one of the groups of major stakeholders of the enterprise whose interests must be balanced by top management, then surely HRM policy decisions cannot be delegated to a functional specialty.

# THE ORGANIZATION OF THE BOOK

Before proceeding, a few words about the organization of *Managing Human Assets* might be useful. Now that we have staked out in general terms the territory we wish to cover in our HRM approach, we will move in Chapter 2 to a conceptual overview of the subject. It is our intent in that chapter to present readers with a set of analytical levers which can be brought to bear generally on HRM issues. We will suggest seven groups of factors—laws and societal values, task technology, unions, work force characteristics, labor market conditions, business strategy, and management philosophy—that need to be considered when making HRM policy choices. We will suggest the four Cs—competence, commitment, congruence, and cost effectiveness—as a way for managers to consider the impact of HRM policy choices. Finally, we will propose that the ultimate consequences of HRM policies be viewed on three levels: organizational effectiveness, employee well-being, and societal well-being.

From there we will move sequentially through each of the four HRM policy areas—employee influence, human resource flow, reward systems, and work systems—and close with an integrative chapter. These chapters are not meant to be exhaustive examinations of the many practice fields such as labor relations or wage and salary administration subsumed under our policy areas. Consistent with the general manager's perspective, we have tried to sketch an overview of each policy area based on our knowledge of relevant personnel and labor relations issues and practices and our experience with the policy issues they raise for general managers. Our hope is that managers will be stimulated to consider and probe the dilemmas, the issues, the problems, and the possibilities for action inherent in the task of managing human resources. Ultimately the effectiveness of human resource management in corporations can only be enhanced by general managers who have mastered a way of thinking about the task of managing the organization's human resources.

# Chapter 2

# A Conceptual Overview of HRM

IF GENERAL MANAGERS are to determine what human resource policies and practices their firm should employ, they need some way to assess the appropriateness or effectiveness of those policies. In this chapter, we will offer some ways of diagnosing not only the impact of management decisions on the human resources of the firm, but also whether the policies that guide those decisions continue to make sense and what changes might be considered in them.

The analytical approach depicted in Figure 2–1 is a broad causal mapping of the determinants and consequences of HRM policies. The HRM map shows that HRM policies are influenced by two major considerations: situational factors and stakeholder interests. By situational factors we mean those forces—laws and societal values, labor market conditions, unions, work-force characteristics, business strategies, management philosophy, and task technology—that exist in the environment or inside the firm. These factors can act as constraints on the formation of HRM policies and can also be influenced by HRM policies. HRM policies are and indeed should be influenced by the interests of various stakeholders: shareholders, management employees, unions, community, and government. Unless these policies are influenced by all stakeholders, the enterprise will fail to meet the needs of these stakeholders in the long run and it will fail as an institution.

HRM policies affect certain immediate organizational outcomes and have certain long-term consequences. Policy choices made by

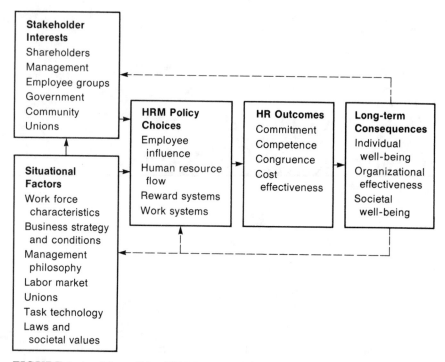

**FIGURE 2-1    Map of the HRM Territory**

managers affect the overall *competence* of employees, the *commitment* of employees, the degree of *congruence* between the goals of employees and those of the organization, and the overall *cost effectiveness* of HRM practices. These four Cs are not exhaustive of the criteria that HRM policy makers may find useful in evaluating the effectiveness of human resource management, but they are reasonably comprehensive.

In the long run, striving to enhance all four Cs will lead to favorable consequences for individual well-being, societal well-being, and organizational effectiveness (i.e., long-term consequences, the last box in Figure 2-1). By organizational effectiveness we mean the capacity of the organization to be responsive and adaptive to its environment. We are suggesting, then, that human resource management has much broader consequences than simply last quarter's profits or last year's return on equity. Indeed, such short-term measures are relatively unaffected by HRM policies. Thus HRM policy formulation must incorporate this long-term perspective.

The HRM map in Figure 2-1 also illustrates the circularity of HRM policy choices. HRM policy choices affect the four Cs and have long-term consequences for individual well-being, organizational effectiveness, and societal well-being. But long-term consequences also affect situational factors and stakeholder interests. For example, protests by mistreated, insecure employees in the society can lead to government legislation regarding fair employment practice or can result in the industrial democracy legislation seen in Europe. Strikes that affect society negatively can influence changes in labor legislation. Poor profitability over an extended period will affect shareholder interest and must inevitably result in changes of HRM policies regarding wages, training, and perhaps employee influence. There are other feedback effects. The central point is that the long-term consequences of HRM policies for individual well-being, organizational effectiveness, and societal well-being will affect those policies and the context within which they are formulated.

How can the analytical framework just presented be used by the readers of this book, including practicing managers?

We find that it is necessary, as a central matter, to clarify who has a stake in the issue at hand, to identify these stakes, and to determine how much power they may be able to apply. These questions are analytically important whether the decision-maker ultimately wants to accommodate or deny the interests of another stakeholder.

One can use other aspects of the analytical framework in various ways. If managers want to understand why their company is currently pursuing a particular approach to an HRM issue, such as an adversarial stance toward labor relations or a policy of lifetime employment, they must analyze the situational factors, both their current force and their historical influence.

On the other hand, managers may want to compare the relevant merits of two HRM policy alternatives, such as a work system with narrowly defined jobs versus one emphasizing whole tasks and team responsibilities. These managers can then attempt to forecast the differential effects of the two systems on the development of competence, the level of commitment, and the like. They can also attempt to extend the forecast another step by asking how good each policy is for the enterprise, the individual, and society. At either the first or second steps of these forecasts, the policy maker may decide that none of the policy alternatives being considered is satisfactory and return to the task of formulating another alternative.

The evaluation of given alternative policies and the formulation of new alternatives involve more than looking at the long-term consequences shown in Figure 2-1. Managers must also examine the question of *fit* among HRM policies—specifically the fit of the policy being reviewed with the other HRM policies and systems. For example, would a proposed approach to designing work systems require a change in the way employees are selected, and is such a change feasible? Managers must then return to an examination of situational factors. How does a proposed policy fit with each of the situational factors and stakeholder interests shown in Figure 2–1? We believe it would be a mistake to follow any analytical process mechanically. Thus we urge the reader to consider only the *spirit* of the foregoing description of analytical steps, and not to regard it as a procedural prescription. Ideally managers could simultaneously consider all of the above factors affecting both the feasibility and desirability of a policy alternative. The actual way a manager considers and reconsiders each of the relevant factors will vary from case to case and from policy maker to policy maker.

We turn now to an exploration of each of the elements in our analytical framework.

## EVALUATING HRM POLICIES
## IN TERMS OF THEIR CONSEQUENCES

We have proposed that the long-term consequences of HRM policies be evaluated in terms of their benefits and costs at three levels: the individual, the organization, and society. Let us elaborate.

It is almost tautological to argue that an organization's HRM policies should be evaluated in terms of whether they promote the organization's goal achievement and survival. An HRM policy may be important because it serves to increase the organization's efficiency or its adaptability, its service performance or its price performance, its short-term results or its long-term results.

It is insufficient to ask only about the organizational outcomes of HRM policies and practices, even if these include human outcomes such as turnover. The well-being of employees must be a separate and distinct consideration. Working conditions can have both positive and negative effects not only on employees' economic welfare, but on their physical and psychological health. The amount of weight managers will choose to give to such consequences, independent of their direct implications for the organization, will depend upon the managers' values and their own conception of the legitimacy of employee claims on the enterprise.

Evaluation of HRM outcomes can also be made on the *societal level*. What have management's past HRM practices cost not only the company and employees, but society as a whole? What are the societal costs of a strike or a layoff? Alienated and laid-off workers may develop both psychological and physical health problems that make them burdens to community agencies funded by the local, state, or federal government. Today employers pass on many of the costs of their management practices to society. Whoever bears these costs, they should be recognized as associated with the HRM policy decisions made by management.

In some areas there is a close coincidence of interests between corporations, individuals, and society. For example, the physical and psychological well-being of employees is gaining importance as a corporate concern. Employees' physical fitness and life-style (at work and away from work), as well as personal health habits with respect to tobacco, drugs, and alcohol are now recognized as contributing to the health care costs of the firm and to its productivity. Johnson & Johnson and Control Data, for example, have launched extensive programs to help employees diagnose their health and develop personal programs for improvements.

In considering whether an HRM policy enhances the performance of the organization, the well-being of employees, or the well-being of society, the four Cs can be considered in the analysis of these inherently complex questions:

1. *Commitment.* To what extent do HRM policies enhance the commitment of people to their work and their organization? Increased commitment can result not only in more loyalty and better performance for the organization, but also in self-worth, dignity, psychological involvement, and identity for the individual.

2. *Competence.* To what extent do HRM policies attract, keep, and/or develop people with skills and knowledge needed by the organization and society, now and in the future? When needed skills and knowledge are available at the right time, the organization benefits and its employees experience an increased sense of self-worth and economic well-being.

3. *Cost effectiveness.* What is the cost effectiveness of a given policy in terms of wages, benefits, turnover, absenteeism, strikes, and so on? Such costs can be considered for organizations, individuals, and society as a whole.

4. *Congruence.* What levels of congruence do HRM policies and practices generate or sustain between management and employees, different employee groups, the organization and community, employees and their families, and within the individual? The lack of such congruence can be costly to management in terms of time, money, and energy, in terms of the resulting low levels of trust and common purpose, and in terms of stress and other psychological problems it can create.

## The Problems of Measurement and Assessment

The four Cs do not provide managers with actual measurement methods and data for assessing the effects of their firm's HRM policies. These methods are numerous, and they differ depending on the level of analysis chosen (individual, corporation, or society). Corporations gather data on the competence of employees through performance evaluation by managers and through third-party assessment of competence by personnel specialists, psychologists, other managers, or assessment centers. When such data are looked at in the aggregate, particularly when a company tries to determine the talent it has available for succession planning, a picture emerges of the depth in technical or managerial competence in the organization.

Data about employee commitment can be obtained by managers in any area of the organization by means of attitude surveys. These surveys can be conducted through interviews and questionnaires administered either by personnel specialists or by outside consultants. Open-door policies and observations of group meetings with employees can also keep managers in touch with their employees' attitudes. The key for any manager is to create conditions for expression of attitudes and open dialogue among various employee groups within the firm. Another source of data—personnel records about voluntary turnover, absenteeism, and grievances—can provide indirect evidence about employee commitment. Taken together, such data might fall short of providing managers with an absolute measure of commitment and congruence, but they can provide a useful overall picture.

Cost effectiveness may appear to be easier to measure, but that appearance can be deceiving. Wages are the easiest to assess, while the long-term costs of certain profit-sharing plans, pension plans, and cost-of-living adjustments are more difficult to assess because of future uncertainties. The cost effectiveness of recruitment and employee development is even more difficult to measure, yet both are an important part of the total employment cost.

Congruence of goals can be more easily identified, particularly when its absence results in an open conflict like a strike. Although the total costs of a strike are difficult to pin down, such an assessment can be part of a total assessment of HRM policies. The existence of more subtle forms of conflict, such as those between managers and subordinates or among various groups of employees, are more difficult to identify. Their costs are even harder to evaluate. Where employees are under union contract, the number of grievances is an indicator of conflict and the administrative costs of those grievances are measurable. But the impact of accumulated grievances on organizational performance is far more difficult to assess.

These difficulties in measurement are exceeded by the difficulties in making judgments about consequences of HRM policies on employee and societal well-being. Various governance mechanisms such as union-management task forces or employee committees (for non-union employees) can provide important vehicles not only for gathering data about human resource outcomes, but for assessing the meaning of these outcomes for various stakeholders. Workers councils and collective bargaining are examples of legislated governance mechanisms that serve the same purpose. Only through participation of stakeholders in assessing HRM outcomes can managers obtain relevant data for an evaluation of the impact of HRM policies and practices on employee and societal well-being.

The problem of assessing HRM outcomes will not be solved easily. The desire to account for human resources as if they were in the same metric as financial resources (dollars) has led to experimentation with human resource accounting systems. These systems have tried to value a person by estimating his or her replacement costs and the investment the firm has made in that person's recruitment, training, and development. Such accounting efforts, while potentially very useful, have fallen short of their promise, at least judging by the fact that they are not widely used. An even more difficult task has been assigning a value to the commitment of employees or the climate and culture of the firm which encourage motivation and growth by its employees. These difficulties are not likely to be overcome soon. In the final analysis, assessment of HRM outcomes is a matter of judgment informed by data from a variety of sources and in a variety of forms (qualitative and quantitative) and evaluated by various stakeholders. A process of outcome assessment must, therefore, bring together a variety of stakeholders (employee groups, management, and union, for example) to discuss the data and to reach a consensus on its meaning.

## THE STAKEHOLDER INTEREST PERSPECTIVE

One way of viewing a company is as a minisociety made up of large numbers of occasionally harmonious, occasionally conflicting constituencies, each claiming an important stake in the way the company is managed and its resources are deployed. Central to the HRM approach of this book is the assumption that general managers must recognize the existence of the many stakeholders and be able to comprehend the particular interests of each stakeholder. In thinking about various HRM policies and practices, then, the general manager plays an important role in balancing and rebalancing the multiple interests served by the company.

Stakeholders in a given enterprise may include owners, government, host communities, workers, labor unions, and the managers themselves. Because the focus of this book is on human resource management, we will pay particular attention to workers as stakeholders. By ''workers'' we include blue-collar, professional, and other white-collar employees. Different employee groups can have different stakes in a particular policy matter. Younger and older workers might find their interests affected in very different ways by company policies relating to benefits and pensions. Black and white workers might feel differently about a company's promotion policies. So might male and female employees. In general employees and management will surely differ with some frequency over such matters as the amount and kind of pay, benefits, and conditions of work. While these are rewards to employees, they are costs to the employer—costs that reduce profits and investment funds.

Why are workers not as concerned as management about corporate profits? Why shouldn't they be more self-regulating in their expectations and demands for monetary and nonmonetary rewards? And why are managers not more understanding about worker needs and more concerned about worker well-being in their decisions? The answers lie, in part, in the different interests of the two groups. Those groups often have different views about the necessary but sometimes difficult trade-offs made within an organization—trade-offs between business goals of efficiency, growth, and investment on the one hand and employee needs for security, equity, job satisfaction, and economic well-being on the other.

Organizations constantly make trade-offs, either implicitly or explicitly, between the interests of owners and those of employees, as well as between various employee groups. Managers are not always aware, however, that such trade-offs are taking place, or even that different stakeholder groups may hold differing views of how those trade-offs should be made. Some managers may be lulled into believing that all stakeholders have the same interests and points of view because the organizational hierarchy has blocked stakeholders from expressing those interests or views. Other managers may be aware of the differences, but may deny the ''legitimacy'' of any viewpoint other than that of owners and managers.

The task of general managers is to recognize the potential for differing—even conflicting—points of view among the various stakeholders over how trade-offs should be made. They must develop a role and perspective that allows them to manage the trade-off process in such a way as to minimize differences between stakeholders and to contain conflict when it arises. For American managers (as contrasted with managers in Europe, for example) such a role represents quite a departure from the traditionally espoused shareholder perspective. While in actuality managers already manage in a way that recognizes shareholders as only one among many groups of stakeholders, conscious acceptance of the stakeholder perspective would put them in an even more neutral position with respect to shareholders to whom they traditionally have felt accountable. Given the make-up of boards of directors and the power of financial institutions, adopting a stakeholder perspective as opposed to shareholder perspective could be very difficult. Our HRM model suggests that changes in contextual factors such as society and legislation would be needed to support movement toward a stakeholder perspective.

## SITUATIONAL FACTORS

The HRM model suggests that HRM policies and practices must be designed and implemented to fit a variety of important situational factors. We do not want to imply that HRM policies should be *contingent* on situational factors, or that they become the dependent variable. To the contrary, we believe that in the long run, all situational factors are subject to some influence by creative HRM policies and practices. Some situational factors are subject to influence by HRM policies in the short to medium term. The use of the term "situational factors" should not imply that these factors are all "outside" the firm. Clearly, unions, laws, societal values, and labor markets are external to the firm in the sense that they are part of the organization's environment; yet they emerge, in part at least, from the human resource policies of the past. Management philosophy, work-force characteristics, task technology, and business strategy are "inside" the firm in the sense that they appear to be subject to more managerial control, yet they are also affected by external business and societal forces. The key point is that at any given point in time—for example, when a general manager is examining current human resource policies and contemplating making changes—all the factors are part of the situation, even the manager's own values and philosophy. More important, all the situational factors must be understood by the general manager as potential constraints created by the past unless specific steps are taken to modify them in the future.

The situational factors are discussed below, beginning with the most important and central of these: work-force characteristics.

### Work-Force Characteristics

What is the nature of people at work? Managers at every level and in every function of the organization convey their answer to this question through their managerial actions: corporations convey their answer through their HRM policies and practices. These policies and practices reflect the *assumptions* of management about employee motivation, capacities, values, potential, and desire for personal development. If the assumptions are not consistent with reality or potential of the work force, HRM policies and practices will not fully utilize or develop employees, resulting in potential loss for both employers and employees. In addition, such policies may create conflict between employees and the organization. Thus, asking what is the nature of people at work may be the most important quesiton managers can address when formulating and monitoring their actions and the impact of those actions on their human resources. But like other important questions, this one has many, sometimes contradictory, answers which depend on the individuals under consideration and their development as human beings.

To simplify the problem of fitting policies to work-force characteristics, corporations typically develop different HRM policies and practices for different groups of employees. Administratively, the work force in most U.S. corporations is typically broken down into four identifiable aggregates: (1) hourly and blue-collar, (2) nonexempt salaried white-collar, (3) exempt salaried professionals, and (4) managers. Within these groupings, of course, there are many meaningful subgroupings such as engineers, clerical personnel, skilled tradespeople, younger and older workers, and so on.

Policy differences should be shaped by valid assumptions about the differences in background, needs, expectations, and educational qualifications that employees bring to their jobs. However, managers must be careful not to differentiate between groups on the basis of invalid assumptions. Distortions are most likely to occur with respect to people at lower levels of the organization. In part at least, policy differences between groups have arisen because managers make assumptions that lower-level people—who are different from them in terms of background, social skills, and values—lack the will and skill to contribute and the potential to develop. This distortion can happen easily because today's managers are often isolated from nonmanagerial employees by organizational practices, hierarchy, and bureaucracy. Managers are no longer promoted from hourly ranks as they once were. Rather, they are educated in business schools where their main contacts are with other prospective managers. The elimination of universal military training has also precluded an enforced opportunity for shared experience with dissimilar groups.

Because it is natural to assume the existence of differences, particularly when hierarchical levels and socioeconomic background make contact and communication difficult, it is especially important for managers to recognize the potential *similarities* between employees as well as the actual differences.

Firms that are effective in human resource management—such as IBM, Charles P. McCormick Spice, Hewlett-Packard, Donnelley Mirror, and Lincoln Electric—explicitly or implicitly adhered to some fundamental assumptions about people when they developed their human resource policies, while also fitting them to more complex realities. For example, McCormick, the architect of McCormick Spice's culture, assumed that all his employees had needs for equity, pay, participation, and security. This assumption guided the human resource policies of his firm in its early years.[1] The assumptions that people want autonomy, want a sense of accomplishment, want to identify with something, want meaning, and want to grow could be added to this list. The power in developing human resource policies in accordance with a few optimistic assumptions about people lies in the capacity of such policies to encourage the selection and development of employees who conform to them.

We do not propose that the list of assumptions above is right or complete. We do propose that effective human resource management involves a tension between some universal truths about what people want or might live up to if given an opportunity (the optimistic view or normative perspective) and the more complex realities of what people are capable of wanting and doing at any given point in time (the realistic view or situational perspective). The former perspective would lead to the view that employee groups are similar and that there are some human resource universals. The latter perspective would reflect the assumption that employee groups differ from one another and that human resource policies must be different for different groups and situations. Without the tension of *both perspectives*, human resource policies will fail to inspire the commitment and competence for which all employees have the potential and they will fail to be practical and workable.

The problem of emphasizing differences rather than similarities is most acute with respect to ethnic minorities and women in the work force. By 1985, women will outnumber men in the work force, and minority groups will be an even larger and more powerful constituency than they are now. Successful HRM approaches in the 1980s and 1990s will depend to a large extent on the ability of all managers in a firm to make valid assumptions about both differences and similarities of these various employee groups.

### Business Strategy and Conditions

An organization's HRM policies and practices must fit with its strategy in its competitive environment and with the immediate business conditions that it faces. If a manufacturing firm operates in a highly competitive environment in which cost effectiveness and efficiency in manufacturing are key, that firm needs to develop HRM policies and practices that encourage cost savings efforts by all its employees. If quality is a key success factor, then HRM policies and practices must encourage concern and involvement of employees with the quality problem. If a professional service firm depends on attracting, motivating, and keeping the best professionals in their field, then that firm must develop HRM policies that bring in the best people, develop their competencies, and offer rewards and other inducements that encourage the right people to join and stay with the firm. Such degrees of competency may be the main factor that differentiates one firm from another.

Unfortunately, the match between HRM policies and business strategy is often poor. One reason for this is that managers often develop business plans and make capital investments without adequate regard to the human resources needed to support those plans. For example, growth plans involving the building of plants or opening of branch offices may take inadequate account of a shortage of managers to run these facilities. The result can be lower returns on investment or even complete business failures. Managers, at least those outside the HR functional area, have typically assumed that human resources are not a constraint and will be available in sufficient qualtity and quality. With increasing managerial and technical complexity and a scarcity of talent, that assumption is often erroneous.

A second reason for the poor fit between business strategy and HRM policies lies in the human resource function itself. That function often develops activities and programs that are not relevant to line management's needs. This problem arises in part from the differences is perspective between short-term, profit-oriented line managers and long-term, people-oriented human resource managers. But the problem also stems from the fact that many HR activities are not developed in close coordination with business planning. HR executives are often left out of the business planning process, frequently because they do not occupy a high level in the organization. Just as regularly, these executives develop policies and practices based on general assumptions about the kinds of behavior and performance required rather than on a careful analysis of the strategy, the tasks that the strategy presents to the organization, and the competencies and involvement required from employees.

Business strategies can also shape the human resources of the firm, the types of people, attitudes, and commitment the firm is likely to obtain. If a company's success rests on promoting a relatively undifferentiated consumer product through advertising and promotion, for example, it needs to attract people whose skills are quite different from those of people in a firm where technology-driven products are clearly differentiated. The latter firm is likely to have longer-range goals, and needs to attract and keep people interested in contributing to these goals. The former is likely to set much shorter-term goals and rely on people attracted to quick results and personal gains. The competencies and commitments of the two employee groups are likely to be quite different. This does not suggest that one business is more desirable than another. It does point out that product/market strategies might constrain the kind of HRM policies and outcomes possible. Since these HRM policies must also fit with management's values, those values must be understood when managers make business strategy decisions. Ideally, then, business strategy should influence HRM policies and practices. At the same time, available human resources as well as managerial and societal values should inform decisions about business strategy.

### Management Philosophy

The HRM policies of an organization are shaped by the management philosophy of its key managers, just as the philosophy of these leaders is shaped by the historical pattern of HRM policies. The relationship between HRM policies and management philosophy is stronger in some organizations than in others, depending on the pattern of development of the organization. If, in the early stages of development, an organization has a powerful founder and leader with a clearly articulated philosophy and set of values, HRM policies are more likely to be internally consistent. This consistency will create a stronger and more pervasive culture with respect to HRM matters. That culture, if sustained over time, will mold new leaders who reflect its underlying values and style.

By "management philosophy" we mean the explicit or implicit *beliefs* of key managers about the nature of the business, its role in society, and how it should be run—particularly how it will treat and utilize employees. A manager's philosophy is shaped by his or her values or assumptions about the role of business in society and the role of people in the business.

In an earlier section on business strategy, we stated that a definition of the business itself may be related to the types of HRM policies and practices the firm can develop. That link is again evident if we inspect the relationship between business philosophy, which shapes strategy, and HRM philosophy and policies. The Lincoln Electric Company's philosophy that profits are a means to an end rather than an end in itself has surely shaped the longer-term strategy of the firm that has placed more emphasis on providing value to the customer than on a growth in sales and profits. This approach led naturally to HRM policies such as employment security, employee stock ownership, and a profit-sharing plan that doubles employee income and distributes to employees approximately half the profits of the firm.

There are numerous examples of corporations whose HRM policies have been shaped in accordance with their founders' business philosophies, among them IBM, Matsushita, Hewlett-Packard, and Mc-

Cormick Spice. That these are successful companies with unique capacities to attract, keep, and involve their employees is not generally in dispute, though the direct link between their success and their HRM policies is more difficult to prove.

It is also not clear how long a philosophy of management and the corporate culture which it shapes can be sustained once the key leaders have departed the scene. For example, Konosuke Matsushita, Bill Hewlett, and Bob Packard are still alive if not very active in their firms. It is also not known how large or how quickly a corporation can grow before its philosophy is diluted and its human resource policies lose their internal consistency. Rapidly growing companies like Hewlett-Packard are facing these problems now.

These questions, while challenging the imagination of managers in diffusing and sustaining a philosophy, in no way weaken the known link between management philosophy and HRM policies. In fact, the importance of that link has been acknowledged in recent efforts to create innovative work systems at the plant level aimed at developing high commitment among employees. These efforts typically involve the definition, in advance of plant start-up, of a philosophy of management, that will guide the design of human resource policies and practices. This process not only helps lead to a consensus among the management team about what the philosophy should be, thereby socializing them into a common view, but it also provides a guideline for future action as new events and realities unfold. Without a stated belief system, short-term pragmatic consideration would dominate HRM policy decisions rather than simply influence them. The result would be inconsistent new policies and an erosion of the philosophy. Thus, a general philosophy allows lower-level managers and future managers to shape new HRM policies and practices that are consistent with the philosophy but pragmatic and relevant to the immediate situation.

If we were to examine the *Fortune* 500 companies, we would undoubtedly find many companies that do not have an articulated philosophy of management, though clearly their HRM policies are an implicit statement of philosophy. Lacking founders who articulated a philosophy, they probably tended to develop HRM policies on an ad hoc basis, with pragmatic considerations or values of the managers at the time dominating policy formulation. For this reason, their human resource policies may not be consistent and may be seen as inconsistent by employees. This lack of consistency probably makes it harder for employees to attach a meaning to their relationship with the firm other than one dominated by their own self-interest. Nor can these employees develop trust in the firm, since trust is based on consistent treatment. Instead, their basis of involvement with the firm will be utilitarian, based on an exchange of work or a service for certain rewards, as opposed to moral, based on their identity with a stated purpose or philosophy.[2] Finally, lacking a clear philosophy or strong culture, the future development of HRM policies is likely to be equally inconsistent and uncertain because key leaders with different philosophies will rise to the top.

Management's philosophy, whether stated or unstated, is not the only way managers shape HRM policies and practices. Their *style* of management—the way they behave, communicate, and interact with others—sends a powerful signal up and down the organization about what they care about. It also helps to shape the organization's HRM manager policies and practices. If managers state their philosophy that employees should be given the opportunity to grow and develop through participation in management, and then make unilateral decisions revising decisions made at a lower level, the credibility of policies that encourage worker participation may be undermined. Similarly, policies that encourage employee development through open and candid discussions of performance with subordinates are not likely to be implemented if upper level managers do not model this process through their own practices.

The lack of consistency between philosophy and policies can also undermine sustained implementation of HRM policies. Managers who have formulated a policy that conflicts with their own philosophy are not likely to sustain follow-up efforts to implement that policy. Only managers with convictions—those whose philosophy and style are both consistent with the policy—are likely to continue to implement and reinforce such a policy.

### Labor Market Conditions

One measure of a firm's effectiveness is the ability of its managers to compete successfully with other firms for financial and human resources. With respect to human resources, that ability is determined by the attractiveness of the company to prospective recruits and current employees, as well as the condition of the labor markets from which the firm draws its supply of people. The boundaries that define the labor markets in which a firm competes may vary dramatically from one group of employees to another. For unskilled production employees, the labor market may be the surrounding community. For professionals and managers, the labor market may encompass all professionals in that category in the nation.

New hires will be motivated to come to work for a company and current employees will stay if they perceive the company's wages, location, organizational climate, advancement opportunities, job security, and working conditions as more attractive than those of other companies. Over a period of time, these factors combine to form a firm's reputation in the several labor markets in which it competes. That reputation becomes an asset or a liability in attracting and keeping employees. For example, a firm that has a reputation for periodic force reductions may have difficulty competing for employees, particularly for employees in scarce supply.

But the ability of managers to attract and keep the people they need also depends on the conditions of labor markets in which they compete, as well as on their firm's HRM policies. Shortages of people with given skills make it more difficult for a corporation to attract and keep people. In cases where it is extremely difficult to find people with the right skills (the current shortage of engineers and skilled blue-collar workers, for example), business plans and goals are affected. In tight labor markets, firms have to offer more inducements than they would otherwise in order to attract and keep people. Of course, the more a company is able to develop and keep its own professionals, managers, and other skilled employees, the less hiring of experienced personnel it has to do. The desire to reduce, as much as possible, the necessity of competing in a tight labor market has led some firms to consider an employment security policy. It has also led firms to intensify their efforts in training and developing their own employees. The shortage of skilled blue-collar workers in the machine tools industry recently caused one firm to reconsider its cyclical pattern of hiring and firing. It attempted, instead, to adopt an employment security policy accompanied by an investment in an apprentice training program.

Managers are well advised to track long-term trends in labor markets, since these trends indicate how difficult and/or expensive it will be to acquire people with the skills their business may require in the future. Information of this kind can help managers assess the viability of their long-term strategic plans. Perhaps more important, it can point to changes that will be needed in educational programming at colleges, trade schools, and professional schools [which will be needed] to assure employers themselves of an adequate supply of people with the right skills. When shortages are indicated, firms can attempt to influence educational institutions to modify their programs and recruit more students in an effort to influence the labor market. Or, business organizations can set up their own internal educational programs. Firms in high-technology fields have been doing both as they have come to realize that there will be a shortage of electrical engineers in the 1980s. Those that recognized the trends sooner and anticipated their needs more adequately will be able to compete more effectively in the labor market and the business.

Trends in the labor market include changes in the participation of women and minorities as well as changing values of the work force that make employees more resistant to arbitrary authority. And the movement of the post-World War II "baby boom" has created a gradual aging of the work force that will place changing demands on HRM policies, particularly in the areas of flow and rewards. These trends, if not anticipated, can present real problems to managers who have not adjusted their HRM policies and practices to fit them. On the other hand, organizations that effect changes in HRM policies and practices in anticipation of demographic trends can gain a competitive advantage by being better able to attract, utilize, and keep a new breed of employee.

In summary, a firm's ability to compete in its labor markets is dependent on its ability to anticipate trends in the labor markets and to prepare to take advantage of these trends through imaginative human resource management policies and practices.

### Unions

Historically, unions have served as a mechanism to provide a collective voice for nonsupervisory workers over such HRM matters as due process, the distribution of rewards, transfers and promotions, and working conditions. Even where employees are not unionized, unions can influence HRM policies. The perceived threat of unionization can lead employers to adopt HRM policies and practices that they might otherwise avoid. Within a company, wage increases negotiated by the union create pressures to increase wages for nonunion employees by a similar or slightly greater amount in order to avoid dissatisfaction that might lead to further union organizing. Firms without any union may feel forced to pay close attention to pay, fringe benefits, employment security, working conditions, promotion practices, and termination practices. If a corporation operates in a heavily unionized community, it must establish some degree of parity between its policies and those of unionized firms, or risk unionization. Nonunion firms like IBM have human resource policies and practices (including grievance procedures, open-door policy, and employment security) that are more generous and costly than those of many unionized firms. Undoubtedly, the desire to stay nonunion was a major factor in designing these policies.

Furthermore, unions influence HRM practices of nonunionized firms indirectly through their political influence. Legislation that has come about, in large part, because of the political clout of unions has imposed certain human resource standards on employers. Occupational health and safety, workman's compensation, and minimum wage legislation are just three examples. In France and Britain, where unions are more closely allied with political parties than in the United States, their influence is even greater and is felt not only in legislation but in government policy with regard to human resource practices. Even though only 35 percent of the U.S. work force was unionized at the peak of union power in the 1960s, unions have had an important effect on human resource policies and practices of all American businesses, unionized or not.

### Task Technology

By "task technology" we mean the way equipment (hardware or software) is arranged to perform a task. Historically, the technology used to produce a product or provide a service has had a powerful and pervasive effect on human resource policies and practices, particularly in manufacturing operations. It has been shaped by the engineer's view of what constitutes a rational and efficient operation. That rational view (heavily influenced by Frederick Taylor and other adherents of Scientific Management, which will be discussed in greater detail in Chapter 6) has traditionally dominated plant layout and the design of jobs. Similarly, the imperatives of technology itself often have determined the nature of work. The machine and the task have tended to constitute the independent variables, while human beings were left to be the dependent variable.

This view of technology has largely shaped the nature of work as we find it in the late twentieth century. It spawned the assembly line, as well as the division of work in which "planning" and "controlling" have been systematically split off from "doing" and assigned to higher levels or staff groups. Even "doing" has been divided still further with the goal of reducing the time and cost of employee selection and training. This trend has led to problems of depersonalization, boredom, and alienation. Such human problems may in part be responsible for the rise of unionization. They are partly responsible for the quality and productivity problems which have become concerns of most U.S. industries during the past decade.

Technology is now also transforming the office. The work of clerical employees, professionals, and managers will be affected as new information technology (minicomputers and word processing, for example) is introduced and becomes an integral part of the work system for these employees.

In the work systems section of the book, we will consider some of management's recent attempts to reverse the trends of the industrial revolution which has increasingly used the principle of division of labor to simplify and routinize factory work. We will also discuss the effect of this new technology on office work: Can it be developed in a way that enhances rather than degrades human commitment and organizational competence? A recognition of human needs has already prompted management to search for more socially sensitive options in job design and task technology in the plant, but it is still an open question whether these options will be extended to the new office technology, or whether an attitude of technological determinism will continue to guide its development.

### Laws and Societal Values

HRM policies and practices in various countries differ in accordance with the unique culture or ideology of each society. By culture, we mean the values or basic assumptions that people in a society or an organization seem to hold about how one ought to think and behave. These assumptions are often implicit and can be inferred from the standards of expected behavior that are informally enforced by the society, organization, or group. These standards of expected behavior are sometimes called "norms." Ideology is a dynamic framework of interrelated values and beliefs that emerges within a society and is used by that society to make its values explicit and give them institutional validity. Thus, ideology is more explicit than culture or norms and can be found in formal statements of beliefs provided by leaders and other prominent societal and organizational members. Ideologies are modified in response to changes in the nature of a society and in the real world in which that society exists.[3] For example, ideology is shaped by the unique historical and political development of the society, and that development is a function of realities such as geography, demography, resource availability, evolution of traditional institutions, and patterns of behavior and the collective experience of the society as it struggles to survive and prosper. The process of ideology formulation is, therefore, a dynamic one: Changes occur as the society is confronted with new realities. The importance of ideology is that it serves as a bridge between universally held values such as survival, justice, security, self-fulfillment, economic use of resources, and self-respect and the means by which those values are put into practice in a particular setting and at a particular time.

It should not be surprising that HRM policies and practices that express the ideology of an organization—which is itself a minisociety—are heavily influenced by the ideology of the larger society. Its managers and employees have been shaped by that ideology and are likely to develop and accept HRM practices consistent with it.

Likewise, it should not be surprising that HRM policies differ across societies because of explicit differences in government policies and legislation governing employer-employee relations. With the exception of Japan, where emphasis on informal understandings and relationships reduces reliance on legislation, most countries have developed extensive legal frameworks specifying the HRM policies and practices that firms are to employ. Legislation governing employer-employee relations develops out of negative experience of employees with HRM practices in the society. These result in political pressures on government to legislate or regulate HRM practices.

Legislation affecting HRM policies and practices includes the legal framework in which unionization and union-management relations occur, wage and hour laws which govern payment of overtime, laws governing occupational health and safety, equal employment opportunity legislation, legislation governing employee pension funds, and income maintenance programs like workers compensation. In Europe, more extensive legislation exists to govern employee relations, including strict rules that restrict the freedom of management to terminate employees and legislation which establishes the rights and framework for employee participation in an enterprise. As with other legislation, of course, the intent of this legislation is quite often not translated into practice. Managers who do not accept the right of employees to participate find ways to circumvent that legislated process, just as employee representatives who do not have experience in business have some difficulty participating meaningfully, even if they have been encouraged to do so. Thus, a society that seeks to influence HRM must, over time, transform the ideology and skills of both managers and employees if real transformations are to occur.

The extent of government influences over HRM practices often depends on the ideology of the political party in power. President Lyndon Johnson's concern for civil rights resulted in an executive order which prohibited federal contractors and subcontractors from employment discrimination on the basis of race, color, national origin, religion, and sex, and required larger employers to develop affirmative action programs designed to increase the representation of women and minorities in the company's work force. Under an administration that was less favorable to the ideology underlying such a program, enforcement obviously would be reduced, as would the effects on HRM practice.

It becomes obvious, then, that HRM policies and practices are not and cannot be formed in a vacuum. They must reflect the governmental and societal context in which they are embedded. For this reason, policies and practices that work in the United States will not necessarily work in Europe or Japan. Similarly, Japanese multinational firms have discovered that not all policies that have been effective in their home country are applicable in the United States. Company housing, slow promotion, or promotion based on seniority, for instance, may not have the same effect outside of the Japanese context. Managers both in and out of an organization's human resource function must understand the culture, ideology, legislation, and regulations of the society in which they operate before formulating HRM policies. A U.S. firm operating in Belgium recently learned that lesson when it discovered that its general manager, accustomed to great freedom in hiring and firing in the United States, cost the company a lot of money in severance pay as he tried to rid his subsidiary of managers he could not or would not learn to work with compatibly.

Just as important, variations in HRM policies and practices across countries offer useful alternatives for U.S. managers to learn from. This comparative perspective allows managers to examine and question the ideology and assumptions that underlie their own HRM practices. Looking at what managers in other countries do can also suggest alternative models for integrating people and organizations. The interest of American managers in Japanese practices and the stimulus for change provided by the success of Japanese management are the best examples of this phenomenon. However, wholesale application of HRM policies from another country must be avoided if good fit with situational factors is to be obtained. By studying other cultures, U.S. managers may also be able to discern long-term patterns that may engulf them in the future. The alternatives may also suggest strategies for dealing with these long-term changes.

## ORGANIZATIONAL ADAPTABILITY

Implicit in much of the discussion here and in later chapters of the book is the assumption that effective human resource management policies and practices lead to increased adaptability, a critical ingredient in the long-term survival of business organizations. This point is discussed more explicitly below.

In the long run, organizational effectiveness means that the firm has been flexible and responsive to its market and social environment. When the market demands lower costs, or product innovation, or improved service, the management of the corporation must sense the need for change and be able to mobilize the support of various stakeholders, employee groups, unions, government, educational institutions, suppliers, and the community to make adjustments in their own expectations and behavior. Effective HRM policies and practices are those that are designed and administered through a process of mutual influence between management and employees and that result in high levels of commitment, competence, cost effectiveness, and congruence. Here is how the four Cs can contribute to employee and organizational adaptability.

1. *High commitment* means that employees will be motivated to hear, understand, and respond to management's communications about changes in environmental demands with their im-

plications for wages, work practices, and competency requirements. The mutual trust will be there to enable management's
message to be more believable to employees and to enable management to be responsive to employee's legitimate concerns as
stakeholders.

2. *High competence* means that employees in the firm will have the
   versatility in skills and the perspective to take on new roles and
   jobs as needed. Through a positive attitude toward learning
   and personal development fostered by policies that encourage
   and reward learning, employees will be more capable of responding to change.

3. *Cost effectiveness* means that the organization's human resource
   costs—wages, benefits, and indirect costs such as strikes, turnover, and grievances—have been kept equal to or less than
   those of competitors, while major adjustments such as the ones
   facing employees in the steel and auto industries have been
   avoided. Once again, only a continual process of mutual influence about the realities of the business and the needs of employees can bring about this outcome.

4. *Higher congruence* than competitors means that the firm has
   shaped work systems, reward systems, and flow policies so that
   there is a higher coincidence of interest among management,
   shareholders, and workers. Furthermore, a process of employee influence in the affairs of the company will also foster
   congruence. In such a climate, changes in policies and practices
   prompted by the external environment are less likely to be perceived by employees as not in their interest. Moreover, the inevitable differences between shareholder interests and employee interests that remain in even the most effective
   corporations will probably be easier to manage because an atmosphere of collaboration and mutual problem solving will
   have been developed between stakeholders. Adversarial relations are less likely to exist.

Effective organizations are also adaptive to changes in their social
environment. Managers in adaptive organizations can sense changes
in societal values and attend to the spirit as well as the letter of laws that
operationalize these values. These changes begin to be reflected in their
management philosophy and practices, particularly their human resource practices. Managers who see themselves as responsible for the
well-being of the enterprise, its employees, and society—i.e., for long-
term consequences as opposed to the more narrow outcomes such as
profit or growth—are more likely to sense and incorporate changes in
societal values into human resource policies. Their HRM policies are

less likely to undermine their relationships with their employees, government, and community.

We believe that the relationship between employers and employees, and the attitudes and motivation of management and labor are very important ingredients in the process of organizational adaptation. Therefore effective human resource management as we plan to discuss it in this book is an important strategy for achieving an adaptive organization.

## SUMMARY

In this chapter we have provided a map of the key factors that have a strong influence on HRM policies and are in turn influenced by them. For example, we suggested that management's assumptions about work force characteristics influence human resource policies just as those policies affect work-force characteristics. Similarly management philosophy, business strategy, labor markets, laws and society, task technology, and unions affect HR policies and to varying degrees are affected by them. For many of these factors—business strategy, task technology, unions, and management philosophy—a two-way process of influence is possible and needs to be strengthened. That is, policies need to be forged with a clearer understanding of the constraints, just as those constraints may be seen as amenable to modification by progressive and well-articulated HRM policies. Other factors, such as laws, society, and labor markets, may be more immutable constraints in the short run, but even they are subject to influence and change in the long run. We characterized each of the situational factors interacting with human resource policies in the belief that a better understanding of their influence will allow managers to design policies that fit the situation and/or change the situation.

The interests of various stakeholders—shareholders, management, employees, government, the community, and unions—must also be an important factor in designing HRM policies and practices. Without attention to the perspectives of all stakeholders, HRM policies and priorities are unlikely to gain their acceptance. In the long run this is likely to result in the failure of those policies and in a loss of organizational effectiveness.

The well-being of the enterprise, society, and employees were suggested as long-term criteria by which general managers ought to evaluate the HRM policies of their organization. The clear implication is that general managers should search for policies that enhance the well-being of all three, not the enterprise alone, which has traditionally been the central consideration. Finally, commitment, competence, congruity, and cost effectiveness were suggested as specific outcomes that help define all three long-term criteria and that should be assessed explicitly in evaluating human resource policies. Innovative companies are explicitly shaping policies to enhance commitment, competence, and congruence, outcomes that in many companies are by-products of human resource policies rather than explicit goals. Such policy shaping increases an organization's capacity to adapt to changes in its environment.

The conceptual framework presented in this chapter offers *a way of thinking*, not a mechanistic tool for analysis. By adopting it, it is hoped managers will be able better to understand the historical roots of HRM policies and outcomes and to develop creative solutions to human resource problems that fit and influence the situation, satisfy the interests of several stakeholders, and reach for improved outcomes for the enterprise, society, and employees.

# Chapter 3

# Employee Influence

EMPLOYEES AND SHAREOWNERS are two important stakeholders in business enterprises. Typically, both groups share a stake in the survival and prosperity of the organization, but employees have an additional stake in the particular policies and other means employed by the organization in pursuing prosperity.

Employees' stakes are, in part, economic: What fraction of the economic pie will go to them as wages and benefits rather than to owners in the form of dividends, or be retained by the enterprise itself for capital investment? And who absorbs certain costs of uncertainty in the size of the pie—for example, employees through layoffs or shareowners through their financing of employment assurances? And how do these economic stakes differ from one employee group to another?

An employee's stake is also psychological: How much dignity is accorded the individual by management's policies and practices? How much status does one have as a factory employee, as a supervisor, as a division controller? How much intrinsic satisfaction does an employee derive from his or her assignments?

Employees also have a political stake in the enterprise. Unless people are self-employed, the work organization will be the setting in which they will spend about half of their waking hours during the 40 to 50 years of work life. What are an employee's rights and obligations within those workplace societies?

In the larger society in the United States, one has certain political rights: to vote on issues and to elect leaders. One is assured the rule of law, not rule by man. One is guaranteed certain rights of privacy, freedom of speech, and assembly. One is assured justice by due process. As citizens we take those rights for granted. These rights have never extended to corporate society. In many ways, employees are expected to leave their citizenship rights and responsibilities at the plant entrance each morning and pick them up again only when departing for the evening. Implicitly, if not explicitly, the employment relationship involves a contract in which an employee accepts a truncated set of political rights. But how truncated?

We believe the most central issue for employees as stakeholders is the question of *influence*: How can they act to improve or protect their economic share, psychological satisfaction, and rights? How is such influence to be exercised?

Management, of course, has a set of concerns different from the ones just expressed which leads them to a different view of the influence question. Top managers must act on their own judgment about the appropriate division of the economic pie, and that judgment often conflicts with employees' preferences. Managers are charged by stockholders with the efficient use of capital, people, raw materials, and energy. Efficiency involves control; control requires direction; direction requires authority. Management's policies and practices in service of efficiency and control may conflict directly with employee "political" rights and indirectly with their psychological needs. Not surprisingly, management historically has been attracted to their own version of political rights, i.e., "management prerogatives." Typically, they have regarded the idea of increased employee influence as subtracting from their ability to achieve efficiency and control.

Society's views of what employees are entitled to in terms of their economic, psychological, and political interests change over time. Indeed, employees themselves have shifting expectations, as do the unions who represent a segment of American workers. Finally, management's own values and their judgments about what is effective management involve shifting standards about how much the enterprise should accommodate employees' interests and especially how much employee influence is desirable. We will explore below how the direction of change has been toward an expectation of greater employee influence. We see no reason why that trend will not continue.

In this book we do not recommend specific answers to the question of how much influence employees should have over organizational objectives, policies, and practices, nor do we answer the question of what mechanisms should be provided to make possible the exercise of employee influence. Answers to these questions vary with circumstances and conditions. We do, however, take the position that managers should have a conscious and well-thought-out policy that addresses precisely these questions of how much influence and by what means. Policies in this area provide the cornerstone for the development of other policies regarding personnel flows, rewards, and work systems. We are confident that managers' objectives in this area are seldom simply to minimize employee influence. They are to provide for some optimum amount of influence. But how do managers decide what is optimal for their organization? What are the costs and risks associated with minimal employee influence? What costs and risks do managers have in mind when they think of "too much" employee influence?

We have used the phrase "employee influence" because it is a label not currently in widespread use by either practitioners or academics, giving us some freedom to offer a definition without contradicting already existing understandings. We should acknowledge, however, that it is related to "participation," as that word is used to describe a style of management in the United States and as it refers to codetermination and other forms of governance in Europe. "Employee voice" is another phrase we use occasionally, although it is not quite as descriptive as "employee influence." "Voice" says that employees' interests will be *expressed* (not necessarily heard and acted upon), while "influence" goes one important step further. Not only will their interests be heard, but there will be mechanisms which allow them to help shape their company's HRM policies.

Our concept of employee influence is intended to be the most generic formulation of the core HRM issue that underpins a number of different institutions or organizational practices, including collective bargaining in the United States, legislated works councils in Europe, Japan's *ringi* system of seeking consensus around management decisions through wide sharing of information, and a variety of other management devices for learning about and responding to the nature and strength of employee concerns.

This chapter will provide an historical and conceptual context for the employee influence issue. It will also outline some alternative ways corporations and societies have chosen to deal with the question of how much influence to give employees, what kind of influence to give them, and what mechanisms, legislated and nonlegislated, are to provide the vehicle for influence.

## THE CHANGING ROLE OF
## EMPLOYEES AND STAKEHOLDERS

To achieve its goals, a corporation must find some combination of motivation and control that will move people toward a common purpose. Historically, control has been exercised primarily through the authority of owner-managers, and later by professional managers representing shareholder interests. Organizations have historically been able to obtain effective control over operations through (1) division of labor intended to achieve efficiency, (2) a heirarchy of authority, and (3) rules and procedures designed to achieve coordination. In the early days of the industrial revolution such detailed control of employee behavior was considered completely legitimate. As George Lodge has pointed out, the legitimacy of such control rested upon an ideology derived from the British social philosopher, John Locke.[1] Lockean ideology placed primary emphasis on ownership of private property (a gift from God) and the unquestioned right of the property owner to exercise authority over how that property was used. The authority of managers, then, was bestowed down the hierarchical ranks from above, ultimately from property owners.

Given that ideological environment, the simple and routine tasks of early enterprises, and the labor market at the time, top-down control worked effectively. Prospective employees had few skills to offer factory employers, nor did these employers require many. Moreover, people lived much closer to the subsistence level than today. Thus, individuals did not have the power that comes from marketable professional and managerial skills which today give "knowledge workers" considerable power to negotiate conditions of work. In Europe a history of aristocracy and class structure conditioned employees to accept authority. In Japan employee compliance with hierarchical control was supported early on by Chinese Confucianism, which emphasized family hierarchy and responsibility to group, and military dictatorship which highlighted the warrior's code of "master above self."[2] In the United States a large immigrant population in the late eighteenth and early nineteenth centuries lacked not only skills and economic resources but also the power that comes from knowledge of language and culture. An implicit economic contract existed between employers and employees whereby employees accepted management's authority in return for the economic inducements of a job and pay. Employees were not in a position to talk of employment security or employee advancement and development. Furthermore, one worked under whatever conditions management specified, including long days, long work weeks, and sometimes unsafe conditions.

The virtually unchallenged authority of management had the apparent advantage of allowing rapid decision making and implementation. There was no time and energy spent in dealing with differences that existed between stakeholders. Employees dissatisfied with conditions of employment turned to labor unions. Some of these, such as Industrial Workers of the World, were militantly socialistic; others, such as the early American Federation of Labor, were interested mainly in increasing the economic share allotted to the craft workers they represented. But the numbers of unionized employees remained relatively small until the Great Depression of the 1930s, when the skilled, semi-skilled and unskilled workers formed industrial unions.

It was inevitable that unilateral management control would lead to problems. For one thing, such top-down controls allow a social and emotional distance to develop between powerful managers and less powerful employees. Those in power, therefore, run the risk of growing aloof and becoming even more insensitive in their relationships with employees. This gap can, in turn, lead to lowered trust and even less willingness to communicate with employees. This sequence of distance, aloofness, insensitivity, and distrust can develop between top management and middle management just as it can develop between a first-line supervisor and production employees. It can develop even more easily between top management and lower-level employees simply because the physical and hierarchical distance is so great and there are few, if any, opportunities for employees to voice their concerns and views about management's goals and means. Middle managers are distanced in the hierarchy from those both above and below them. Hence they are blocked from fully understanding the concerns and demands of employees below them, and from communicating upward the concerns and demands that they are aware of for fear of upsetting top management and being branded as disloyal. Add to these problems the different interests of management and employees that exist to begin with and it becomes clear that a potential for conflict is ever present.

Just as importantly, unilateral control can create dependence which in turn can increase resentment and distrust towards management and the organization itself. It has been argued that the developmental imperative for all human beings is to move from dependence (a condition of childhood) to independence and then interdependence (a condition of mature and healthy adulthood). Stated another way, human beings strive to be involved and to gain influence over their lives to the extent that they are psychologically ready to do so and to the extent that economic or organizational conditions enable them to do so. Hierarchical organizations have been said to impede this developmental process by placing too many controls on employees, thereby making them unnecessarily dependent.[3] The consequence of this dependency can be that employees are less willing to take responsibility for their work or the performance of the organization. Thus, with the exception of those who are rapidly promoted upward, bureaucracy may prevent the development of ''involved'' and ''responsible'' employees who would be assets to a corporation.

The limitations of hierarchical control have led naturally to a search for alternatives. Dissatisfied employees have sometimes attempted to gain some influence over their well-being by organizing unions. Spurred by dissatisfaction with the conditions of employment and the relative powerlessness of workers, societies have responded with legislation that enables employees to unionize more easily or that creates institutional mechanisms for worker representation on boards or councils. These mechanisms are intended to empower employees to influence affairs over which management has previously had more complete control. In other instances, societies have also legislated minimum standards for safety, employment security, employment opportunity, and other working conditions. Finally, spurred by the high costs of employee-management and union-management conflict, by increasing evidence that employees are now less willing to accept unilateral directives, by the desire to avoid unions and preclude further legislative initiatives by the society, or, in some cases, by progressive values, management itself has instituted reforms in its own practices. Corporations in Europe, the United States and Japan have experimented with a variety of innovations aimed at turning adversarial relationships with unions into cooperative ones and at giving employees more direct influence over their work and the human resource policies of the firm. Thus, a redefinition of management's prerogatives and employee rights has slowly been taking place in this century.

## LEGISLATED EMPLOYMENT STANDARDS AND EMPLOYEE PARTICIPATION

In democratic societies employees are also voters. When they are otherwise unable to satisfy what they consider to be legitimate aspirations for minimum wages, income security, safe working conditions, fair treatment, or equal employment opportunity, they have recourse through political means.

### Legislation and Regulation

European countries have enacted legislation to define minimum standards of employment more frequently than the United States or Japan. In many countries it is difficult to dismiss an employee without an extensive process of review by the government and the payment of high severance costs. Those requirements often in effect create an employment security policy. Only when whole industries or corporate survival is threatened are exceptions negotiated between companies and government.

In many western European countries, the national government legislates many of the matters that are dealt with by collective bargaining in the United States. After consulting with the affected parties, the national government legislates employee benefits including paid vacations, holidays, sick leaves, hospital and medical care, as well as payment for death, retirement, severance of employment, and increased size of family.

While in Europe national laws cover much of the substance of labor relations, United States collective bargaining law leaves a great deal to be determined in the bargaining process. Unlike European labor agreements, for instance, U.S. contracts usually include actual wage rates as opposed to minimum rates; benefit plans such as length of vacation, vacation pay, holidays and holiday pay, and supplementary unemployment benefits; and local plant and individual worker matters like discipline, promotions and demotions, layoffs, seniority rights, plant safety, and grievance and arbitration procedures. It can be said, then, that while U.S. laws tend to cover the *process* of labor relations, European laws often deal with the *substance* of that relationship.

Governmental legislation and regulation have increasingly been moving beyond the process of labor relations. Equal employment, health and safety, and minimum wage are some examples that have already been mentioned. Government regulatory agencies may lead companies to create their own influence mechanisms (job posting, for instance, which allows employees some influence over their career development, or affirmative action committees to which employees may appeal decisions on the basis of perceived inequities). These agencies also serve as external mechanisms to which employees may appeal as a means of influencing decisions.

### Worker Representation on Boards or Councils

Several European countries, including Norway, Denmark, and the Netherlands, have legally established a dual system of providing worker influence. Unions engage in collective bargaining and political lobbying, while elected workers councils are given certain governance powers—ranging from the right to be informed and consulted to the power of codetermination—over the workplace. Such councils are generally elected by employees of a particular plant, with larger multiplant companies having a central workers council as well.

A 1972 West German law, for example, requires that employees sit as representatives on permanent works councils that are granted legally defined rights such as the right to be thoroughly informed on human resource matters, the right to contest planned dismissals, and the right to advise and consent on such issues as employment, transfer, classification, and the wage framework. Other German laws call for labor codetermination by providing for worker representatives on supervisory boards (boards of directors) which meet a few times a year and have general responsibility for policy decisions. In large German steel companies, for instance, the boards consist of five representatives of employees, five of stockholders, and one neutral member elected by the rest of the board. The employee representatives include two members from the works councils and three from the union. In other German industries, codetermination grants just less than equal representation to employees on management boards. While supervisory boards do not run day-to-day operations, they do review corporate strategy and human resource policies, and appoint the management board, the top management group in German corporations.

Historically, unions in the United States have shied away from the notion of participation on corporate boards of directors, preferring to maintain an independent and adversarial position. An important exception to this rule is the agreement worked out between the United Auto Workers (UAW) and the ailing Chrysler Corporation to place then UAW president Douglas Fraser on the company's board of directors. Another exception is the agreement of several unions to make wage and work rules concessions to Eastern Airlines in return for employee stock ownership and four seats on its board of directors.[4] It is too early to tell whether these and other moves toward employee representation on boards of directors will be merely an exception or a trend forced upon seriously troubled companies seeking greater involvement of their unions and increased commitment of employees to reductions in labor costs.

How effective are legislated mechanisms for employee participation in giving employees real or "felt" influence? The degree of real influence is partially determined by legislation and varies from country to country. But it is also a function of how much management seeks to involve employee representatives actively in decisions, and here actual practice varies widely, from attempts to utilize participation mechanisms actively to efforts by management to minimize their power and influence. In addition, the business knowledge and group-process and decision-making skills possessed by worker representatives will affect their influence and, indirectly, the influence of employees.

As for the amount of "felt" participation by employees, some studies have shown that feelings of participation do *not* necessarily increase because legislated mechanisms for participation exist. Workers may feel as distant from their representatives as they are from managers. It turns out that skill in communicating with employees is as important for employee representatives as it is for management.

We can now return to the question of whether employee representation on boards of directors in the United States is an anomaly forced by economic crisis or a model that will be followed by less troubled companies. If these governance models are to be followed by other companies, they must provide those companies with a competitive edge by improving cost effectiveness, congruent (less adversarial) relationships, and commitment. These outcomes are likely only if management can develop a genuine stakeholder perspective and the skills to engage in a process of mutual influence. At the same time, union and employee representatives must acquire the requisite business knowledge as well as the process and political skills needed to manage their constituencies. The absence of requisite knowledge and skills by labor and a genuine stakeholder perspective and process skills by management underlies the problems sometimes experienced by legislated participation in Europe.

### Partial or Complete Employee Ownership

In 1975 the South Bend Lathe Company was saved from closing when its 500 employees borrowed money from the federal government and bought shares in the firm through an employee stock ownership plan (ESOP). Such loans are possible under legislation aimed at making employee ownership easier. About 3000 firms, mostly small companies, have begun similar ESOP plans by turning some or all of their stock over to employees. A 200-employee picture frame factory in Somerville, Massachusetts operates under an employee stock ownership trust in which employees control all voting and nonvoting stock. More recently, General Motors' employees in Clark, New Jersey purchased a 43-year-old bearing plant from the company in order to prevent the plant from shutting down.[5] Unable to negotiate a 35-percent wage reduction with the union, management offered to sell the plant to employees under a plan that would loan employees money for the purchase and guarantee a specific order level from GM for three years. Only a third of the employees agreed to become owners, but they immediately took a 35-percent pay cut. Is the ultimate mutuality of interest between employees and shareholders made possible by employee ownership the only condition that enables such reductions in labor costs? What are the implications of this for corporate survival and responsiveness to competitive forces?

Partial or complete employee ownership theoretically allows employees the opportunity to exercise complete influence over the way the company is managed. Whether the shareholders will put mechanisms in place that allow various stakeholder groups to influence business goals or human resource policies is thus determined by the employees themselves. However, recent research suggests that employee ownership does not automatically lead to enhanced employee influence and labor-management cooperation.[6] A recent strike by the employee-owners of the South Bend Lathe plant provides dramatic real-world evidence that unless management possesses attitudes and skills in involving employees, and employees are willing and able to become involved, employee ownership will not result in greater influence. "Felt" influence does not increase with the increase in economic and legal power.

Increases in congruity, cost effectiveness, employee commitment, and competence do not necessarily result.

## COLLECTIVE BARGAINING

Given the problems of unilateral control that were discussed earlier, it is not surprising that employees have attempted to protect their well-being through collective action. Feeling the inherent limitations of an "individual contract," employees organized into unions which served as a counterbalance to the dominant force of management. In the United States the modern trade union movement was born in 1886 with the creation of the American Federation of Labor (AFL). As president of the AFL from its founding to his death in 1924, Samuel Gompers indelibly marked and helped shape not only that union, but the entire labor movement. Gompers based his organizing efforts for the AFL on the tenet of "bread-and-butter" unionism. Others might talk about reforming the American economic system; it was the bread-and-butter issues of wages and working conditions that would propel the AFL. George Meany, who presided over the AFL when it merged with the Congress of Industrial Organizations in 1955 and who led the AFL-CIO through nearly the next three decades, agreed with Gompers's approach. "We accept without question," he said, "the right of management to manage with reasonable consideration, of course, for the rights of workers to a fair share of the wealth produced . . . .. [T]he only reasonable difference of opinion between American labor and American management is over the share the worker receives of the wealth that he helps to produce. That, of course, is the simple basic reason for the trade union instrumentality. We want to have a say as to what that fair share for the worker should be."[7]

It was not until the Great Depression of the 1930s that political support developed for legislation that would protect a union's right to organize and collectively represent the workers. The National Labor Relations Act (1935) recognized workers' rights to bargain collectively over such issues as wages, hours, and conditions of work. It guaranteed covered employees complete freedom to select the bargaining agent of their choice. And it made any attempt by employers to dominate or otherwise interfere with the formation or administration of any labor organization an "unfair labor practice." Finally, the Act created the National Labor Relations Baord (NLRB) as an independent federal agency to oversee the proper functioning of the law's provisions, and to issue rulings and directives.

It was this law, more than any other single act, that shifted economic power in the United States away from the exclusive domain of management to be shared by blue-collar workers. With the federal government as overseer, the law created three power bases—management, unions, and government—which would now act as countervailing forces. Management would speak for the interests of shareholders, unions would protect organized workers, and the government would attempt to seek a balance between the two on behalf of the "common good."

In the aftermath of severe labor disputes that followed World War II, Congress passed the Labor-Management Relations Act (Taft-Hartley), which defined unfair labor practices as applying to unions as well as management. Another provision allowed the president to issue a "cooling-off" injunction (a temporary back-to-work order) when a labor dispute in private industry imperiled the national health and safety. The law also specifically outlawed closed shops (an agreement that permits the hiring of only union members), and allowed individual states to pass their own laws banning union shops (an agreement which stipulates that while anyone may be hired, union membership is a requirement for continued employment). Since the passage of the law in 1947, twenty states, all of them in the South and the agricultural Midwest, have enacted laws to ban union shops.

The important point here is that U.S. society, along with other societies, has supported the institutional mechanism of collective bargaining by which employees can exercise influence. The collective bargaining process may take place at the plant, company, or industry level and even at the national level in some countries.

Representatives of management and those of the union sit across from each other at a bargaining table and hammer out agreements that provide for due process by specifying a grievance procedure, that define pay systems, and that establish procedures which govern transfer, promotion (usually by seniority), apprentice programs, and termination. Some unions have negotiated provisions limiting management's latitude with regard to contracting out work, introducing labor-saving technology, and transferring work from one unit to another.

In the United States, most contract negotiations cover a particular plant or company. Thus, the United Auto Workers negotiate separately with General Motors, Ford, and Chrysler. There are some exceptions to this; steel, for instance, negotiates as an industry. In the case of a large company like General Motors, the national contract is supplemented by local agreements between individual plants and their local unions which deal with the specific working conditions at that plant.

If management and union negotiators fail to reach an agreement, the union is free to strike and management is free to lock out employees. Because sit-down strikes are illegal, management personnel may enter a plant during a strike and attempt to operate the facility. The federal government can offer the assistance of trained labor mediators, but those mediators cannot impose an agreement. Once a contract is signed, both strikes and lockouts may be prohibited by that contract. There is always the possibility of wildcat strikes (local strikes unauthorized by the national union) or illegal lockouts of employees. However, nearly all contract disputes are settled through some sort of grievance or arbitration procedure. Unions and management typically write into their contract a provision for final and binding arbitration.

The National Labor Relations Act provided the NLRB with two main functions: to oversee free and secret elections by employees to determine their bargaining agent, and to prevent and remedy unfair labor practices by employers and unions. But before the NLRB ever becomes involved, unions must undertake a process of seeking support among the employees of a company or industry. During such an organizing campaign all managers, not just those specializing in labor relations, must be aware of the legal environment that governs their actions as well as the activities of the union.

The union organizer, with the help of some in-plant supporters, asks employees to sign a card authorizing the union as their bargaining agent. The union must secure the signatures of at least 30 percent of the employees before going to the NLRB with the request for a representational election. Many union organizers, however, will not seek an election until the percentage of employees who have signed cards is significantly higher than the 30 percent required by law. Those cards are not binding on the employee. In the election itself, employees who signed union cards are free to vote either for or against union representation.

Employers may waive the necessity of a representational election. If they wish to challenge the union's petition for representation, however, they must file their own petition so stating with the NLRB. The NLRB will then determine whether or not the employees are covered by its jurisdiction (government employees are excluded from NLRB coverage, along with agricultural laborers, domestic servants, and independent contractors). The NLRB then moves in to oversee the election.

One of the most critical early decisions to be made by both sides—management and union—is the definition of the bargaining unit. The Taft-Hartley Act prohibits the inclusion of supervisors. Beyond that, the employer and the union can reach their own agreement, or turn to the NLRB to make that determination. The NLRB has broad discretion to select an employer—or industrial—unit, a craft unit, a plant unit, or a subplant unit. The NLRB also sets the date for the election, usually 15 to 30 days after verifying the signatures.

During the organizing campaigns, employers are legally free to oppose the union's efforts (and they usually do mount a vigorous antiunion campaign). Employers may not, however, engage in any tactics which the NLRB determines would prevent employees from making a reasoned choice. Thus, employers cannot use economic power to coerce employees. They cannot threaten employees with reprisals like loss of job or benefits as an inducement for not supporting the union drive. Neither employers nor unions can make last-minute (24 hours prior to election) campaign speeches.

Studies indicate that employer campaigns against union representation are rarely effective when they engage in economic fear tactics. Such tactics rarely change attitudes, but rather tend to reinforce the pro-union attitudes of employees already convinced of their employer's hostility toward the employees.[8] A more effective tactic by employers emphasizes the uncertainties of union representation, and holds out the promise—vague, lest NLRB rules be violated—of improved and enlightened working conditions. Unions, on the other hand, often try to build on already existing dissatisfaction with working conditions, and work to reassure workers that they will not lose any benefits they have already won in changing from a nonunion to a union shop.

The NLRB-supervised election gives employees a choice between one or more bargaining representatives and no bargaining representative. Once an agent receives a majority of the valid votes cast, that agent becomes the *exclusive* bargaining agent for that unit. After the NLRB certifies the winner, the employer must bargain with that agent in good faith. (What constitutes "good faith" is sometimes difficult to determine.) Either side can appeal the results of an election, however, first to an NLRB regional director, then to the board itself. If the NLRB determines that an atmosphere existed in which it is reasonable to believe that the free choice of employees was interfered with, they may set aside the results and call for a new election. On the other hand, they may certify the results and order the parties to negotiate. If either party fails to comply, the board may seek an order from the United States Circuit Court of Appeals, at which time the contesting party may present its arguments to the court. Such appeals can be used as a tactic in the organizing campaign. By utilizing all available appeal channels an employer can drag out the organizing process for well over a year in an attempt to sap union strength.

Once the bargaining units are certified, the employer and the union must bargain in good faith over wages, hours, and other conditions of employment. Any dispute over the precise meaning of "other conditions" will be determined by the NLRB. The National Labor Relations Board recognizes five broad areas of unfair labor practices by employers:

1. Interfering with, coercing, or restraining employees in the exercise of their rights to join (or not) or assist labor organizations.

2. Assisting, dominating, or contributing financially to labor unions.
3. Discriminating against employees in order to discourage union membership or encourage it, except as provided by a valid union security clause in a collective bargaining agreement.
4. Discriminating against employees because they have filed charges or given testimony to the NLRB.
5. Refusing to bargain in good faith with the representatives of the employees.

Likewise, the NLRB recognizes eight major areas of unfair labor practices on the part of unions:

1. Coercing or restraining employees in their choice of a bargaining representative.
2. Coercing or restraining employers in their choice of a bargaining representative in collective bargaining.
3. Causing an employer to discriminate illegally against an employee.
4. Refusing to bargain in good faith with an employer.
5. Engaging in secondary boycotts.[9]
6. Charging excessive or discriminatory initiation fees.
7. Engaging in featherbedding (receiving payment for work which is not performed).
8. Engaging in organizational or recognition picketing.

Unfair labor practices charges are filed with the regional NLRB director, and the ensuing appeals process is the same as that outlined above for the appeal of election results.

Though collective bargaining agreements provide influence mechanisms only for the workers who actually belong to the unions (a minority of the work force in the United States), they serve as an indirect mechanism for all employees. The perceived threat of unionization leads some employers to adopt human resource policies they might otherwise not adopt. Some nonunionized firms have grievance procedures, open-door policies, and employment security provisions that are motivated in part out of a desire to remain nonunion.

Unions also provide employees with influence over legislation. Unions support candidates and lobby directly for legislation favoring employee well-being. Many human resource standards, including occupational, health and safety, workman's compensation, and minimum wage laws, have been legislated partly as a result of union influence.

# MANAGEMENT INITIATIVES

Management's response to unions or legislation has typcially been resistance, since these mechanisms are usually seen as reducing management's freedom. But this response is not universal, and some managers
today are looking for ways to make collective bargaining more constructive for all stakeholders. We will return to the alternative management policies toward unions after we examine some trends in direct
employee participation.

## *Employee Participation in Work Itself*

In the past 20 years there have been an increasing number of managerial innovations in shop (and office) floor participation. Employees
in such innovative organizations are given greater responsibility and
authority for making decisions about the task itself than is common in
most organizations. This involvement is accomplished by reversing the
historical trend toward more division of labor and giving employees or
groups of employees more responsibility for a "whole task." Thus,
employees gain more control and influence over work goals and methods, a sharp reversal from the historical pattern of hierarchical control.
Innovations in work systems have been applied in Europe and the
United States. A variation of this approach, found most often in Japan,
is to bring employees together in groups which identify prodution
problems and make suggestions for solving them. Such groups are
called "quality circles" or self-management groups and are increasingly finding their way into U.S. companies. This trend will be ex-
plored in detail in Chapter 6 on work systems, because these innovations also affect the content and organization of work.

Employees who are given increased responsibility for their tasks do
not have more influence over corporate human resource policies such
as pay or employment security. There may still be conflict between
managers and workers over these matters, particularly if managers are
making unilateral decisions. Employers hope that participative mechanisms will create a greater coincidence of interests between employers
and employees, thereby increasing trust, reducing the potential for
conflict, and increasing the potential for an effective mutual influence
process on matters such as pay, employment security, and other working conditions.

Some companies introduce participative methods at the shop floor
in the hope that a greater congruence of interest will make it less likely
that workers will organize. However, when union avoidance is the objective to the exclusion of developing a genuine process of mutual influ-

ence between management and employees, participative methods are likely to fail. Similarly, in unionized shops work participation is unlikely to be effective if those unions are not involved. Unions will see such participation as a threat to their existence, while employees are likely to suspect that these developments are a management ploy. In short, worker participation in the task itself is likely to be a more successful nonlegislated mechanism for employee voice and influence if it is accompanied by union-management collaboration when a union exists.

### Management Provisions for Employee Voice

Some managers have unilaterally increased employee influence by creating mechanisms by which employees may have a stronger voice in the corporation's affairs. In the last decade Caterpillar Tractor, Northern Electric Ltd., IBM, Pitney Bowes, and McCormick, among others, have installed two types of mechanisms:

1. Ones that aim at ensuring due process for employees who have grievances.
2. Ones that enable employees to suggest changes and innovations in management practices which will increase fair treatment or enhance efficiency.

Such mechanisms can be seen as a way to balance the goals of justice and efficiency in the absence of a countervailing force such as a union. In effect, management creates a check-and-balance system over its own decisions in the conviction that checks and balances are needed over their natural tendency to take primarily the shareholder perspective or to emphasize business outcomes at the expense of human outcomes. Sometimes, management may create mechanisms for employee voice without being fully committed to the concept of greater influence for employees. Recommendations and suggestions are not acted on, or no provision is made for judicial review (that is, for review of grievances by third parties not involved in the dispute or otherwise biased in their perspective). In these instances the credibility of such mechanisms quickly erodes, creating a level of distrust that may be actually higher than it would have been without the installation of these mechanisms.

Mechanisms for employee influence may require direct contact between employees and managers or they may provide indirect information through surveys, ombudsmen, or employee relations personnel. While indirect means offer anonymity and protection to employees, they limit the ability of management and employees to understand first-hand each other's perspectives. Such mutual understanding has the potential for transforming the attitudes of both parties.

The following are examples of mechanisms for employee voice:

1. "Speak up" or feedback programs. Employees may telephone a special number to raise questions or voice concerns, or may write letters to a designated company representative.
2. Special councils where management and/or employees regularly get together to talk about problems. Agendas are submitted by employees and management.
3. "Sensing groups" in which managers meet periodically with small random samples of employees to hear their concerns or suggestions and to communicate company policy and goals.
4. Open-door policy and other formal grievance systems in which employees may complain to a manager who is not their immediate supervisor. Typically, a formal and preplanned process for review of the complaint is part of such a policy.
5. Task forces of employee groups (women or minority caucuses, for example). They can be commissioned to review corporate personnel policies including pay, affirmative action, promotion policies, and the like.
6. Employee relations personnel and ombudsmen located throughout the organization, accessible to employees to deal with grievance or concerns and to expedite their solutions.
7. Attitude surveys conducted by questionnaire or by an employee task force to diagnose problems and make suggestions to management. Management commits to respond publicly.

Historically, nonlegislated mechanisms for influence have been adopted by companies in order to avoid unions. There are instances of other companies, like McCormick Spice, that have adopted mechanisms for employee influence out of the deep convictions of their founders that employees have ideas that can contribute both to improved productivity and to employee satisfaction.

### Union Relations Policy

What policies do management in the United States adopt toward unions attempting to organize their workers and toward unions that already represent their workers? And what are the policies and preferences about relationships that union officials bring to collective bargaining?

Many of the companies in industries that have developed largely since World War II, such as the computer industry, have remained nonunion. They have adopted human resource policies and management styles that are relatively responsive to employee needs. Their history of growth has been an asset in this respect—producing both advancement opportunities and employment security. Other companies, such as Eastman Kodak, Delta Airlines, and Gillette have also been successful in keeping their work force nonunion, largely because of responsive human resource policies and practices. By and large, the companies that are today totally or predominantly nonunion intend to stay that way.

A very different pattern exists in most of the industries that developed before or during the 1930s and 1940s, when industrial unionization activity peaked. These industries include steel, automobile, rubber, glass, and mining. Almost all companies in these industries accept that they must deal with unions in their existing facilities. However, their actual labor relations may range across a spectrum from "conflict" or "containment-aggression" to "accommodation" or even "cooperation."[10] In these heavily unionized industries, when a company established a new plant in the 1960s or 1970s, it often considered the option of trying to keep the plant nonunion, and many companies have been successful in doing so. For example, the U.S. tire companies typically deal with the Union Rubber Workers in their older plants, but they also have several relatively new tire plants that have not been unionized. The labor relations dilemma for these managements is that if their collective bargaining relationship moves toward the collaboration end of the spectrum, the union appropriately asks, "If we can trust each other and solve problems to our mutual advantage in these older plants, why do you try to keep us out of the new plants?" Or more pointedly, they ask, "If you are so dedicated to keeping us out of the new plants, how can we trust you in the old ones?" This issue became increasingly salient in the GM-UAW relationship in the 1970s and was finally resolved by an agreement between the parties in 1979 which virtually assured the UAW that any new plants opened after 1979 would be union plants. How will this issue be handled by managements of other companies who, like GM in 1979, wish to evolve more collaborative relationships?

There is a third category comprising a small number of companies that have some unionized facilities but many more facilities that are not organized, and which have in recent years adopted a policy of converting unionized facilities to nonunion status whenever possible. They can do this legally only by implementing positive HRM policies and hoping employees will see the union as unnecesary or undesirable. The law precludes active encouragement to employees to seek a decertification election. HRM policies that have decertification as their ultimate objective have met with very limited success to date, but a growing number of companies with a moderate fraction of their work force already unionized are considering this policy. Will this policy trend continue and become a major factor in the United States? Will it be successful? What revisions in their HRM policies will these managments regard as most instrumental to this labor relations objective?

A fourth, considerably looser grouping of companies fits into no convenient national pattern. Industries like supermarkets, building construction, maritime, and health care often involve multiple unions and follow regional or even local patterns. Public employment (except for federal employment) is sensitive to differing state and local laws. Employers in these industries, no less than in those industries with stronger national or industry-wide patterns, must make decisions on the nature and type of relationship they wish to see evolve from collective bargaining.

In general terms, it can be said that we are witnessing two opposing trends on the part of companies that currently are partly or predominantly unionized. On the one hand, a growing number of managements are attempting to structure a closer partnership with their unions—this involves accepting the legitimacy of the union role in a larger set of enterprise issues. On the other hand, a smaller number of companies are trying to decertify the unions they have whenever possible. Both sets of policy objectives are rationalized by their adherents in terms of increasing the competitiveness of the company through an increase in operational flexibility and a decrease in disruptive conflict.

That leaves a residual group of unionized companies—mostly those whose collective bargaining relationship can be characterized as containment-aggression or accommodation and who have no present plans to change their relationship pattern. Will these companies join one of the trends? How will they decide which?

How do the unions view efforts by management either to increase employee participation or to initiate more cooperative union relations?

In the United States, some union leaders are seeking influence over less tangible issues like the design of new technology, the design of work itself, relations between workers and their supervisors, and more broadly defined conditions of work. The president of the Communication Workers of America (CWA), Glenn Watts, believes that the time has come for unions to insist upon influence over the quality of working life for their members. "For many years there have been problems that we have not been able to take care of," Watts said. "Our members were expressing concern about things that went well beyond wages and benefits." The Teamsters are also beginning to reject the notion that management's participation and influence over non-bread-and-butter issues is inherently manipulative to the detriment of the interests of the workers. "The view that participative management is manipulative is old thinking," explained an officer of the Teamsters' Honeywell local in Minneapolis.

Not all union leaders accept the notion of increased influence in nontraditional areas. The independent United Electrical Workers (UE), for instance, say they "reject participation in any of these employer-generated groups which bypass our regular union structure with the goal of—by use of advanced psychological techniques—brainwashing workers into making suggestions that will result in speed-up, combination of jobs, downgrading and layoffs."

The UE's views of employee participation and union-management cooperation on noneconomic issues reflect the fears of some union leaders that cooperation with management will dilute the militancy of union leaders and rob members of a strong voice speaking for their own interests. Others may fear that employee participation will lessen the need felt by employees for a union and thus erode the union's base.

Traditionally, collective bargaining has been viewed as essentially adversarial in nature and distributive in intent. That is to say, two parties with inherently conflicting interests about how the economic pie should be divided—the key content matter of collective bargaining— engage in a show of power to determine the distribution of that pie. Necessarily, then, the more one side wins, the more the other loses. But, as the statements of union leaders cited above indicate, there are signs of interest in the United States on the part of some union leades as well as management in finding an alternative to such exclusively adversarial relationships and to engage in mutually beneficial problem solving. This urge, as we have already indicated, is especially apparent among companies facing a competitive crisis where joint problem solving may become a matter of survival. In such cases, joint union-management problem solving is acknowledged as a general goal by both union and management, but is engaged in separately from the collective bargaining process. This separation can reassure a union that its traditional role is not being threatened, while allowing them to participate in improvements in work life. Joint agreements between General Motors and the United Auto Workers (UAW), Ford and the UAW, and the Basic Steel Conference and the United Steelworkers of America all carefully separate quality of work life, employee involvement and labor-management participation activities—both in structure and content—from collective bargaining. Thus, collective bargaining deals with matters still considered to be distributive (wages, benefits, etc.), while joint committees composed of union officers and management representatives concern themselves with such matters as improving attitudes, sharing information about the competitive environment and the welfare and concerns of employees, redesigning the work environment, and—by implication at least—improving productivity and saving jobs.

General Motors structurally reflected this division between the cooperative quality of work life (QWL) approach and the more traditionally adversarial labor relations approach by placing QWL under its personnel function while keeping collective bargaining as part of labor relations. But an alternative pattern has already emerged within the auto industry. The cooperative initiatives with the union that Ford began in 1980, labeled "employee involvement," have been taken within the labor relations department itself. And the special collective bargaining in 1982 that led to a new contract first at Ford, then at General Motors, reflected an attempt to apply cooperative problem solving to the usually distributive bargaining process.

The movement from adversarial to cooperative relationship, which has affected a small minority of companies in this country, has gone further and affected more industries in Japan. During the post-World War II period, bad economic conditions, labor-management strife, and a desire to isolate radical factions within the trade union movement led to successful efforts by both moderate union leaders and management to cooperate. In exchange for employment security, many of these moderate labor leaders were willing to make concessions to management on such matters as flexible assignment of workers, worker involvement in problem solving, and other productivity-enhancing practices. Through extensive consultation on labor-management committees, many Japanese unions have exercised considerable influence on what has traditionally been viewed as prerogatives of management: quarterly production schedules, work-force levels for given jobs, and worker assignments, for example.[11] Different forms of worker and union influence that have emerged in Europe will be discussed below.

The high level of mistrust between managers and union officials in many American plants is one reason why managers prefer to have nonunion operations: it liberates the attention of supervisors for matters other than conflicts with the union. Historically, American unions have been too good at the adversarial role. When they meet management head-to-head in our industrial workplaces, the unions often prevail. As a result, management has tried to avoid the contest by being nonunion. The severe recession of the early 1980s, when many unions agreed to concessions, has resulted in a significant break with the general trend of unions winning higher wages through tests of strength with management. It is too early to know whether this experience will result in less adversarial relations or even cooperative union-management relations in the future. Much probably depends on management's posture toward unions whose bargaining power has diminished and on the capacity of union leaders to be creative in defining and selling to their members a new role for unions in a context of cooperative union-management relations. If management and unions seize the occasion to forge a new relationship, union-management cooperation of the type seen in Japan may well become the model. If union leaders continue to see an adversarial relationship over economic issues as the only role or if management uses its increased strength to weaken unions, then adversarial union-management relations will continue and management will continue to try to operate on a nonunion basis.

The desire to be nonunion is an aspect of American industrial relations that European (except British) and Japanese managers often fail to understand. American managers seem to them to be obsessed with being nonunion, when their own experience in Europe and Japan suggests that union relations can often be managed successfully just like other aspects of business. But European and Japanese managers by and large do not confront the presence of strong and militant unions on the shop floor as American managers do. Instead, the pressure of militant European and Japanese unions is felt primarily in the outside political environment, or at the industry-wide level in collective bargaining. The combination of militant trade unionism with a strong base is apparently unique to Great Britain and the United States.

The important point is that historically the emergence of unions and collective bargaining has, not surprisingly, resulted in an adversarial relationship and the use of power (strikes, walkouts, etc.) as the primary means of exercising influence. As the costs of this relationship to both parties begin to outweigh the gains, efforts begin toward accommodation and even cooperation, particularly on noneconomic issues that are more easily subject to problem solving. It is an open question as to how far this trend will go. Undoubtedly that will be determined by its utility to management, workers, unions, and society as a whole. A number of questions will be asked continually as this general trend continues:

1. Does cooperation enhance the influence of all parties? At what point, if any, does it erode the power of unions or management by coopting their perspectives to the point where their stakeholders' interests are no longer represented?
2. On what issues (pay, working conditions, supervision, business strategy, etc.) is cooperation and problem solving possible, even necessary? On what matters must union-management relationships continue to adhere to traditional negotiation and bargaining where economic power is the final arbiter?

3. If a mix of labor relations strategies (cooperation and adversarial) is necessary, how can such an inherently unstable mix be managed? What structures and processes are necessary, and what skills do union leaders and managers need to possess to sustain a mixed relationship?
4. At what level in the hierarchy of the labor relations system—plant, corporation, industry, or national—should or can various issues be dealt with (for example, pay, economic security, supervision, and technology) and how will these choices affect the mutual influence process between unions and management?

### Considerations in Developing an Employee Influence Policy

There is a striking contrast between the employee influence practices of the 1800s and the practices that have emerged as a result of collective action by employees, government legislation, and management response and initiatives. While hierarchical authority representing shareholder and management interests continues to be an important source of social control in organizations, the limitations of hierarchy have forced a search for other mechanisms of social control, ones that recognize the legitimacy of other stakeholders. There is no reason to believe that the trend toward corporate governance which relies on mutual influence processes rather than hierarchical authority is likely to change. The success of Japanese companies and some companies in the United States and Europe in implementing a process of mutual influence adds weight to the hope that such shared influence may well help bring various stakeholders together in a mutual understanding of the realities facing each other and the enterprises as a whole.

Experience tells us, however, that mutual influence mechanisms do not always lead to desired outcomes. Highly participative mechanisms exact their own price from management and employees both. Managers may feel that their traditional prerogatives are being threatened, their authority over subordinates diluted. They may feel torn between the organization's long-range and often vaguely stated goals of improving productivity through participation on the one hand, and the short-term, more clearly defined and understood financial goals set by the organization on the other. Managing in an environment where employees are frequently consulted and involved can be tremendously costly in terms of time. Managers will find more and more of their work days being spent in committees or talking with union leaders, individual employees, or groups of employees. The skills demanded of a manager in such an environment differ considerably from those expected in a highly hierarchical setting. Supervisors become facilitators and decisions they previously made unilaterally become consensual. This lack of control and the high level of uncertainty and ambiguity make some managers feel uncomfortable. Others may need a significant period of time to adjust to the new demands being made upon them and to learn the new skills required. Still others may not be able to adjust at all. Companies may therefore face the dilemma of what to do with a manager whose economic performance in the past has been excellent but whose ability to function in a more participative environment is limited and whose limitations are blocking progress.

The impact of alienation, frustration, and boredom on employee well-being is relatively well-known. But systems that involve employees in decisions to which they have not previously been a party extract their own costs. Employees are required to shed their dependent role and become more interdependent. They must attempt to understand other stakeholder perspectives, acquire new knowledge about the business, and take responsibility for the enterprise as a whole. All of this requires employees to adjust and develop in ways that have the potential for adding stress, the kind of stress—uncertainty, ambiguity, complexity, and competing demands of company and family, for instance— more traditionally associated with management-level personnel.

Power and politics, too, may become a major barrier to greater mutuality in the stakeholder influence process. Because they want to retain their position of power, formal or informal leaders of stakeholder groups (managers, union leaders, etc.) may urge members of their group to hang on to older perspectives and block the development of new perspectives. Sometimes, aspiring leaders may ''whip up'' support for themselves by encouraging an adversarial relationship with other stakeholder groups. Changes in relationships and in the development of a mutual influence process between stakeholder groups may be blocked until circumstances reduce the appeals of such leaders or they have left the scene. Recognizing the political realities of various stakeholder groups and managing those realities become additional difficulties in implementing a process of mutual influence.

These potential barriers, and others, make any policy of increasing employee influence difficult to implement. Failure along the way, caused by the inability of stakeholder groups or their representatives to develop attitudes and competencies consistent with an emerging process of mutual influence, can cause major regression, higher distrust, and the reemergence of conflict. Indeed, as the organization depends more and more on an emergent culture which supports a mutual influence process and less on hierarchical control, managers fear that failures invite anarchy.

It is clear that managers' decisions about what employee influence policies to pursue must rest on balancing the opportunities of more participation by employees against the difficulties and risks of implementation. Ultimately these risks can only be reduced if the manager is persistent over time and willing to nurture a gradual evolution rather than a rapid revolution. That persistence will depend on the manager's own values and convictions.

If major change in an employee influence policy is dependent at least in part on management's values and convictions, a real dilemma is created, one that presents a major barrier to increasing employee influence. The willingness of managers to initiate and persist in such change efforts rests upon their assumptions about work-force competence and responsibility. If individual members of the work force are assumed by managers to be uninterested or incapable of making useful, intelligent, and informed decisions about the well-being of the organizations that employs them, then these managers are unlikely to want to initiate efforts to increase employee influence. Unfortunately, managers' assumptions about the capacity of employees to participate in decisions are likely to be pessimistic because their assumptions are shaped, in part at least, by their experiences in organizations that do not afford employees opportunities to participate and influence. Thus, a self-fulfilling prophecy develops in which employees are not offered an opportunity to influence because of pessimistic management assumptions, and those assumptions are formed by past practices which have left employees dependent and unskilled in the participative process.

This dilemma is one of the causes of the slow and uneven pace of change in employee influence. Organizations that have begun to transform their employee influence policies have typically started the process by allowing managers so inclined to experiment in outlying plants, branches, or divisions. By allowing them freedom to shape a new culture, models are created in the organization which can be used to educate other managers. That educational process can occur as less progressive managers visit the leading-edge organizational units or are transferred to them to learn by working in those units. In this way, change can be diffused to other parts of the organization as managers whose assumptions have been transformed by their experiences in model units are sent elsewhere in the organization. Because changes in employee influence involve a change in culture, experimenting in a few organizational units and diffusing change through socializing and transferring managers has been a part of most major change efforts. Of course if the changes start at the bottom or middle of the organization, there are potential conflicts between the emergent pattern of employee influence at these lower levels and more traditional values concerning employee influences that may remain among many top managers and staff groups. These conflicts in values can slow progress and cause regression.

Most organizations that are engaged in transforming patterns of employee influence create a network of change agents, whose full-time responsibility is to support the changes through consulting, teaching, counseling, and coaching their managers. These change agents may be personnel specialists, organization development consultants from either inside or outside the firms, or line managers who have been temporarily assigned to support the change. Ford Motor, for example, has assigned 150 individuals as full-time employee involvement coordinators. The theory underlying this approach is that individuals so assigned, properly trained and properly supported by higher level managers, can sustain a commitment to new values and assumptions more easily than managers who are embedded in day-to-day operations. By consulting with target organizations, they encourage managers to change because they represent living symbols that the organization is changing, and that new assumptions, values, and skills are called for.

Finally, transformation in employee influence policies has typically involved extensive educational programs for managers, supervisors, and employees. This investment in education has both real value in transmitting skills and symbolic value in serving notice that a change process is underway.

Implementing a change in employee influence typically involves several of these approaches, all of them aimed at creating new experiences for managers and employees and thereby changing assumptions and values.

## SUMMARY

Employees and employers will have different views on how to split the economic pie, on how much involvement employees should have, and about management prerogatives and employee rights. Originally employers had almost total authority over the disposition of these questions. But the trend in democratic societies has been toward more employee influence through collective bargaining, legislated mechanisms for worker participation, and management's initiatives to allow more employee participation. This trend has come about as employees, voters in democratic societies, exert political and social pressures to create more mechanisms of influence. Whatever the means, general managers should consciously decide what their employee influence policy is, and how much influence employees should be given.

Historically, aggrieved employees have organized themselves into unions to develop a collective voice about pay and working conditions. In the United States, the National Labor Relations Act and the National Labor Relations Board have empowered the government to maintain a balance of power between unions and management, making possible a process of mutual influence through collective bargaining. Management's approach to union relations can materially influence whether those relations are collaborative or adversarial, thus affecting employee influence. In many societies legislation specifies how much and what kind of influence employees should be given. In Europe, laws direct codetermination through employee and union representation on supervisory boards (boards of directors in Germany) and workers councils. In the United States, equal employment legislation gives employees a voice through regulatory agencies that enforce the law and through the threat of court action. The U.S. government has also enacted legislation which helps employees buy out their company's stock under certain circumstances, making it possible for them to become owners and elect board members. Though economic ownership would seem to make it possible for employees to have a lot of influence, in reality the extent of their influence is determined by management's and workers' skills in participation.

Unions and legislation have created pressures which have resulted in management initiatives to give employees more influence through involvement in decision making on the shop floor, through various task forces and committees, and through due process mechanisms. In some cases managers have initiated efforts to give employees influence because of their belief that this is the best way to maintain a competitive and adaptive corporation. General managers in these companies have developed a conscious policy to provide employees with more influence through participation and/or cooperation with unions.

Important questions remain about the future of employee influence in business organizations and about union-management cooperation. Does cooperation enhance the influence of all parties or can one party be coopted? Can cooperation in some areas coexist with competitive bargaining in others? Moreover, there are many problems in maintaining a process of mutual influence between employees and employers. Skills and competence of employees, union leaders, and managers are crucial to its success. The process is vulnerable to self-serving actions by leaders who can reduce trust and re-ignite suspicion and hostility. For this reason, most organizations engaged in the process of increasing employee participation and influence employ several approaches in concert to move change along. They develop model organizations, they create a network of internal and external consultants to support the change, and they invest in education and training.

# Chapter 4

# Managing Human Resource Flow

THE MORE DYNAMIC the environment (rapid changes in market and technology), the more a corporation must be concerned with managing the flow of people *in, through,* and *out* of the organization. Growth requires recruitment, development, and promotion of an expanding pool of competent managers and technical specialists. Increasing competition in mature industries may require fewer employees—ones with a different mix of talents, capable of responding to different environmental demands. Strategic decisions concerning how an organization will respond to its environment must be matched by equally strategic decisions concerning how the organization will manage the flow of employees. Not having the right skilled workers or managers when they are needed can seriously undermine the success of strategic business choices. Just as damaging is a surplus of human resources which can be costly to the corporation and potentially damaging to the sense of well-being of employees. Unfortunately, the problem of ensuring that the right people are available is not merely a problem of forecasting personnel requirements, difficult as that task is. The availability of needed talent is also a function of the corporation's capacity to attract, keep, and develop the people it needs. These tasks require that management adopt a social capital perspective (see Chapter 1). Employees are treated as investments which if properly supported and developed can yield a long-term stream of benefits to the organization, not as variable costs to be hired when the organization is growing and laid off when the organization is retrenching (though clearly cost effectiveness must be of continuing concern).

A corporation's continually changing requirements for types and numbers of people are sometimes poorly matched with concurrent employee needs for stability and opportunity. The objective of human resource flow policies is to meet the corporation's current and future force requirements and employees' career needs at the same time. Obviously, these objectives may be in conflict. Unions are often formed as a result of conflict between employers and employees about these very issues. Therefore, human resource flow policies must reflect management's values about the relative importance of organization and employee needs.

## THREE PERSPECTIVES IN MANAGING FLOW

We are suggesting that flow policies can be approached from the point of view of the *individual* employee and of the *organization*. Increasingly, these policies must also reflect the interests of yet another stakeholder: the organization's host *society*. These interests are imposed upon the organization through government legislation and regulatory agency policies concerned with such matters as employment, promotion, termination, and retirement. Though the role of government differs from country to country, its involvement reflects the fact that corporate policies on human resource flow have a profound effect on people's economic and psychological well-being, and therefore have an effect on the economic and social well-being of society as a whole. Thus, flow policies can be examined and evaluated from the perspective of the *individual*, the *organization*, and *society*.

### *Individual Perspective*[1]

The term "career" is too often seen as applicable only to the lives of managers and professionals, and not to the lives of nonexempt white- or blue-collar workers. Typically, the term connotes upward mobility and aspiration. From that perspective, an assembly line worker or a restaurant waiter is not thought of as having a career. As a result, corporations focus career development efforts on their professionals and managers, while ignoring blue-collar workers. Since human resource management applies to *all* employees, a broader concept of career seems to be in order. From this broadened perspective, careers may be viewed as "a series of separate but related experiences and adventures through which a person, any person, passes during a lifetime.''[2] Careers can be long or short, and an individual can pursue multiple careers either in sequence or at the same time. In this sense, the concept of career becomes a shorthand notation for a particular set of activities with a natural, unfolding history—involvement over time in a given role or series of roles. Moreover, career includes both an individual's work and family experiences, as well as the interaction between the two.

An individual attempts to gain control of these ''separate but related'' experiences so that they fit an emerging self-concept (self-perception of unique competence and values). At the same time, that self-concept is progressively shaped by work and family experiences. Central to this broader definition of careers is the component of identity. As Erik Erikson has said, identity is never gained once and for all, but is achieved throughout life.

Individual careers develop from an interaction between the competencies and career goals an individual brings to the organization and the work experience the organization provides. To the extent that the organization provides opportunities for the individual to use and develop his or her personal competence while moving through various jobs, functions, and levels, the individual will grow and experience career satisfaction.

Organizations may respond to strategic requirements for certain skills by altering the types of opportunities they provide. For example, a strategic decision to develop more generalists rather than functional specialists must be accompanied by human response policies that provide opportunities for and encourage multifunctional experiences. Multifunctional experiences also provide an opportunity for individuals to clarify their career goals and to decide whether this developmental direction is personally satisfying. Thus, varied experiences act to clarify a person's career goals as well as develop them.

It should be clear that career development is an organic, unfolding process rather than a mechanistic, preprogramed one. Each career experience leads to a new understanding of self as new successes or failures redefine how individuals see themselves, their potential, and their limitations. Each experience therefore reshapes an individual's career aspirations. Major failures can lead to career crises which arise from job choices that do not fit the individual's core competencies and personality. Understanding and managing a process that avoids major failures but makes possible personal learning and growth is critically important if organizations are to develop their employees while at the same time giving them career satisfaction. It is generally accepted that the more control an individual has over career choices, the more the individual is likely to choose a career path that fits his or her core competencies and values, thereby ensuring satisfactions and growth. Historically, individuals had little control over their life's work. Career choices were determined by one's station in life, one's family, and one's society. Most organizations gave employees little control over their careers, preferring to make placement and promotion decisions without consultation. It has become increasingly clear that this practice cannot continue, given the desire and power of today's employees to exert more control over their careers.

One example of this desire and expanding power to control one's own career can be seen in today's "knowledge workers." With marketable skills gained through education rather than through apprenticeship, they have the ability and the interest to exercise substantial control over their careers. With the growth in demand for knowledge workers (skilled labor, professionals, and managers), these individuals will have to be allowed increasing control over the entire course of their working lives, such as becoming established, being promoted, undergoing job changes, reaching a leveling-off point, being fired or laid off, and facing eventual retirement. As we shall see, organizations, too, want control over these events and for this reason a continual tension exists.

This broad concept of career implies that it is impossible for organizations to apply a single definition to what desirable career development is. For managers and professionals, it may be an opportunity to develop and advance, though advancement may be defined differently by an engineer and an achievement-oriented business school graduate. For many blue-collar and white-collar workers, employment security and stability may be more important, while security may be of lesser importance to managers and professionals. Further, assessments of career needs are complicated by changes in career aspirations that take place throughout a person's life.

Effective human resource flow policies and practices must allow a continual process of *matching* individual career needs and organizational requirements. Of course, to the extent that an organization develops an interactive process, it not only allows individuals who want to exercise career choices to do so, but it also arouses desires to make career choices in employees who may not otherwise have thought they had such control their lives. In this regard, such policies can shape the amount of influence employees may come to want over their careers.

It is important to note that employees' perspectives may differ between cultures. Do Japanese workers have different career needs with respect to rapid promotion and do they desire less control over their careers than American workers? We do not know the answer to this and other specific questions about cultural differences, but we do know that cultural and organizational forces shape views of careers just as personal forces do.

### Societal Perspective

It is no longer possible for managers to develop human resource flow policies and priorities without considering the societal perspective. That perspective can be said to impose itself on the organiztion in one of three ways: through the shifting values of the work force, through the impact of outside institutions, and through regulation and labor union policy.

SHIFTING WORK FORCE VALUES.    Complicating the problem of managing human resource flows is an apparent shift in social values away from a view of work as the single most important aspect of life, and toward a view that work is only one of many facets of life. Strategic decisions concerning internal movement and career development of employees can no longer be made without taking into account this growing emphasis on both self-development and family development. Employees no longer automatically accept job assignments that their employers consider important for their development if these assignments conflict with personal and family needs. Similarly, blue-collar workers no longer accept as given the fact that they must and should work overtime. As educational levels increase, blue-collar workers may grow dissatisfied with the same routine job for the duration of their careers. Flow policies that give these workers opportunities for career progress will become more important. These trends probably apply most to economically developed countries where standards of living are high and security needs have been met, freeing individuals to seek fulfillment of other needs. However, good cross-cultural data are not available.

OUTSIDE INSTITUTIONS.    The emergence of knowledge workers as a growing proportion of the work force makes organizations increasingly dependent on educational institutions. Not only do these institutions control the number of people that will be available to corporations, they often create and define career paths in society through program decisions. These institutions also socialize people within particular career paths. The expectation and values of the students they turn out may or may not mesh with organizational realities. When they do not, frustration and turnover are often the result. The current shortage of engineers in high-technology companies, and the frustration of pharmacists with their roles in large pharmaceutical chains are only two examples of such mismatches between the programs of educational institutions and the needs of business. An interactive process between educational institutions and business is required so that educational institutions will be able to shape and modify their programs to business needs so that corporate human resource flow policies will mesh with educational realities.

GOVERNMENT REGULATION AND LABOR UNION POLICY. Government bodies and labor unions are increasingly responding to the needs of people for employment security. There is growing research evidence that the unemployment that results from corporations that treat labor as a variable cost creates psychological stress and social dislocation. Losing one's job can increase family problems, endanger emotional health, and increase the likelihood of alcoholism, drug abuse, psychiatric disorders, cardiovascular disease, and even suicide.[3] In Europe, high severance pay requirements and other legislative restrictions on an employer's freedom to terminate employees have resulted, in part at least, from an awareness of such negative costs. Under the restraints imposed in many European countries, managers will have to manage in a way that stabilizes employment and offers more security. An American firm operating in Belgium recently found that it could no longer afford to tolerate its subsidiary manager's policy of terminating employees he perceived to be ineffective. The costs of termination were just too high. Instead, that manager had to learn to obtain effective performance through better selection and management methods.

As the cost of termination increases, or the flexibility of management decreases—through either government legislation, social pressures, collective bargaining agreements, or explicit unilateral policy decisions by employers—management will have to give increasing attention to deciding which employees to hire in the first place and efforts to train, retrain, or otherwise develop their already available human resources. This has been true for some time in Japan, where approximately 30 percent of the work force—those in large corporations—have lifelong employment, and it appears to be the direction in which some United States corporations are also going.

On the other hand, legislation is often used to open career paths that historically have been available to only a privileged few. Work-force, welfare, and unemployment policies affect the careers of people and the supply of people available to firms. Similarly, licensing and standardization of occupations in various states and industries affect corporate selection and training policies. In the United States, equal opportunity legislation has and will continue to have significant effects on hiring, internal placement and promotions, and termination practices. Selection methods and performance evaluation systems are being challenged in the courts on the grounds of their validity and objectivity. Class action suits, brought against companies by the Equal Employment Opportunity Commission (EEOC) on behalf of groups of employees, can end in settlements worth millions of dollars. The most celebrated of these suits, involving the EEOC and AT&T, ended in a consent decree costing the company $33 million. There has also been an increase in the number of lawsuits that employees in the United States are bringing against corporations claiming unjustified discharge.[4]

The emergence of legislation and regulations governing flow policies reflects the recognition by society that corporate actions have profound effects on the well-being of people and society as a whole. Layoffs, for example, have economic consequences for the communities in which they occur. Because of strong family and community ties, some unemployed workers will remain in their city or state instead of looking for work in other sections of the country. Layoffs thus often place the greatest financial burdens on the communities that can least afford to carry it.

When social and government agencies are burdened by the social and psychological problems resulting from layoffs, *all* citizens end up paying an economic and social price. Though less dramatic, flow policies that do not allow personal development and utilization of employees' talents also reduce the quality of life and have social consequences. For example, Kornhauser found that employees in dull jobs are less involved in family and community affairs.[5]

We may say, then, that human resource flow policies can have significant negative social consequences. On the other hand, they can contribute to the career development and life satisfaction of employees, thereby enhancing societal well-being.

### Organizational Perspective

Managing human resources flow has historically *not* been a major strategic consideration in running a business. Many of the jobs required in business organizations were unique to individual companies and could be acquired only through experience within those organizations. Because of the relatively slow pace of change, skill requirements did not change much over time. Many jobs such as accounting or management had not yet emerged as professions, and there were few technical and professional schools to supply needed talent. Government was relatively uninvolved in employment issues. There was also a large supply of labor willing to move from agriculture to the factory and office.

All of these factors have changed. The emergence of the knowledge workers in the labor force, rapid changes in technology and business practices, the increasing need for generalists, more complex organizations, the emergence of minorities and women, mobility of the work force, and the greater involvement of government have made the management of human resource flow policies a more important consideration. Rapid change can result in costly excess work force, while rapid growth can mean insufficient workers. The unavailability of an experienced plant manager is clearly as critical to the success of an operation as the unavailability of capital resources. From the organization's perspective, effective flow policies should lead to the following outcomes:

1. Availability of the right number of personnel with the needed mix of competences in the short and the long term.
2. Development of people needed to staff the organization in the future.
3. Employee perception of opportunity for advancement and development consistent with their needs.
4. Employee perception of relative security from termination due to factors beyond their control.
5. Employee perception that selection, placement, promotion, and termination decisions are fair.
6. The lowest possible payroll and people-processing costs possible to meet the objectives above.

Finally, it should be understood that policies concerning recruitment, selection, promotion, and termination of employees are the means by which institutions can shape a philosophy of management; they are often the implicit means by which a corporate culture is formed. Not only do people become socialized through their experiences with flow policies, they also come to recognize the qualities of behavior that will be rewarded with promotion, and they come to form views about management's concern for their well-being.

## HUMAN RESOURCE FLOW POLICIES, SYSTEMS, AND PRACTICES

As the discussion so far has indicated, human resource flow must be managed strategically so as to match organizational needs with the career aspirations of employees. This must be done within the constraints imposed by social institutions, and with the well-being of society in mind. At best, managing human resource flow is imperfect. Some people will always be insecure or unhappy with the opportunities afforded them. Every organization has considerable "noise levels" associated with these issues. Similarly, the best personnel planning process may not deliver the people needed by the firm because employees do not grow as expected or because business projections do not materialize. However, major discontinuities can be avoided and employee satisfaction can be increased by more deliberate planning and examination of particular policies, practices, and systems and their relationship to each other. We now turn to a discussion of some of the strategic issues that general managers must consider in managing human resource flow.

## 1. Managing Inflow

Recruitment decisions about where and how to recruit can have an important impact on the composition of the work force, its ultimate fit with the corporation's needs and culture, and employee turnover. These decisions affect all of the four Cs: competence, commitment, congruence (conflict), and cost effectiveness.

Problems in recruiting, particularly for certain professional and technical talent, arise when educational institutions fail to yield an adequate flow of qualified graduates. The recurring shortage of engineers, for example, results from fluctuations in the supply of engineering graduates and experienced engineers (which in turn are related to demographics and past educational patterns), and from fluctuations in the overall demand for engineers.[6] While it is not our purpose to present a detailed discussion of the identification and selection of recruits, we can point to several methods that organizations can use to ensure an adequate supply of talent:

1.  A decision to locate facilities in the proximity of educational institutions that graduate people with the needed competencies or in industrial centers that already employ such people can increase the availability of talent.
2.  Human resource functions can provide schools, particularly schools from which they recruit, with forecasts of future personnel needs.
3.  Corporations can develop their own educational institutions, as Wang Laboratories and General Motors have done.
4.  An organization that develops a good reputation as an employer in such areas as employment security, compensation, employee relations, and opportunity for challenging work and growth can increase its capacity to attract recruits.
5.  Corporations can establish ongoing relationships with universities by assigning key executives to coordinate recruiting and by donating time, equipment, and people to those schools.
6.  Corporations can use visits and summer jobs as a way of identi-

fying talent and involving students early in their schooling, perhaps several years before they are ready to enter the job market.

## Criteria for Judging Recruiting Effectiveness

Recruitment policies need to be considered as part of an organization's overall strategy for two reasons. The first and more obvious reason is that recruitment seeks to provide the organization with people who have the talents needed to achieve strategic goals. But recruitment will also have significant impact on long-range employment stability and turnover. Employee turnover is both disruptive and costly. It is well known that the most important reason for turnover within the first several years of employment is unmet expectations, and these disappointments are often a function of the recruitment process itself. Managers motivated to attract scarce talent tend to discuss only positive elements of the job and company while glossing over less attractive realities. They do not help the prospective employee to assess realistically the fit between personal skills and goals and the job and the organization. A more open process of communicating organizational realities would yield employees who were satisfied with their careers. New hires would be more highly motivated to adapt themselves to organizational realities. The likelihood of fit in expectations, skills, and core values between themselves and the organization would be higher because more self-selection would take place. Some companies have found that training line managers to conduct recruiting interviews can improve the effectiveness of recruitment. The interviewee can also take some responsibility by asking hard questions and testing for fit between him- or herself and the organization.

The discussion above suggests that the recruitment and "joining up" process should not be looked at only from the point of view of its impact on cost effectiveness and congruence or conflict. Recruiting can be an important strategy for shaping the culture of the organization. It is at the time of recruitment and entry into the organization that an implicit "psychological contract" begins to be formed between employee and organization. Prospective employees receive many signals about what the company expects, just as company recruiters make many judgments about the fit of the prospective employee with the company.

Understanding these transactions can help general managers understand the culture of their organization. Reshaping these transactions can help them develop their organization in desired directions. For example, the choice of which managers in the corporation will recruit and make final selection decisions will affect who enters the orga-

nization, and what their competencies, predispositions, values, and expectations will be. It is for this reason that key line managers often
involve themselves in recruitment interviews. They want to influence
the inflow of personnel because they know it is a major lever for shaping the company.

## 2. Managing Internal Flow

Once employees have been recruited, their flow through the organization—transfers, job assignments, promotions, and demotions—must
be managed so that their competence is developed to meet corporate
needs, while at the same time they satisfy their own career aspirations.
We will now discuss key considerations in managing internal flows: the
velocity of personnel flow, the assessment and measurement of performance effectiveness, and the development of employee skills and
competencies. Each of these considerations must be viewed in terms of
its impact on organizational effectiveness and employee and societal
well-being.

### Velocity of Personnel Flow

By velocity of personnel flow, we mean the rate at which employees move from job to job. Velocity may be examined for horizontal
movement (lateral transfers) and vertical movement (promotions). It
varies widely between different employee groups in the corporation.
Historically, middle and upper middle managers have moved from job
to job rather frequently; the average time in a job being as low as two to
three years in some corporations. Among clerical workers or techni-
cians, the average time in a job may be far higher, say five to ten years.
Similarly, managers in mature industries are likely to be in their jobs
far longer than managers in growth industries like high technology or
health care. Finally, velocity for different employee groups will vary
across time periods. For example, the postwar baby boom will lead to a
large population increase in the 35 to 50 age category between 1980
and 1990. That increase will be accompanied by a relatively slower
growth in middle management jobs, resulting in fewer opportunities
and slower upward movement.

CORPORATE STRATEGY AND VELOCITY.    Any given velocity may
have positive and negative outcomes with predicatable benefits and
costs, and these must be balanced by the general manager. The important point is that velocity is part of managing human resource flow and
it warrants monitoring. Naturally, flow velocities are sometimes be-

yond control of management—demographics, for example, will affect velocity. But managers make some decisions that have consequences for human resource flow velocities but are not immediately recognized to have such effects. For example, strategic decisions concerning how rapidly a corporation grows will affect flow velocities. Too often, market opportunities are considered far more important than human resource considerations in determining a growth strategy. The potential consequences of insufficient human resources on profitable growth and the effects of rapid growth on quality of life need to be weighed.

Decisions about how many employees are to be recruited each year also affect velocity, as well as the availability of trained personnel in the future. Uneven recruiting from year to year, often brought on by economic cycles, can force rapid movement and promotion for one cohort of entering employees and too-slow movement for another. Such uneven recruiting patterns result in an uneven supply of talent to replace retiring employees or feed growth. Companies with lifetime employment that promote only from within have learned that steady recruitment is necessary to assure a balanced distribution of age and skill in the work force.

In evaluating the strategic impact of velocity decisions, managers can consider the impact of their decisions on the following HRM outcomes:

1. *Satisfaction and commitment.* Satisfaction of employees with career development will increase if upward mobility in the corporation becomes more rapid. Lateral transfers also seem to have a similar effect. These in turn are likely to increase commitment to the organization because employees see a bright future in terms of personal rewards.
2. *Competence.* A curvilinear relationship probably exists between velocity and the development of employee competence. That is, slow movement of personnel (laterally or vertically) is likely to result in too few opportunities for employees to broaden their skills and their perspective of the enterprise—that is, to develop as generalists. On the other hand, the type of very rapid personnel movement that is experienced in rapid growth companies can easily result in individuals progressing faster than their capacity to develop and demonstrate skills. The result can be failure for the individual (the well-known Peter Principle) and a resulting loss of investment by the company.
3. *Motivation.* There is also a curvilinear relationship between velocity and motivation. Too many years in the same job will reduce motivation, as the challenge that comes from efforts to

master a new task declines.[7] On the other hand, insufficient time to master a task not only leads to the inadequate development mentioned above, but may prevent individuals from developing a sense of competence and a continued desire to achieve.

4. *Congruence.* Slower advancement can lead employees to question the fairness of the decision-making process in the corporation. The consequence can be litigation by employees, particularly women and minorities. On the other hand, high velocity can be so demanding that quality of life suffers, particularly in relationships with family. Personal stress and higher divorce rates are not uncommon among employees in rapidly growing high-technology companies. Similar symptoms have been found among blue-collar employees in new plants that are attempting to increase commitment by having employees rotate jobs, take more responsibility, and assume accountability.

5. *Costs.* High flow velocities are more costly. An employee who has been on the job a short time is less effective. Also, the costs of training and transfers are high and getting higher. Finally, the risks of employee failure and costly mistakes resulting from inexperience must be considered.

### Defining and Evaluating Employee Effectiveness

The management of personnel flow through the organization requires continual judgments by managers about potential effectiveness of recruits and employees. Poor judgments translate into failure for the individual, immediate costs resulting from poor performance, and long-range costs associated with missed opportunities to promote employees who have potential. Too many bad personnel decisions can leave an organization without adequate backup personnel to fill openings created by promotions or retirements. The cumulative impact of poor individual judgments will ultimately impair the ability of the organization and its subunits to meet their strategic and business goals.

The biggest problem in selecting and evaluating effective employees is the subjective nature of the process. Except for education, academic performance, and specific technical skills, it is hard to measure the characteristics that are assumed to be predictive of performance: motivation, cooperation, ability to make decisions, initiative, ability to work under pressure, capacity to develop, and capacity to supervise. Even when attempting to be objective about whether a candidate possesses certain qualities, a manager sees the candidate through his or her own personality, past experiences, and values. Managers tend to hire people in their own image. While such an approach may ensure smooth boss-subordinate relationships, it may not ensure effectiveness, particularly if the biases imposed on the selection process—temperament, dress, social mannerisms, etc.—are not in actuality related to performance. Since managers' values and predispositions are subtly shaped by the culture of the organization, the potential for systematic bias throughout the organization is high.

One of the by-products of managers hiring in their own image has been systematic discrimination against minorities and women. Government has responded to this discrimination with legislation such as the Civil Rights Act of 1964, requiring employers to hire and promote women and minorities in proportion to their presence in the larger population. If they cannot do this, employers must prove that their personnel decision-making process is baed on job-relevant selection criteria. While some corporations have always had an interest in developing good and fair selection and evaluation procedures, government legislation and the potential for costly court decisions have stimulated a wider concern about this problem.

Unfortunately, efforts to develop objective employee evaluation procedures have not met with great success. To be sure, psychological testing, assessment centers, and improved performance appraisal systems have contributed to some improvements in the judgments that can be made. But these methods have not changed the fact that it is fallible human beings who fill out appraisal forms or integrate information from tests and third-party assessments into their decision-making process. We suggest that the task of evaluating performance be approached with realistic expectations. Countless corporations have experienced a common pattern when new procedures for selecting and evaluating employees are established: an initial period of enthusiasm is followed by general disillusionment as problems become evident. Finally, another new method is developed to solve those problems, and the whole pattern repeats itself.[8]

At best, the *methods* of selection and evaluation will be imperfect in their capacity to measure performance and potential and in their capacity to meet tests of objectivity and fairness. This suggests that more emphasis be placed on the *process* of selection and evaluation and how it is embedded in the larger organization, and on the amount of influence employees have on that process. Such influence can come through the participation of employees in the definition of effectiveness and through their direct involvement in evaluating prospective employees, peers, and bosses. Employee effectiveness traditionally has been defined and evaluated exclusively by management, but consultation with employees can give managers the opportunity to improve their own judgments with relevant information and improve employee perception of fairness.

With this perspective in mind, we now proceed to a discussion of two major questions that must be addressed in managing the selection and evaluation process: what is effectiveness and how will effectiveness be evaluated?

WHAT IS EFFECTIVENESS?    That question must be addressed at two levels of analysis: the immediate job for which a person is being considered, and the culture of the organization in which that job is situated. Except for some blue-collar, clerical, and technical positions that are relatively easy to define, insufficient attention has been given to identifying the requirements for job success. As a result, typical specifications call for certain academic standing and work experience. These specifications have the virtue of being measurable. Unfortunately, they may not be relevant. Most selection processes, particularly those for higher-level jobs, tend to be based more on general parameters and subjective assessments than on defined characteristics that are assessed with objectivity.[9]

A clear statement of job responsibilities is also not entirely helpful because these cannot always be translated into the skills, abilities, and knowledge that the individual must possess. Managers concerned with improving selection and promotion decisions must invest time and energy, both of which are quite costly commodities, in specifying the task segments of a job and translating these into the specific skills and knowledge required to perform the job. Personnel departments can help. But if the resulting definition of effectiveness is to be truly relevant to the organization's task, managers must be involved in the definition process.

Effectiveness, particularly in managerial positions, is also a function of the organization's culture. Over time, many characteristics and ways of doing things come to be valued by the organization and are implicitly or explicitly taken into account during selection and promotion processes. General managers must attempt to define as explicitly as possible what individual characteristics are valued. Personnel specialists can help by researching the characteristics that distinguish effective and ineffective performers as defined by judgments of the corporation's managers. This research process makes it possible for managers to examine these characteristics for their relevance to business strategy and organizational effectiveness and helps them identify irrelevant biases or important omissions. It allows top management to determine if their philosophy is adequately represented in personnel decisions and to take appropriate action if it is not.

Organizations that rely on a strong culture of shared traditions and beliefs for achieving employee commitment must be especially concerned about selecting and promoting individuals with characteristics that fit that culture. Such organizations can sustain their culture only if they maintain a fairly high degree of homogeneity of values. They are, therefore, likely to emphasize personality and management style as significant dimensions, perhaps more than technical skill. Of course, by doing so they may discriminate against certain employees, and take the risk that their biases violate legislative guidelines or society's values.

So far, little has been said about results—sales, costs, profits, market share, number of units produced, etc.—as a criterion of effectiveness. This is not because we believe that the attainment of results is irrelevant, but because results are not the *only* criterion of effectiveness, even when they are espoused to be the primary criterion for promotion and compensation decisions. When first introduced, quantitative measures of results were thought to be the way to make performance evaluations more objective. However, such measures do not always reflect important dimensions of performance nor are they always within the control of employees. Thus, ''process'' dimensions of effectiveness (those having to do with *how* the job is done) are often introduced in personnel decisions. Furthermore, the accomplishment of results at one level is not always a good predictor of whether an employee will be able to function effectively at higher levels in the organization.

Figure 4–1 illustrates this point. Individuals who achieve results *and* exhibit the behaviors, attitudes, and characteristics that experience suggests are effective and/or that managers believe to be effective are clearly effective performers and possess the potential to rise in the organization. Individuals who do not obtain results and do not fit are rarely retained by organizations because they do not appear to have the potential to succeed. It is the individuals in the other two quadrants who present dilemmas for organizations. Those who do not achieve results but do fit behaviorally are sometimes promoted well beyond their level of competence. Organizations that attempt to identify high-potential employees early in their careers are subject to this error. These individuals may be promoted so rapidly on their *assumed* potential that they never master either the business management or technical task. On the other hand, some employees are not promoted despite a consistent record of results because they are not judged to possess the skills required for higher-level positions and/or because they do not fit the culture. For example, some successful plant managers or successful deal-makers in banks do not understand how they could have been passed over for promotion, given their job performance. What they do not understand, and what has not been made explicit by their organizations, is that certain behavioral skills and personal styles are as strategically important to the organization as are quantifiable and measurable technical skills. Because they do not know what these behavioral skills and style characteristics are or how strategically important they are relative

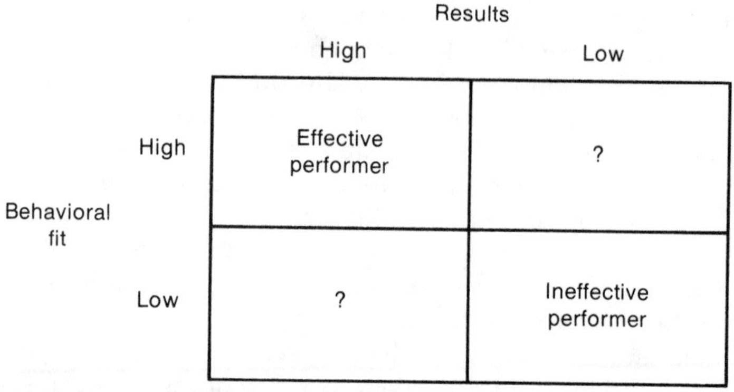

Results

|  | | High | Low |
|---|---|---|---|
| Behavioral fit | High | Effective performer | ? |
| | Low | ? | Ineffective performer |

**FIGURE 4-1    Effectiveness Dimensions**

to results, these individuals are unable to develop them or make the decision to seek other employment—an argument for explicitly defining and communicating behaviors associated with effectiveness.

If behavior is to be a criterion, attention must be given to the question of fairness as viewed by employees. Employees who do not believe that the criteria being utilized are relevant will either leave the organization or protest by seeking legal redress or union protection. In the past, management has dealt with this problem by commissioning personnel research studies to establish the objectivity of effectiveness criteria. But this approach still leaves the power for defining effectiveness with management. An alternative approach may be to allow employees more influence in selecting managers or peers as a way of giving them influence in the definition of effectiveness. Peer ratings, which have been shown to be good predictors of effectiveness, probably gain their validity because peers possess information about each other that superiors may not possess. Some of the most innovative work systems in the United States involve members of work teams in the selection of new employees, although getting employees to rate their peers is difficult and requires extraordinary maturity and interpersonal competence. Employee task forces may be involved in defining effectiveness for their group, department, or plant, creating the standards that will guide personnel decisions in the organizations as a whole. Employee influence in defining effectiveness can only work, however, if employees and management share common goals.

HOW WILL EFFECTIVENESS BE EVALUATED?    Organizations face two sets of evaluation problems: evaluation of *prospective* and of *current* employees. Even if effectiveness has been adequately defined, managers must still assess the extent to which individuals possess certain characteristics. The most common methods for doing this are the employment and performance appraisal interviews. Because both methods have been shown to be subject to bias, they have been supplemented with other methods:

1. Structured interviews
2. Interviews or performance evaluations by multiple managers/evaluators
3. Checklists of derived characteristics as guides to the employment and performance appraisal interview
4. Paper-and-pencil tests of ability, intelligence, personality, and interest
5. Clinical assessments by psychologists or consultants
6. Internally administered assessment centers and performance tests that ask individuals to perform tasks under simulated conditions

These methods structure the assessment process so that information gathered is more reliable (less subject to errors in measurement) and more valid (the information is relevant and predicts effectiveness with greater accuracy) than is the information collected in employment and appraisal interviews alone. The predictive power of these additional assessment techniques is established by one of two types of validity studies. Either the characteristics being measured have been shown to be correlated with the present performance of current employees (concurrent validity), or scores on tests or evaluations are correlated with later performance on the job or advancement in the organization (predictive validity). Another method for determining the validity of an assessment procedure is to examine whether the knowledge and skills being assessed represent adequately the actual content of the job (content validity). These methods of validation have all been subject to challenge in the courts. Of the three methods, content validity is most likely to be upheld by the courts. If more than one of the approaches to validation described above have been used, the organization's assessment methods have generally been upheld.

Many corporations prefer not to use either paper-and-pencil tests or assessment centers during recruitment for fear that applicants will resent being subjected to such an evaluation process. Some companies use these methods to help evaluate the potential of existing employees, while others may attempt to increase objectivity (validity) through multiple appraisals, checklists of relevant characteristics, and the use of in-depth clinical interviews by psychologists or personnel specialists. Self-selection by prospective and present employees is a method that is underused by corporations. If employees are informed candidly and in some depth about the characteristics that are required for success, they will eventually select jobs or career tracks that are realistic given their talents and aspirations.

Discussions about the validity of various testing and measurement tools have usually been the province of staff specialists. However, we are suggesting that general managers need some familiarity both with the general concept of validity and with the specific applications within their organizations. More structured and well-researched methods of assessment can improve the organization's probability of selecting the right people for specific jobs when effectiveness has been defined. What is less clear is the impact of these methods on the relationship between the individual and the organization. Do applicants or existing employees who are subjected to the various impersonal selection procedures resent them and, as a result, decide to go elsewhere? If so, what kind of people are alienated by these procedures, and how do they differ from those who are not? Would an emphasis on self-selection as opposed to formal selection procedures demonstrate an organization's commitment to informed choice and self-control over career? If so, how would this emphasis affect who decides to take a job and how that individual subsequently relates to the corporation? These are all questions that general managers, as well as testing and measurement staff specialists, must weigh.

The challenge to managers is to take advantage of available measurement and testing technology, while not losing sight of its effects on how recruits perceive and later relate to the organization. The companies most successful in their use of sophisticated assessment methods have usually avoided using results in a rigid manner. It is important to recognize that the more openly and regularly assessment results are discussed with inside or outside candidates, the more trust candidates have in those results.

Evaluations of employee effectiveness and potential are usually performed by supervisors and then used by management to make personnel decisions. An enormous amount of time, money, and energy has gone into the development of different performance appraisal systems. While improved appraisal systems may better reflect job content, successful implementation still rests largely with the managers involved in the process. And a significant number of managers resist evaluating their subordinates. When controls force them to evaluate, they provide ratings of questionable validity. In response, some corporations have adopted forced distributions in rating employees. Quotas mandate a fixed percentage of employees that will be placed in each of the rating categories from poor to excellent. This type of forced distribution, however, is resented by managers and subordinates alike. It has the potential for damaging the self-esteem of individuals, particularly since studies have shown that a disproportionate percentage of employees rate themselves as high performers.

Research evidence and experience suggest that managers assign more accurate performance ratings when those ratings are not used to make personnel decisions and/or when they are not made available to subordinates. Because evaluations of performance are a matter of judgment, managers are naturally concerned about negative impacts on pay, promotion, and job security. They also prefer not to discuss these ratings with subordinates, because they do not want to damage relationships. If they have to justify the ratings or if personnel decisions about pay, promotions, or terminations are to be made as a result of their judgments, ratings tend to be less valid.

For this reason, it has been recommended that evaluation for administrative purposes (pay and promotion) be kept separate from evaluations for career development purposes. Developmental evaluations should be performed at different times from pay and promotion assessments, and the results should not be placed in personnel files. By separating these two evaluation processes, it is hoped that evaluations for administrative purposes will be more accurate, while performance feedback discussions will be open, but not overly evaluative.

There are no easy solutions; it is unlikely that the evaluation problem will ever be completely resolved. The most creative solutions have concentrated on the *process* rather than the *method* of appraisal and on *developing manager ability and motivation to evaluate accurately and communicate* this evaluation openly to subordinates.

### Employee Career Development

There are really two major concerns that a human resource flow policy must address when considering ways of managing internal flow. The first, addressed above, is the question of how to define and evaluate performance effectiveness. Consistent with the social capital perspective of HRM introduced in Chapter 1, we would also suggest that internal flow policies need to address the matter of employee and career development. After selection, employee development is one of the key methods available to corporations for ensuring the mix of skills needed to be competitive in the future. It is a form of investment which is directly related to the corporation's capacity to be flexible and adaptable to changes in its environment. In short, employee development is a key strategy for organizational survival and growth.

Far from taking a coherent and strategic approach to employee development, many corporations engage in scattered, uncoordinated, or even inconsistent developmental activities that are poorly suited to the developmental needs of individuals or to the corporation's strategic needs. Training departments plan programs and market them internally in accordance with their perceptions of developmental needs, which do not always coincide with the strategic goals of the company or individual employee needs. Employees are often transferred or promoted on a timetable dictated by organizational needs, not by their own readiness. Participation in a training program may not coincide effectively with the need for education created by a job transfer or promotion. Assessment, feedback and counseling methods are rarely coordinated to maximize the learning and development of the individual. This lack of coordination between centralized practices and the individual's needs can reduce development, because as we stated at the beginning of this chapter, individual development is an organic unfolding process, not a mechanistic one.

The challenge, then, is to *stimulate* and *guide* an essentially individual developmental process in a way that is consistent with corporate needs. Some corporations operate with few centrally planned career development programs, while others have chosen to centralize and control the process to the detriment of individual choice, growth, and career satisfaction. The most effective approach is for general managers to create a context that encourages employee development in directions that meet corporate needs but does not overdetermine the speed or direction of any given individual's development.

We have said that the *career development* process encompasses *a series of experiences* that stretch individuals to learn new knowledge, attitudes, and behavior. Through this process, employees can determine if they have the core competencies to master the task. If they do not, they obtain feedback that the career directions chosen are not the right ones. If they do master the new experiences or jobs, the resulting sense of accomplishment confirms the direction chosen and sustains it as long as the experience continues to be satisfying. Employees must, of course, stay in their jobs long enough to obtain closure, to see the results of their efforts. This cannot happen when the velocity of movement in the firm is too rapid.[10] It should be clear that the most important developmental experiences are job and task experiences. This fact is not always reflected in the mix and sequence of developmental tools used by corporations. Education and training, which are not always sequenced to complement a special assignment, seem to work best when job experiences have motivated an individual to learn needed knowledge, and when they are accompanied by feedback on performance and counseling from a respected supervisor.

When the slow growth of a firm precludes promotions as a means of providing growth experiences, job enrichment—the redesign of work to include more responsibilities—is used increasingly to stimulate development and reduce costs. Enrichment is usually applied to traditionally fairly narrow blue-collar jobs, but it can also be applied to middle management, where too many jobs and levels have increased costs and reduced opportunity. Lateral transfers are another method of providing an opportunity for development and growth short of promotions.

Figure 4-2 illustrates the multiple tools that must be properly mixed and sequenced by the supervisor and employee working collaboratively to enhance the employee's development. Organizations need to inventory these tools in order to make them known to managers and to develop plans to help managers use them. Education programs are easier to inventory than job enrichment programs, which is why they are more frequently used. But it is the competence of supervisors in performance appraisal, coaching, counseling, modeling, and supporting that is the key to a program's success. Therefore, if career development is to occur in an organization, general managers must find ways

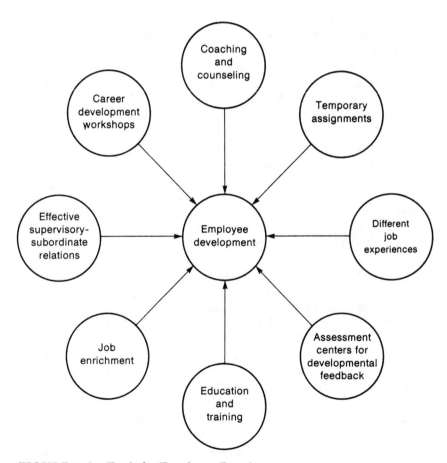

**FIGURE 4-2    Tools for Employee Development**

to select, train, and reward so as to build these elusive developmental skills. Some corporations are supplementing the supervisor's role in coaching and counseling with a staff of personnel specialists trained in this task. Career development workshops and assessment centers are also utilized to provide participants with a guided experience in exploring their interests and aspirations.

Perhaps the most important but underutilized part of the developmental process is follow-up. When developmental plans are created by a supervisor and submitted to the personnel department, it is essential that the company follow up to determine what the result has been. As we shall see, the key to follow-up is a continuous forum for discussing the potential of employees and their developmental needs.

We now turn to a brief examination of the context that general managers might create to encourage employee/career development, and discuss some of the elements of that context.

PHILOSOPHY AND REWARDS.    In some companies few resources are available for education and career development, and supervisors do not spend much time discussing performance or doing career planning. In others, such as AT&T, Exxon and IBM, considerable emphasis is placed on these activities. Exxon's chief executive officer, Clifford Garvin, meets frequently with the corporate compensation and executive development committee to discuss the top 250 executives in the company.[11] For a career development process to be encouraged centrally but not overly controlled, managers throughout the corporation must share a belief that employee development is important and will be rewarded. This shared belief must be articulated by the organization's leaders. They must provide a model for effective career development in their relations with subordinates and they must explicitly and visibly reward managers for developing people.

CAREER OPPORTUNITY INFORMATION.    In order to ensure that employee development is successfully meshed with an organization's strategy, it is essential that the organization encourage employees not just to develop, but to develop in directions required by that strategy. Are technical skills likely to become less valued in the next five years as compared with general management skills? Will the company be placing more emphasis in the upcoming years on the interpersonal and behavioral skills of its managers? Is it likely to need a more aggressive sales force? Will competitiveness hinge on low costs, efficiency, and productivity? It is not only important for organizations to be able to answer such questions, but the answers must also be *communicated* to employees. Only through such communication will employees have some idea of what skills will be valued in the future and what experiences are considered important in developing those skills.

To do this well, corporations should project the types of jobs and skills requirements they estimate will exist in the future given their business strategies. Will the competitive edge in the future be obtained through production, sales, or technical work? What mix of skills is likely to be valued, to fit evolving corporate strategy and culture? Just as important, what have been the career paths to general management or technical management in the past? Estimates of future growth can never be totally accurate, but employees should be encouraged to think about what paths successful people in various careers have followed and how these paths might change in the future. Information can be disseminated through publications, training programs, and the audio-visual medium.

CAREER PATHS.   The career paths a corporation makes available to its employees have an important influence on the extent and nature of their development. One way to characterize career paths is in terms of whether they encourage functional or technical specialization, or whether they encourage cross-functional mobility. Investigations of companies that have not adapted well to competitive pressures, those in the steel industry for example, show that these companies have developed few generalists capable of becoming general managers, product managers, or program managers. Individuals were brought in at the bottom of a function and promoted within it, causing them to retain a specialist's view.[12] A strategic emphasis on adaptation to new competitive demands might suggest an emphasis on cross-functional mobility in order to break down barriers between functions, develop individuals who understand the views of other functional specialists, and develop employees committed to the solution of business problems.

We are not advocating that all firms adopt cross-functional career paths, nor that all individuals be encouraged to take them. Along with the benefits described, there are some costs. Some depth of functional and/or technical expertise may be sacrificed. It is important, however, for corporations to make conscious policy choices about how much cross-functional or divisional mobility they desire, consistent with other strategic choices concerning the direction of the corporation.

In each organization, there are some career paths that are more valued than others. The valued track can be managerial (referred to as cross-functional above), or it can be technical. Typically, managerial jobs are more valued for the status, power, and monetary rewards associated with them. Attracted by these rewards, individuals in technical or sales jobs often attempt to switch careers and seek managerial positions despite the fact that their skills and/or interests may lie in their technical specialties. A firm needs to examine the career decisions that its internal job market encourages to determine if these decisions are consistent with its strategy and needs for employee competence.

Traditionally, blue-collar workers and white-collar clerical and technical employees have not had much opportunity to progress to more challenging jobs. Locked into their stations, their on-the-job enthusiasm and capacity for learning and growth declines. In response, some companies have attempted to stimulate growth and commitment through job rotation or job enrichment. Others have designed skill-based pay systems that align rewards with learning and development. We will explore some of these efforts in later chapters.

Companies also need to consider the opportunities for upward mobility that they provide to blue-collar and white-collar clerical and technical employees. A two-class society has been created in many companies, lowering cooperation and commitment to common goals. The removal of artificial barriers to advancement such as the requirement of a college degree is one method of increasing employee competence and commitment. Other ways of increasing the corporation's human assets include providing education and training (or the opportunity to seek it), and providing job experiences that allow lower-level workers to gain the knowledge, attitudes, and behavior required to join the managerial class.

CAREER AUTHORITY AND CONTROL.    We discussed earlier the importance of individual control over the developmental process. There are three principle means by which the corporation can provide individuals with control over their careers.

First, a company can develop a cadre of *personnel development specialists* to whom employees may go directly to discuss their career goals and receive information about realistic career possibilities. These specialists typically are involved in helping managers find candidates for open positions, so they are aware of opportunities. They provide an employee with an alternate route for career management if his or her boss is ineffective or too controlling. But these specialists also serve the corporation, which means they play the difficult role of representing both employees *and* the company in personnel transactions.

Second, employees can be asked to fill out an *inventory of skills and job preference*, which can be cross-referenced for use in job searches.

Third, a system of *job posting* allows employees to apply for other positions in the company when they become vacant. An increasing number of companies are using this method in an attempt to give more direct career control to employees. It calls for employees to respond to announcements (postings) of positions and to be considered just as if they were external job applicants. The personnel department may screen applicants for a job before giving the hiring manager a list of potential candidates. The hiring manager interviews applicants, decides who to hire, and provides feedback to successful and unsuccessful applicants. Job posting has been adopted widely, particularly for lower-level jobs, because it appears to solve the problems of control. The courts and regulatory agencies such as the EEOC have looked favorably on job posting as in indication of affirmative action and nondiscrimination, one reason why an increasing number of corporations are adopting the system. However, job posting does not ensure fairness. In some cases, supervisors have decided who they want to hire before posting, making the interview a sham. Furthermore, the screening process is subject to bias. Finally, unless the company is willing to explain to employees why they have been rejected, the system may simply raise expectations and then dash them. Despite its weaknesses, job posting has potential for giving individuals some control over their careers, provided the corporation is open and willing to invest in the method by giving supervisors the proper training.

These three approaches to managing internal flow are not mutually exclusive. Together they offer an opportunity for giving an increasing amount of career control to employees; but that control will not be felt until corporations are able to change the paternalistic attitudes of managers concerning employee influence over their careers.


## 3. Managing Outflow

A company may attempt to improve its mix of competencies rapidly by increasing the outflow of personnel through early retirement programs and/or layoffs of the lowest performers. Early retirement increases the percentage of younger personnel who management often believes are more flexible in adjusting to a changing business future than older, more entrenched employees. At the same time, personnel reductions allow for a rapid lowering of payroll costs, which can improve profitability in the short term. In the United States, this scenario has been used by companies in many industries as a response to recession and competition. Pressured by the quarterly earnings expectations of investors, corporate management has used work-force reductions as a major strategy for maintaining earnings and dividends expected by investors, stock analysts, and financial institutions. It has been one of the primary means by which mature industries such as autos, steel and rubber have attempted to cope with international competition in the early 1980s.

As we have already mentioned, legislation in some European countries and a social contract between unions and management in Japan have placed significant constraints on layoffs in those countries. Some restrictive legislation on terminations and layoffs is also beginning to be seen in the United States, suggesting that American managers will find it increasingly difficult to use personnel outflow as a strategic response to competitive pressures. Individual rights and the welfare of society will become more important considerations. Under the Age Discrimination in Employment Act of 1967, as amended in 1978, older employees are protected from forced retirement prior to age 70. In some states there is no upper limit. "There is a tremendous increase in employee lawsuits, particularly over age, sex and race discrimination and unjustified discharge," says Robert Conken, president of the American Arbitration Association.[13] These pressures will modify the policies of U.S. firms toward more caution in layoff and terminations, ultimately moving them closer to the full employment model.

The *central strategic dilemma* for managers is how to balance the needs and rights of employees for employment security with the requirements of the corporation to use personnel outflow as a means of cost reductions and renewal. Research evidence and experience demonstrate that employees who become insecure because of work force reductions are less productive and less committed to the organization.[14] The best tend to leave after the economy turns around. On the other hand, unless corporations take extraordinary care in the selection, training, and internal movement of personnel, legislative barriers to outflow can erode competitive position. How can corporations and society obtain the benefits of employee security without incurring the costs of overstaffing and stagnation?

LIFELONG EMPLOYMENT/TERMINATION FOR POOR PERFORMANCE. Lifelong systems, such as those at IBM and Hewlett-Packard, guarantee employment only if performance is maintained. If performance declines, so does pay, and employees are pressured either to improve their performance or to reexamine their relationship with the company. Terminations occur for poor performance on a case-by-case basis and not when a recession and profit squeeze provide a convenient excuse. This policy requires continual attention by management to performance and a willingness to confront problems.

LIFELONG EMPLOYMENT FOR A CORE GROUP.    If a corporation cannot offer employment security to all of its employees, it may still choose to offer it to some of them. The number of employees is based on the lowest employment level economic circumstances are likely to force on the corporation. Ford Motor and the UAW agreed in their 1982 contract to institute such a policy at two experimental plants, subject to worker approval, for the life of the contract. The assumption is that it is better to remove job security as an issue for a core group (at these two Ford plants, 80 percent of the work force) who can then be asked to waive restrictive work practices and to participate in improving productivity. This policy does not deal with the potential obsolescence of the core group nor is it known what effects the policy will have on relations between protected and unprotected employees.

DOWNWARD AND LATERAL CAREER MOBILITY.  One means of achieving a better balance between required job skills and job holders without termination is to utilize downward and lateral mobility, particularly late in a person's career. A division manager may move down to head a function from which he or she came, or a salesperson who has been promoted to management may welcome returning to sales again if he or she is given proper status and recognition. Companies that de-emphasize hierarchical position and emphasize professional competence as a source of power are more able to move employees out of managerial positions with dignity.

CAREER RENEWAL.  Companies can encourage individuals to leave oversupplied positions and move to undersupplied positions through effective training and development programs. Job retraining for laid off employees is a variation of this concept. Both Ford Motor and General Motors have negotiated with the UAW to undertake an extensive job retraining effort for laid off employees; the programs will be managed and funded jointly as part of the 1982 contract.

EARLY RETIREMENT.  By offering special financial inducements, many companies have increased the outflow of personnel they consider unable to adapt to a realignment of the firm. Usually the inducement is retirement at an earlier age without a reduction in pension. The employee is able to retire at age 55, but will receive benefits he or she would have received at 62 or 65. The individual is then free to pursue a new career if he or she so chooses, and the firm can offer promotions to those they believe to be more competent to perform in the future. This is the single most popular option for managing outflow used today by American firms to revitalize themselves in the face of international competition.

WORK-FORCE REDUCTION THROUGH ATTRITION.  Given the short-term severance and outplacement costs of work-force reductions, the savings in salaries are often overstated, particularly if cuts are not assumed to be the only way of eliminating poor performers. If one adds the costs of lower productivity and commitment, a case can be made for reducing the work force through attrition in conjunction with training and lateral or downward mobility.[15] The attrition alternative is not sufficiently considered, because a cost-benefit analysis is rarely conducted (particularly with regard to the impact on organization effectiveness). In times of adversity, finance and control functions, with their relatively short-term focus on quarterly earnings, gain power at the expense of the human resource function which takes a long-term perspective.

OUTPLACEMENT.    A recent survey[16] found that 40 percent of the companies in its sample use outplacement firms that take over immediately after a person has been terminated and help him or her launch a job search. While outplacement service is typically offered only to higher-paid executives, there are examples of firms providing extensive outplacement counseling for a broader spectrum of employees terminated in a work-force reduction. Providing outplacement services demonstrates a sense of responsibility by the firm to those terminated, to the public, and to the remaining employees. In moderate recessionary periods, outplacement can result in better adjustments to termination and even salary increases in new positions.[17] If individuals are supported economically during the unemployed period, they may find their way to satisfying second or third careers or to organizations that fit them better. If outplacement works in this way, it can provide firms with a less costly alternative to guaranteed employment while still offering *career security* to individuals.

CRITICAL POINT REVIEWS.    If an effective outplacement process allows separation without severe psychological or economic trauma, then why not induce employees to reexamine their places in the firm periodically instead of waiting for an economic downswing to force reexamination? This is the approach taken at Corning Glass Works. Every five years, bosses and personnel development specialists conduct reviews to determine whether it makes sense for an individual to remain with the firm given his or her needs, available opportunities, and the firm's view of his or her potential. A joint decision to stay or leave is agreed upon. Since both parties are presumably committed to the decision, separation, if it occurs, is less painful and more amicable. The firm's reputation in its labor markets is not damaged and it can go on to provide opportunities for other employees.

In summary, policies affecting personnel outflow need to be considered as part of an organization's overall strategy, since they will have a major impact on the commitment of employees and on the ability of the firm to be competitive. A combination of the policies and practices outlined above may make it possible for firms in the United States, where legislation has not yet restricted managerial freedom with respect to layoffs and termination, to find a path that balances employees' needs for reasonable employment security with the corporate need to maintain a quality and quantity of personnel consistent with being competitive.

## FAIRNESS IN MANAGING HUMAN RESOURCE FLOW

Every society must deal with the problem of justice. Unless citizens believe they are treated fairly and have the opportunity for their grievances to be adjudicated, they will not be committed to that society; conflict and disintegration will result. Corporations as mini-societies are not exempt from the need to deal with the problem of fairness, particularly with respect to managing personnel flow. There are few issues on which employees or prospective employees feel more strongly than unfair practices with respect to hiring, promotion, and termination. The perception of the fairness of these policies is thus as strategically important to the organization as the particular system and procedures selected to implement the policies. For that reason, we suggest that general managers, as well as staff specialists, need to give careful consideration to the fairness of their human resource flow policies.

Unfortunately, attitude surveys taken over the last 25 years show low employee satisfaction with advancement and a dramatic and consistent decline in feelings of fair treatment.[18] Barely 50 percent of managers and less than 25 percent of hourly and clerical workers felt that their chances of getting ahead were good. When combined with the dramatic decline in perception of fairness by employees (less than 25 percent of clerical and hourly employees rated "fairness" as good or very good while less than 50 percent of managers did), major problems are indicated.

Why is there such a decline in employee perception of fairness? It is quite likely that company practices have not gotten worse; indeed, they may even have improved. With the passing of equal opportunity legislation and greater emphasis in society on the rights of membership, employees are more sensitized to their basic rights and more willing to articulate them. The ever increasing number of legal suits being brought against companies with regard to hiring, promotion, and termination supports this and makes it quite evident that management cannot ignore the fairness issue.

## The Legal Side of the Problem

In the United States, employers must comply with two major sets of regulations governing equal employment practices: Executive Order 11246 (as amended) and Title VII of the Civil Rights Act of 1964 (as amended). These provisions establish criteria by which discrimination is judged, notably comparing the selection ratios of minorities or women with those of whites or males and comparing numbers of minorities and women in the work force with their representation in the population of the community. Thus, intent to discriminate does not necessarily have to be proven (although recent Supreme Court rulings have made proof of intent a more important factor). In many other instances, the government can require employers to develop affirmative action programs (AAPs) aimed at redressing imbalances. It is not our intent to go into the details of these laws or the means by which the government enforces them. The reader can go to other sources for a complete discussion of these specific issues.

## Due Process Mechanisms

It *is* our intent to emphasize the importance of equal employment opportunity laws and regulations in the United States and to point to the consequences of their existence and of noncompliance with them. The consequences are not only financial, though the $33 million consent decree between AT&T and the federal government illustrates that a great deal of money can be at stake. These laws represent a new standard by which employees and the community can judge a corporation. If management calls itself an equal opportunity employer, employees will feel more unjustly treated if they perceive discrepancies in actual practice than if management had not made such a claim. Under these circumstances, employees will feel much more strongly that changes must be made, and they will feel empowered to confront management directly, knowing they have legal recourse if no action is taken.

Management must create a mechanism for determining if complaints are valid and for resolving the problems if they are. This calls for an industrial jurisprudence, a process management can create for resolving grievances before grievances get to a court of law. David Ewing, who has studied how companies handle disputes, found few have appropriate means through which nonunion employees can voice a complaint or file a grievance.[19] There are several types of complaint resolution processes that seem to work in the few companies that have them. Control Data and Polaroid use panels of managers and/or employees, who hear both sides of the case and decide what correction if any must be made. Bank of America, General Electric, and Massachusetts Institute of Technology employ trained investigators or ombudsmen to work out solutions. Donnelly Mirrors and Pitney Bowes use elected employee councils to discuss problems and devise solutions. Companies without due process mechanisms run the risk of expensive legal suits and of arousing distrust among employees. A perception is created, whether justified or not, that management does not value fairness. With that perception comes dispute and legal action, beginning a vicious cycle.

## Management Enforcement and Organizational Culture

There is little doubt that fair treatment of employees cannot spring from legal constraints alone, though these have provided the pressure for change in standards of fairness. (Prior to regulation in the United States, most corporations did not have effective affirmative action programs.) Nor can fairness be obtained by the written policies of top management that have followed legislative pressures. Only the sincere belief of management in certain standards of fairness for all can result in a persistent top-down effort to enforce the standards and thereby change the values of managers throughout the corporation. The following strategies have to be employed in concert to achieve the needed changes in attitudes and behavior throughout the corporation.

1. *Clear articulation of top management values and philosophy* on fairness issues. What is meant by fairness? In particular, what constitutes a fair process?
2. *The setting of clear goals* for hiring and promoting women, minorities, and other underutilized groups. Achievement of the goals must be rewarded and nonachievement must have negative consequences. Experience suggests that only companies that have such goals have had some success in enforcing standards of fairness.
3. *The creation of corporate policies and systems* that encourage fairness. These might include information systems to track the number of women and minorities who were hired, promoted, terminated, and who left voluntarily. They might also include performance appraisal and bonus systems that incorporate fairness considerations.
4. *The development of due process systems* for resolving complaints about hiring, performance evaluation, promotion, and termination decisions. The more power employees or their repre-

sentatives are given to help adjudicate disputes (for example, the elected committees of Pitney Bowes), the more likely it is that change will occur and that perceptions of fairness will result.

5. *Awareness training* for employees, particularly women and minorities, which helps them clarify and articulate their career goals and teaches them how to utilize due-process mechanisms.

6. *Training and development* for managers and supervisors aimed at helping them understand the characteristics of a fair process and developing their skills in managing fairly a number of critical processes, including selection interviews and decisions about performance appraisal, pay, promotion, and termination.

Fairness cannot be measured by results alone, since various stakeholders in the corporation will apply different values in defining a standard. Therefore, efforts to institutionalize fairness must concentrate on defining an open and participative *process* for making human resource flow decisions and resolving disputes that will surround them. Ignoring or suppressing different views or disputes will have a negative impact, leading inevitably to dissatisfaction, turnover, low commitment, a poor public image, and lawsuits. If feelings of unfair treatment are widespread in a democratic society, they will result in legislation that further reduces managerial freedom and flexibility.

## MANAGING FLOW STRATEGICALLY

There are many systems and practices that must be orchestrated to manage the flow of human resources (see Figure 4–3). The personnel function plays a central role in designing and administering many of the practices, but general managers are the only ones who can be responsible for articulating the philosophy that must guide the design and administration of these systems. Without such an articulation, human resource flow practices will not be internally consistent, nor will they support the firm's strategy or culture.

At the beginning of this chapter we made the point that personnel flow patterns *into, through,* and *out of* the organization can have a profound impact on the security and career development of each employee, on the competence level and mix of talents of employees in the aggregate, and on the well-being of the community and society as a whole.

It is a general manager's responsibility to take a leadership role in deciding on a flow pattern and designing policies and systems that take these three areas into account. It is in this sense that we refer to human resource flow as a policy area. The process of continually discussing

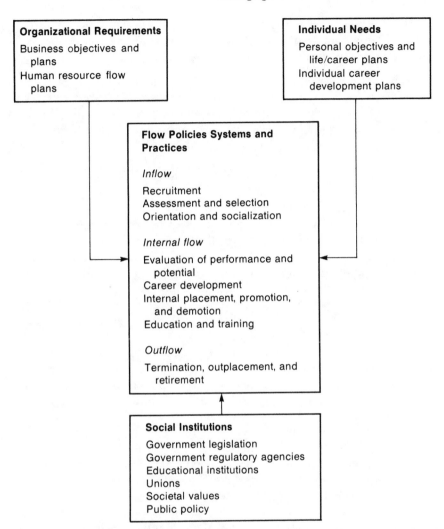

**FIGURE 4-3    Human Resource Flow**

Source: Based on ideas from James Walker, *Human Resource Planning* (New York: Mc-Graw-Hill, 1980).

and monitoring who is being hired, transferred, promoted, terminated, or retired and the way these decisions fit the needs of the individual and the company are also responsibilities of the general manager.

*Alternative Flow Patterns*

There are three basic types of human resource flow patterns that may exist in an organization, and a fourth type that is a mix of the first three. Each of these patterns has different effects on employee well-being, organizational effectiveness, and the role of the corporation in society. The four types of flow patterns are:

1. *Lifelong employment system.* People usually enter the organization at the bottom and stay with the organization throughout their careers. The bottom may be defined differently for different employee groups. Blue-collar employees enter at the lowest job classification in the company, while MBAs are hired for entry-level exempt positions. No one is laid off as a result of economic cycles, but people may be asked to leave because of poor performance, depending on the company and on national practices. Large companies in Japan operate under this system. A select group of their employees are not discharged because of poor performance; instead, they may be sidetracked to less important jobs.[20] Hewlett-Packard, IBM, and some other high-technology companies have a lifelong employment system, but poor performers can be terminated on a case-by-case basis. In Europe, companies are forced to operate under this type of system because legislation makes the costs of termination prohibitive, particularly for older employees.

2. *Up-or-out system.* Employees enter at the bottom and move up through the organization through predetermined tracks until they reach the top rank, which offers full partnership in the organization and usually tenure. Inability to be promoted through any of the ranks along the way or to the highest rank usually means that the person must leave. This system has high levels of turnover at the bottom and relative stability at the top. Big Eight accounting firms, law firms, some management consulting firms, and university faculties are examples.

3. *Unstable in-and-out system.* Employees enter at any level in the organization, depending on the organization's need, and may be asked to leave at any level or point in their career because of economic conditions, poor performance, or lack of fit with new management. Sometimes, employment contracts exist for given periods to ensure individuals some stability. While this type of system is not restricted to any industry, it tends to be found in industries where performance is thought to be a function of the individual (rather than the group) and is highly variable (often due to factors outside the control of the individual). The entertainment industry (sports teams and network television) and many retailing organizations are examples. In-and-out patterns are found in the blue-collar work force where poor economic conditions trigger layoffs and good economic conditions result in hiring.

4. *Mixed patterns.* There are few corporations that are clear-cut examples of one of the above. Large Japanese companies have lifelong employment for their core employees while using an in-and-out system for temporary workers and women. Some companies operate a lifelong employment system for top management, but an in-and-out system for middle and lower management. Furthermore, flow patterns shift over the life cycle of an organization. In the United States, mature companies under competitive pressure from Japan have moved from de facto lifelong employment for management to an in-and-out pattern in an effort to revitalize. Big Eight accounting firms, also under competitive pressures, are outplacing low-performing partners and hiring experienced professionals, thus moving towards an in-and-out system.

In most cases, the choice of patterns selected by an organization is less reflective of a coherent set of management attitudes and values than it is of the economic environment in which that organization operates. If demand for a company's products is subject to severe economic fluctuations, the company is more likely to adopt an in-and-out flow pattern, subjecting employees to layoffs when poor economic conditions prevail. On the other hand, a company in a rapidly growing industry may adopt a lifelong employment policy simply because it has never had to face severe economic decline. If the labor market has a large supply of needed talent, in-and-out flow patterns develop since they allow the firm to replace employees relatively easily. Choices about flow patterns also reflect societal values which can be imposed through legislation restricting the freedom of managers to terminate. Finally, flow patterns may be shaped by the philosophy of a corporation's founders. The belief of James Lincoln that workers should not suffer for the mistakes of management resulted in his adoption of well-known lifelong employment policy at Lincoln Electric.[21]

### Strategic Implications of Flow Pattern Choices

The situational factors that have shaped successive managerial decisions about hiring, promotion, and terminating employees also shape the ideas of the corporation's managers. Over time, a human resource flow pattern is institutionalized. Managers who know they will be asked to reduce employees at some point may be more careless about who they hire and how tightly they control headcount. They may purposely build a reserve of excess employees as a buffer against eventual cuts; this decision, in turn, makes reductions inevitable. The problem with this process is that it does not take into account the effects that institutionalized flow patterns have on the relationship between the organization and its employees or the relationship of the corporation to society. A more strategic approach to human resource flow patterns would suggest that an organization's general manager, supported by the expertise of his or her human resource staff, should weigh carefully the impact of such choices on a broad spectrum of key strategic outcomes, including employee commitment and competence, organizational adaptation and culture, the impact on interdependence and cooperation, and the relationship between the organization and its host society.

EFFECTS ON EMPLOYEE COMMITMENT.    Employees who know that terminations or layoffs may come any time the economy takes a downturn will think differently about their relationship to the organization than employees who know they have a job until retirement. Stories about "bloody September" or the "guns of August," when large numbers of employees were terminated, shape employee expectations and commitment. Insecure employees are likely to be more calculating about the relationship, deciding to stay only so long as their career needs are met quickly. Employees who expect to be with the company until retirement are likely to take a longer-term view of their relationship to the organization. They may be willing to accept slower promotions or temporary setbacks in their career aspirations without lowering commitment. Up-and-out firms may be successful in obtaining high levels of motivation from younger employees who seek promotion, but are likely to incur problems of motivation or "burnout" among senior employees. Thus, different flow patterns and the policies about employment security, advancement, or demotion that shape them cause employees to develop different rationalizations for why they are working and why they are working for a particular company. Are they working to accumulate rewards such as money and promotion that they can take with them to another company or are they working to contribute to an institution from which they will retire? Different flow patterns create quite different "psychological contracts" between the individual and the organization.

We are *not* saying that flow patterns themselves can create high commitment in an organization. We are saying that some flow patterns (notably in-and-out and up-or-out patterns) make it difficult for employees to develop long-term commitment to an organization, even when other factors such as satisfaction with work, pay, and working conditions may make commitment desirable. Thus, some flow patterns may make it more difficult for managers to develop commitment and competence in employees. Lifelong employment creates a base for building commitment and competence, assuming management can develop effective policies in the areas of employee influence, rewards, and work systems.

EFFECTS ON EMPLOYEE COMPETENCE.    The flow pattern of an organization affects how its managers think about the general task of managing. An in-and-out system fosters an emphasis on *selection* as opposed to *development*. If there are no constraints or identifiable costs to hiring and firing, why invest efforts in developing employees? On the other hand, if firing employees is difficult or costly, managers will become more careful in selection and will invest more in development. That developmental approach may increase the competence of employees as well as change the relationship between the organization and the employee. Employees who believe they are receiving an opportunity for development often feel a greater sense of commitment to the organization.

EFFECTS ON ORGANIZATIONAL ADAPTATION.    Flow patterns may also affect the organization's adaptive capacities. Some American managers argue that periodic work-force reductions force managers to weed out dead wood, and provide opportunities to reshape the organization with a new breed of employees. This is one method for managing change. The argument suggests that organizations with in-and-out flow patterns are likely to have more diversity among employees. It is generally accepted that diversity contributes to innovation. Newcomers, not yet socialized by the organization, see old problems in new ways and propose different solutions. It is widely speculated that Japanese companies may not be as innovative as American companies, because of their lifetime employment system. Diversity can, however, be built into firms with lifetime employment if they systematically recruit people with different backgrounds and traits. On the other hand, in-and-out and up-or-out systems are likely to experience problems with adaptation because new people moving rapidly through lower levels do not have the power or network of relationships to create major changes or cannot afford to take risks.

EFFECTS ON CULTURE.    Each organization has its own cultures, a set of shared beliefs and values that guide employee behavior. However, organizations differ in the strength of their corporate cultures. Culture is so pervasive in some organizations that it is an extremely powerful force in shaping behavior, while in other organizations values are not as widely shared and have less of an impact on employee behavior.

Flow patterns affect the *strength of a culture* because they determine how long employees will be with the organization, learning and transmitting a set of beliefs. In an in-and-out system, turnover may be so high that employees do not stay long enough to be fully socialized, or there may be an insufficient number of long-time employees to transmit traditions. Developing a culture in an organization with an in-and-out system is like trying to fill a can with water when it has holes in it. Without employment stability it is difficult, perhaps impossible, to maintain a strong culture.

Strong cultures develop more easily in lifetime systems because employees are more likely to identify with the organization and want to become socialized. Furthermore, a stable pool of senior employees can help with the socialization of new members. An up-or-out system can also develop a strong culture, but the burden of maintaining the culture falls on a relatively small number of senior employees. Managers of high-commitment work systems who want to use culture as a means of social control and want to develop a clan-like organization will have to consider these factors in choosing a human resource flow pattern.

Flow patterns can also influence *the type of culture* that an organization develops, particularly with respect to how power is distributed. An up-or-out system is likely to develop two cultures: senior partners who have made it and have the power, and juniors who have not, the latter being dependent on seniors for approval and ultimate promotion. In a mixed system, employees who have lifetime employment will have more power than those who are not expected to stay or be promoted.

EFFECTS ON INTERDEPENDENCE.    Cooperation in organizations may occur because formal structures direct people to work interdependently. Matrix structures, task forces, special coordinating roles, and reward systems can be used to encourage collaboration between interdependent groups and individuals. But interpersonal relationships can be a more powerful means than formal structures for encouraging cooperation. Senior employees in lifetime employment systems and partners in up-or-out systems develop a network of relationships that make it easier to coordinate interdependent parts of the organization. In Japanese companies cooperation is achieved in the absence of many formal structures because their lifetime employment system allows relationships to develop. Thus, organizations that rely on interdependence to achieve their goals might consider how their human resource flow patterns contribute to this objective.

ROLE OF CORPORATIONS IN SOCIETY.    In-and-out flow patterns reflect different assumptions about the role of the corporation in society than do lifetime employment systems. The former assumes that employees exist for the purpose of helping the corporation make a profit. The latter assumes that the corporation exists to provide stable employment and a meaningful existence for workers. These assumptions are usually implicit. Only occasionally do managers explicitly ask what the purpose of the corporation in society is. Are profits an end or a means to some other end? James Lincoln, the founder of Lincoln Electric, and Konosuke Matsushita, the chairman of Matsushita, were explicit in their beliefs that profits were merely a measuring device, and that the corporation had a higher purpose in society—that of providing a useful product of service to customers and meaningful employment to labor. Lifetime employment fits that concept. Similarly, European legislation regarding the termination rights of employees reflects the implicit belief of those societies that the purpose of the corporation is to provide employment and that profit is not an end, but a means. American managers, on the other hand, usually operate under the assumption that profits are the primary goal of the corporation. Not surprisingly, systems have been developed to fit that belief.

It remains to be seen what impact more intensive international competition will have on the corporation's role in society and on employment security. Will competition force companies and societies to reexamine lifetime employment systems and move closer to the American model? Or will they find ways to remain adaptive while maintaining lifetime employment? What will happen to the predominant American models of in-and-out systems? Can they be adapted to meet the employee's needs for security and the corporation's needs for higher commitment and lower employment costs in recessionary periods?

DECIDING ON A FLOW PATTERN.    The discussion above suggests that human resource flow patterns can affect employer-employee relationships in several important ways, just as they reflect management's implicit assumptions about the purpose of the corporation. However, in many corporations, flow patterns are shaped in a reactive way by the situational forces in the history of the company. This suggests that general managers would be well advised to examine their human resource flow pattern, the rationale underlying it, and its consequences for some of the variables we have discussed. A strategic decision to change the flow pattern might then follow, and that decision could contribute significantly to reshaping all four HRM outcomes: commitment, competence, congruence, and cost effectiveness.

Examination of flow patterns could lead to policy innovations that combine the advantages of both lifetime employment and in-and-out systems and nullify the disadvantages of both. For example, if lifetime employment provides a sense of security for employees but could lead to an obsolescent work force and high costs in a recessionary economy, might it not be possible to obtain both psychological security and the flexibility that management seeks by providing *career*, not *job* security. Company outplacement support, discussed earlier in this chapter, reflects such a strategic decision.

*Designing Flow Policies/Systems*

The choice of a flow pattern will probably emerge from a careful examination and discussion of many of the policies and issues discussed in this chapter. When and how should recruiting be done? How should employee effectiveness be defined and evaluated? How should this information be used in personnel decisions and career development? What systems and practices should the company adopt for developing employees, and what philosophy should guide this process? What philosophy and policies should guide outflow?

These are questions that should be answered explicitly by general managers with the help of key managers and human resource specialists. When a system for examining and shaping flow patterns is lacking, an organization's history and its immediate problems will shape these patterns in ways that may not fit the company's strategic needs.

There is no magic system for designing flow policies. General managers must orchestrate an ongoing process of discussion with key line managers and human resource staff executives about what policies are needed. This dialogue should be based on the following:

1. A data base of information providing some indication of how the flow system is working; for example,

   - Number of qualified "backups" for each management position
   - Turnover rates (voluntary and involuntary)
   - Average tenure in a job
   - Average number of functional experiences of key executives and high-potential middle managers
   - Sales dollars or profit per employee
   - Amount of dollars spent in training and education
   - Types of education programs
   - Compliance with affirmative action goals
   - Employee satisfaction with advancement, personal development, and influence on career decisions
   - Number of hourly and salaried nonexempt employees promoted one, two, or more levels.

2. Appraisal of the values that managers have about employee development, security, and effectiveness.

3. Clarificaiton of corporate strategy—what kind of a firm have we been and will we be in the future? What are the implications for types of people, functions, specialties, and roles we will need?

4. Ongoing dialogue with stakeholders, employee groups (i.e., blacks, women, production employees, managers), union lead-

ers, community social agencies, and federal equal employment compliance agencies about hiring, promotion, and outflow patterns.

5. Task forces of employees assigned to study specific flow issues (e.g., employment security, development of engineers, image of the company at key universities, and so on).

6. Analysis of characteristics, functional competencies, values, and management style of those being promoted most rapidly in the company. Do these fit management's vision of the company 15 to 20 years from now?

7. A similar analysis of those who are leaving the firm voluntarily. Are these people the company can afford to lose given its values and its vision of the future?

A top management group should take time periodically to examine the type of information described above to answer the questions suggested. Some companies have commissioned audits by outside consultants. The consultants collect information by examining records and conducting interviews, then report to top management. Some of the data can be supplied by the human resource function, particularly by a competent personnel research department. With this type of information in hand, top mangement and key line managers should engage in a dialogue to clarify for themselves corporate strategy and philosophy. In the final analysis, flow policies reflect the assumptions of top management about human competence and development in the context of business reality.

### Planning Human Resource Flow

If you are the general manager of a rapidly growing, high technology company, your continued concern is that an adequate supply of managers and engineers will be available to allow the company to expand to the potential created by the market. How would you determine numbers and types of employees? How would you determine who stays and who goes? The answers to these questions can only emerge from a flow planning process, which may be formal or informal, quantitative or judgmental, long- or short-term. The plan may be aimed at assuring a supply of employees in all categories (i.e., engineers, production personnel, secretaries, managers), or it may be aimed at only one or two critical groups such as engineers and managers. Finally, the planning process may encompass the entire company or just a smaller group of key executives and technical personnel. Regardless of the focus, the process encompasses the same basic steps.[22]

1. *Forecast* the number and types of employees that will be needed (labor demand) and the number and types of employees that

will be available in the organization (labor supply) assuming certain rates of turnover, transfers, and promotions.
2. *Program* recruiting, employee development, and/or outplacement to deal with anticipated shortages and surpluses.
3. *Evaluate* the effectiveness of personnel programs in dealing with surpluses and shortages, and revise the plan where necessary.

A quantitative forecast of demand can be made by using certain leading indicators that have a demonstrated relationship to personnel requirements (for example, ratio of sales to sales personnel). The problem with this approach is that it assumes the future to be an extrapolation of the past, an unwarranted assumption in a rapidly changing environment. Alternatively, management can try to project the implications of changes in markets, technology, and strategy for the structure of the organization and the strength and size of certain functions and roles. From this, a forecast of personnel needs can be developed, particularly one that highlights changes in requirements. Management groups that engage in this qualitative forecasting process often find many side benefits such as a clarification of strategy, changing functional roles and relationships, and emerging structural arrangements. The demand forecasting process can lead management to address difficult organizational issues before serious problems develop.

Effective demand forecasting requires a blend of quantitative and qualitative approaches, using each to check and inform the other. Table 4-1 illustrates a typical format for forecasting labor supply, whether arrived at quantitatively or judgmentally.

While the procedure for forecasting supply is well established, the effectiveness of the procedure depends heavily on good personnel data. Even when performance evaluation data are obtained, managers may not always report accurately their assessments of subordinates or their intentions to fire or promote if they don't know how this data will be used. Nor do companies know exactly who is planning to quit. Through an examination of historical patterns, some estimates may be made but these are highly problematical. This is why *aggregated forecasting*, which projects supply for a group of employees using sophisticated models, does not usually yield very useful information, though it may be of some value as a check on a *disaggregated approach to forecasting supply*. This approach, commonly referred to as succession or replacement planning, relies on the personal knowledge of managers to estimate who might quit or retire and who should be promoted or terminated. In replacement planning, managers are asked to designate individuals whom they regard as *backups* for their or other key jobs. Individuals are chosen on the basis of their experience and evaluation of performance and potential. By comparing demand estimates and supply estimates, a

**TABLE 4–1  A Forecast of Labor Supply**

| JOB CATEGORY | (1) Beginning inventory | LOSSES | | | GAINS | INTERNAL MOVES | | (8) Anticipated internal supply |
| | | (2) Retirements | (3) Quits | (4) Others | (5) Transfers in | (6) Promotions out/in | (7) Demotions out/in | |
| --- | --- | --- | --- | --- | --- | --- | --- | --- |
| 1 | 136 | 4 | 0 | 11 | 3 | 0/13 | 0/0 | 137 |
| 2 | 255 | 2 | 18 | 0 | 3 | 13/26 | 0/0 | 251 |
| 3 | 291 | 1 | 29 | 0 | 8 | 26/39 | 0/0 | 282 |
| 4 | 357 | 0 | 36 | 0 | 0 | 39/0 | 0/0 | 282 |
| | 1,039 | | | | | | | 952 |

SOURCE: Adapted from Herbert G. Heneman, Donald Schwab, John A. Fossum, and Lee D. Dyer, *Managing Personnel and Human Resources: Strategies and Programs* (Homewood, Ill.: Dow Jones–Irwin, 1981), Fig. 7–2, p. 13.

shortage or surplus may be identified for each category of employee within the company to which the process is applied. Action plans are then devised by line managers to deal with filling gaps or terminating employees.

The critical link in the flow planning process is *follow-up*. Even after managers have established procedures, development programs do not always follow. If individuals who were to receive specific training or job experiences do not, the company will find itself lacking the needed technical and managerial talent. These are ''soft'' programs that are difficult to define, preprogram, and measure. Increasingly, corporations are finding that flow planning needs to be tied to the strategic planning process. These corporations will not accept a business plan from a manager unless it provides a flow analysis. When these plans are reviewed periodically and managers are rewarded for their accomplishment, they are more likely to be implemented. If the corporation wishes to reward managers who successfully develop people, it is important that follow-up include not only a monitoring of activities (training programs, recruitment programs, etc.) but also developmental results (the number of successful technical or managerial personnel promoted from a unit).

In addition to its analytic nature, succession planning is also a *subjective process*. Employees who are candidates for promotion in the in the eyes of one manager may be viewed negatively by other managers applying different standards. In any case, succession in a corporation must be agreed to by a number of key managers, all of whom will have to work with the person in question. For this reason many companies (for example, Hewlett-Packard, GM, IBM, and GE) have developed a committee process for reviewing key managerial personnel at every level of the organization. At Exxon, as mentioned earlier, the chief executive officer heads a compensation and executive development committee which meets frequently, sometimes once a week, to review development of top Exxon executives. Composed of Exxon board members, the committee discusses each executive's performance and examines developmental needs. To insure continual flow of managerial talent, the committee compares the performance and potential of all executives and makes decisions about who are the most likely successors to key jobs and what experiences they need to succeed. The same development committee system is replicated at each subsidiary, where the president of that subsidiary has his or her own committee. At Hewlett-Packard, the top management group uses three-day sessions more than once a year to discuss each key executive in the company. At General Motors ten vice-presidents and group executives also meet regularly to probe the effectiveness of each executive in a pool of 600 managers. Does the executive seem to be developing at the rate expected? What is the job contributing to the person's ability? Is it rounding out the person as intended? Should an individual be given more responsibility or be moved to another division? If so, who would be put in that executive's place?[23]

A succession review process for key managerial and technical personnel can be established at every level of the organization, starting at the bottom and moving up. If such a process is led by line managers and is regularly scheduled, the message to managers is clear: Flow planning and human resource development are important in this organization! When combined with information from more quantitative aggregate planning, a flow planning process can be developed that will insure the numbers of people and talent mix that the company requires to be competitive in the future.

## SUMMARY

Managing the flow of people *in*, *through*, and *out* of the corporation is a human resource policy area of strategic importance to corporations. Policy decisions in this area require that general managers adopt more than just an enterprise perspective. They must also understand the perspective of the individual, particularly in regard to what constitutes career development and satisfaction. Additionally, they must develop a societal perspective, which involves an understanding of changing worker values, educational institutions that supply prospective recruits, legislation, government regulatory agencies, and union policy.

To assure the right numbers of employees with a mix of skills required to implement corporate strategy, corporations must design appropriate policies and practices for managing employee inflow, internal flow, and outflow. A number of important questions and issues must be addressed to develop effective flow policies. How can employees be recruited that will fit the corporation's needs and culture? What is the optimum velocity of personnel flow through the corporation consistent with good employee development and the strategic needs of the corporation? How is employee effectiveness defined and how shall it be evaluated? How can an organizational context be created that will encourage employee development? What mechanisms and processes can corporations install to meet employee expectations for fairness in connection with hiring, promotion, and termination decisions? Finally, should the company terminate, retire early, or otherwise encourage employees to leave when profits drop? What alternatives exist to this policy?

The sum total of flow policies and practices create a flow pattern. We have identified four types of patterns: lifelong employment, up-or-out, in-and-out, and a mixed pattern of all three types. Each has a quite different impact on important outcomes such as commitment, competence, and organizational culture and adaptibility. General managers must make strategic choices about the flow pattern they want and the policies and practices that will be needed to support their choice. Such strategic choices will be a function of competitive realities, stakeholder interests, and management's values with regard to employee development and security. A continuous process of examining values, the effects of current flow policies, and the future goals of the firm will allow managers to shape flow patterns and policies.

One ongoing responsibility of general managers is to be involved in planning and managing personnel flow within the context of existing policies. How many managers, professionals, specialists, or skilled workers will the firm require to meet its business goals? What mix of recruiting and employee development programs will be needed to serve those needs? Who are the managers and professionals with the highest potential to succeed incumbents in key positions? These are questions that should be addressed as part of the business planning process. Many corporations create special forums where key managers at each level of the organization discuss key people, their potential, and their developmental needs. General managers who create such forums for discussion signal their own concern for developing the corporation human assets and encourage a social capital perspective throughout the corporation.

# Chapter 5

# Reward Systems

THE DESIGN AND management of reward systems constitute one of the most difficult HRM tasks for the general manager. Of the four major policy areas in HRM, this is where we find the greatest contradiction between the "promise" of theory and the reality of implementation. Organizations sometimes go through cycles of great innovation and hope as reward systems are developed, followed by disillusionment as these systems fail to deliver. Organizations must reward employees because in return they are looking for certain kinds of behavior: they need competent individuals who agree to work with a high level of performance and loyalty. Individual employees, in exchange for their commitment, expect certain extrinsic rewards in the form of promotions, salary, fringe benefits, perquisites, bonuses, or stock options. Individuals also seek intrinsic rewards such as feelings of competence, achievement, responsibility, significance, influence, personal growth, and meaningful contribution.

Employees will judge the adequacy of their exchange with the organization by assessing both sets of rewards. The attention of both employees and employers tends to focus on extrinsic rewards, because these rewards are easily defined, measured, and compared across people, jobs, and organizations. Intrinsic rewards, on the other hand, are less clearly definable, discussable, comparable, and negotiable. Union-management negotiations, for instance, rarely deal with intrinsic rewards even though these intangible rewards are often at the root of the

113

conflict between management and labor. Workers who have routine jobs may feel powerless to influence their work or the conditions of work. Wage demands can mask this fact, so that increased pay serves to compensate for the inadequacy of intrinsic rewards. Likewise, the dissatisfaction of a manager or a professional with his or her progress up a pay scale may reflect a deeper dissatisfaction with growth in responsibility, career, and power. Increases in compensation may reduce conflict for a while, but they will not resolve the fundamental problem.

Complaints about compensation and other extrinsic rewards may thus mask problems in the relationship between employees and their organization: the nature of supervision, the opportunities for career development, and employee influence and involvement in work itself. When conflict over pay erupts, general managers would be well advised to undertake their own careful diagnosis of the situation, rather than assuming that the problem should be "handled" by staff specialists in compensation. Such a diagnosis may well point to problems in the other three HRM policy areas. If this is the case, an increase in compensation and the resulting increased cost to the organization will not resolve the underlying conflict. We are not saying that conflict over wages does not have validity or that money is unimportant. We are saying employees sometimes compensate for their dissatisfaction with intrinsic rewards by demanding improvements in extrinsic rewards, particularly pay.

The capacity of an organization to deliver intrinsic rewards through innovations in work systems, employee influence, and human resource flow policies may have marginal effects on the negotiation of extrinsic rewards. Delivering intrinsic rewards through innovative policies will probably not lower compensation costs; in fact, it may call for higher compensation. However, it may stimulate employees to increase commitment and develop their competence, leading to positive effects on effort, indirect labor costs, innovation, and flexibility in the work force. The net benefits of such outcomes to the organization can be quite high even when considered against the cost of higher compensation.

Tying pay and other extrinsic rewards to performance may *reduce* the intrinsic motivation that comes when individuals are given freedom to manage and control their jobs.[1] By making pay contingent upon performance (as judged by management), management is signaling that it is they—not the individual—who are in control, thus lowering the individual's feelings of competence and self-determination. Intrinsic motivation decreases when a person's behavior becomes dependent on a reward that someone else controls, or on the threat of sanctions. Intrinsic motivation also decreases when pay decisions provide individuals with negative feedback about their performance on an intrinsically in-

teresting activity. Therefore, managers must decide whether intrinsic or extrinsic reward systems are to be the primary means for motivating employees. Moreover, managers must be careful to prevent
pay and other extrinsic rewards from interfering with intrinsic motivation.

This chapter will deal primarily with the design and management
of compensation systems. Intrinsic rewards will be discussed in Chapter 6 on work systems, where we will explore in some detail how work
may be organized to stimulate intrinsic motivation. In this chapter intrinsic rewards will be discussed only as they interact with the design of
compensation systems. These systems warrant specific attention because they present difficult choices to general managers. Furthermore,
compensation systems are the primary subject when employees or unions negotiate with employers. Finally, money is important to employees. Dissatisfaction with pay can easily lead to negative effects on employer-employee relations in other policy areas.

The central thesis that we will put forward is that while compensation systems can be managed to improve cost effectiveness and avoid
conflict, they have only limited potential for developing commitment
and competence. On the other hand, compensation systems can and
sometimes do interfere with innovations in the other HRM policy areas. Our point of view runs counter to much of management theory
and practice in the United States (though not in Europe and Japan).
We are suggesting that the design of a compensation system should
rarely be the place to start in solving business and human resource
problems, though it will always be an area that will have to be managed
to complement other HRM changes. Top-down design of reward systems, particularly those systems aimed at controlling behavior through
pay-for-performance incentives, can often hurt an organization's
HRM efforts more than it can help. (We are not talking here about
participative approaches to designing new pay systems which, in effect,
are changes in employee influence.)

## THE REWARD SYSTEM CHALLENGE

In manufacturing firms, payroll costs can run as high as 40 percent of
sales revenues, while in service organizations payroll costs can top 70
percent. It is not surprising, therefore, that general managers take a
great interest in payroll costs and how these dollars are spent. In the
steel and automobile industries for example, payroll costs for production, clerical, and management personnel are generally regarded as
one of the factors affecting the competitiveness of these industries.
Comparing a firm's total payroll costs to the payroll costs of the compe-

tition is one way to assess the competitive position of the firm. It can and should guide management in its policies regarding compensation levels and its positions in collective bargaining.

Despite the enormous amount spent on wages, commissions, cost of living increases, bonuses, and stock options, many studies have shown that in most organizations 50 percent or more of the employees are dissatisfied with pay, and that this percentage is increasing. In 1973, 48 percent of a representative national sample of employees felt they received "good" pay and fringe benefits; by 1977 the percentage had declined to 34 percent.[2] Pay is a major problem in many organizations and there is a continual "noise" level about its adequacy and equity. A recent summary of survey findings by a major opinion polling organization concluded that a majority of employees come to work each day believing that their wages are unfair, that pay increases are unfair, and that any improvement in their performance is unlikely to result in better pay. This is somewhat less true of managers than of clerical, professional, and hourly employees. Satisfaction with fringe benefits is typically higher, but even that dropped in the 1970s to a rate slightly better than 50 percent.[3] These findings are particularly disturbing when one considers that pay has been consistently found to be one of the most important job factors to individuals, usually ranked first or second among all levels of employees. Thus, employees are dissatisfied with the very reward that appears, based on their stated preferences, to have the potential to influence powerfully their willingness to work and to stay with a company. Not surprisingly, the tremendous amount of time and energy expended in dealing with dissatisfaction with pay systems represents a major administrative cost to organizations.

The source of the problem seems to be a contradiction between the *theory* of pay systems and the *reality* of pay practice. Managers in the United States (not so much in Europe and Japan) espouse the importance of paying for individual performance. Similarly, research has shown that employees are more satisfied with pay when it is based on performance.[4] With the exception of those who are unionized and perhaps those who work for the government, American employees seem to accept pay for performance as a basic principle which should govern the distribution of money. The belief in pay for performance is undoubtedly rooted in national culture, which stresses individualism. Yet there is considerable evidence that in many organizations pay is not based on performance. For example, a survey of *Fortune* 500 companies showed that 42 percent used no formal system for assessing the performance of professional and technical personnel, while 41 percent used single rate compensation systems for blue-collar workers so that wage increases could not be based on individual performance but only on general increases, job promotions, or on subjective performance judgments.[5] Without a formal appraisal system it is inevitable that employees would question the equity of pay decisions. Other surveys have indicated that at top management levels, company *size* (measured by sales volume) is the primary factor in determining the pay of the top executive and that pay differentials are then built downward to determine wages of lower-level executives. Corporate performance such as return on equity seems to have no relation to compensation rates for chief executive officers.[6] The gap between espoused beliefs of managers and employees and actual practices undoubtedly causes some of the general dissatisfaction with pay.

Even in firms with a pay-for-performance system, there seems to be a large gap between the promise of these systems and the reality of practice. The most sophisticated pay-for-performance systems designed specifically to motivate employees often end up with significant flaws. Either they do not motivate employees, or they bring about unanticipated and dysfunctional behavior. A frequent consequence of individual pay-for-performance systems is competition between employees when cooperation is desired. In other instances, the measure of performance is invalidated by changes in the firm's business environment. Sales volume may become less important and return on equity more important as a firm moves from an environment of market expansion and resource slack to one of fierce market share competition and scarce resources. In still other situations, the chosen performance criteria may be subjected to the influence of environmental forces beyond the individual's control, or the performance may be negatively affected by interdependence with other individuals and departments. Inflation may erode the value of a merit increase; or increases may be based on performance criteria that are never explained to subordinates.

Some well-designed pay systems simply fall prey to low trust between supervisors and employees or to inadequate communication skills by managers. Employees may discount or even resent merit or bonus awards if they do not believe in the fairness of decisions. The level of pay itself, or its equity with the labor market, may be questioned because employees do not know enough about how the organization has determined pay grades. The result is potential conflict betweeen human resource personnel who are attempting to enforce the pay system and line managers who want to pay salaries which they believe are appropriate.

The still strong support for individual pay-for-performance systems in the United States is based on more than the lingering belief on the part of managers and workers that pay should be based on individual performance. The potential of rewards for motivating behavior, substantiated by many examples where its absence has caused lower

performance or its introduction has temporarily improved performance, provides the impetus for a continued search for better reward systems. The remainder of this chapter will discuss the theory of reward
systems and a review of the problems. The final section will discuss the
policy implications in the rewards area.

## THE THEORY OF PAY AND BEHAVIOR[7]

A body of experience, research, and theory has been developed about
the way in which money satisfies and motivates employees. These theories seem to validate the general assumption of managers that money
can be used to motivate employees, but they also suggest cautions, limitations, and contingencies that are often either forgotten or are difficult to implement in practice. Some of the problems described above
are the result.

### Pay Is Important to Individuals

Virtually every study on the relative importance of pay to other
potential rewards (extrinsic and intrinsic) has shown that pay *is* important: it is consistently ranked among the top five rewards. In fact, in
more than one-third of 45 studies conducted, pay was ranked number
one as a valued reward. An opinion polling organization, reviewing
data from the past two decades, found that pay and benefits were
ranked first or second in importance by employees in every job classification (see Table 5–1). Because it is so important, pay has power to influence people's membership behavior (where they go to work and
whether they stay) and their performance.

**TABLE 5–1   Top Five Work Values**

| RANK | MANAGERS | PROFESSIONALS | CLERICAL | HOURLY |
|------|----------|---------------|----------|--------|
| 1 | Pay & benefits | Advancement | Pay & benefits | Pay & benefits |
| 2 | Advancement | Pay & benefits | Advancement | Security |
| 3 | Authority | Challenge | Supervision | Respect |
| 4 | Accomplishment | New skills | Respect | Supervision |
| 5 | Challenge | Supervision | Security | Advancement |

SOURCE: From William A. Schiemann, "Major Trends in Employee Attitudes
Toward Compensation," in Schiemann (ed.), *Managing Human Resources/1983 and Beyond*. Printed with permission from *Managing Human Resources/1983 and Beyond*. Opinion Research Corporation, Princeton, NJ. © 1984.

However, the importance of pay and other rewards is affected by many factors. Money, for example, is likely to be viewed differently in early, middle and later career because needs for money versus other rewards (status, growth, security, etc.) are different in each stage. Another imporatnt factor is national culture. United States managers and employees apparently place much more emphasis on pay for individual performance than do their European counterparts. European and Japanese companies, on the other hand, rely more on slow promotions and seniority, as well as some degree of employment security. Even within a single culture, shifting national forces may alter people's needs for money versus other rewards. High inflation tends to encourage people to emphasize the importance of money, while periods of slow growth or unemployment place a greater premium on intrinsic rewards or employment security.

### Rewards and Employee Satisfaction

There are some general conclusions to be drawn about the relationship between rewards and employee satisfaction. Since dissatisfaction among employees can lead to turnover, absenteeism, and withholding of effort, organizations seek employee satisfaction to maintain or improve organizational effectiveness. But employee satisfaction with pay is not a simple matter. Rather, it is a function of a number of factors which organizations must learn to manage:

1. The individual's satisfaction with rewards is, in part, a function of *what is expected and how much is received*. Feelings of satisfaction or dissatisfaction arise when individuals compare the nature of their job skills, education, effort, and performance (input) with the mix of extrinsic and intrinsic rewards they receive (output).

2. Employee satisfaction is also affected by *comparisons with other people in similar jobs and organizations*. In effect employees compare their own input/output ratio with that of others. People vary considerably in how they weight various inputs in that comparison. There is a tendency to weight more heavily those things in which they excel, certain skills or a recent incident of effective performance.[8] Individuals also tend to overrate their own performance compared to that of their supervisors. For example, it has been found that many employees rate their performance in the eightieth percentile.[9] Given the fact that an organization cannot pay everyone at the eightieth percentile, it is not surprising that many employees feel they are being underpaid relative to others in the organization. The problem of unrealistic self-ratings exists in part because supervisors in most organizations do not communicate a candid evaluation of their

subordinates' performance to them. Unless supervisors have exceptional communication skills, such candid communication to subordinates seriously risks damaging their self-esteem. The real dilemma is that failure to communicate a candid appraisal of performance makes it difficult for employees to develop a realistic view of their own performance, thus increasing the possibility of dissatisfaction with the pay they are receiving.

3. *The misperception of the rewards of others* is a major source of dissatisfaction. There is evidence that individuals tend to overestimate the pay of fellow workers doing similar jobs while underestimating their performance (a defense or self-esteem building mechanism). Misperceptions of rewards and the performance of others also occur because organizations do not generally make available accurate information about salaries or performance levels of their employees. Managers are understandably reluctant to publish information on individual salaries and performance appraisals. Such information is likely to reveal some inequities in the pay system, and could also lead to dysfunctional competitiveness between employees. Nonetheless, it is not surprising that, given the known tendencies toward misperception, the lack of such information leads to the perception of inequities.

4. Finally, overall satisfaction is *the result of a mix of rewards*, rather than any single reward. The evidence seems to be clear that intrinsic rewards and extrinsic rewards are both important, and that they are not directly substitutable for each other. Employees who are paid well for repetitious, boring work will be dissatisfied with the lack of intrinsic rewards, just as employees paid poorly for interesting, challenging work may be dissatisfied with extrinsic rewards.

### Pay and Membership Behavior

Companies that give the most desirable rewards will be best able to attract and keep people, particularly the better employees. Substantial rewards lead to higher satisfaction, which is generally associated with lower turnover, though turnover is also a function of the labor market and the economy. It is for this reason that companies like IBM intentionally position their total compensation packages at the high end of the market range. High total compensation does not, however, ensure that the best employees are retained. To do this, a company must also pay its better performers more than it pays poorer performers; and the difference must be significant (recognizing that the significance of the difference is a subjective judgment on the part of individual employees).[10] A less than significant differential will result in feelings of inequity when better performers compare their input-output ratio with that of poorer performers. A well constructed and administered pay-for-performance system will then result in retention of better performers, and the turnover of the poorer performers—those the organization may want to lose despite the significant replacement costs incurred. An operational test of a company's success in doing this is to correlate individual employee satisfaction with performance ratings. A low correlation or a negative one indicates problems. The problem may be in the design of the pay plan; it may also be in the administration of that plan. Later in the chapter we will examine some of the problems that can occur in administering a pay-for-performance system.

### Pay and Motivation

From the organization's point of view, rewards are intended to *motivate* certain types of behavior. But under what conditions will rewards actually motivate employees? Important rewards must be perceived to be tied to effective performance in a timely fashion. In other words, individuals will behave in a way that will lead to rewards they value. Motivation depends on the situation and how it is perceived by employees, but the needs people do or do not possess will make them more or less susceptible to motivating situations. For example, individuals with a high need for achievement are more likely to be motivated by situations that provide them an opportunity to satisfy that need than individuals whose need for achievement is low. A person who has a high need for money or advancement will be more motivated to perform in a situation that provides monetary rewards or promotions than an individual who is low in these needs.

An expectancy theory model (Fig. 5–1) has been developed to suggest the conditions necessary for employee motivation:

1. Employees must believe that effective performance (or certain specified behavior) will lead to certain rewards: for example, attaining certain results will lead to a bonus, or a certain performance will lead to approval or disapproval from peers or supervisors.
2. Employees must feel that the rewards offered are *attractive*. Not all rewards are equally attractive to all individuals because of differences in needs and perceptions. Some employees may desire promotions because they seek power while others may want a fringe benefit such as a pension because they are older and are concerned about retirement security.
3. Employees must believe that a certain level of individual effort will lead to achieving the corporation's *standards of performance*.

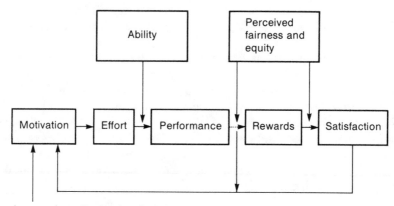

A person's motivation is a function of:

1.  Effort to performance expectancies
2.  Performance-to-reward expectancies
3.  Perceived attractiveness of rewards

**FIGURE 5–1    The Expectancy Theory Model**

SOURCE: Adapted from Edward E. Lawler, *Pay and Organization Development*, ©1981, Addison-Wesley, Reading, Massachusetts. Pg. 21, Table 2.2. Reprinted with permission of Addison-Wesley.

> Unless employees believe that their efforts can have a reasonable probability of affecting performance—e.g., the profit level of a factory or the introduction of a product—they see no reason to exert the effort.

The expectancy theory model's conditions for motivation are shown in Figure 5–1. The model suggests a highly instrumental view of motivation. Motivation to exert effort is triggered by the prospect of desired rewards: money, recognition, promotion, and the like. If effort leads to performance, and performance leads to desired rewards, the employee is satisfied and motivated to perform again. Motivation can be sustained over time only if successive experience in the organization leads the person to believe that this sequence is repeatable (that is, to *trust* the reward system), that his or her efforts can affect certain performance outcomes, and that the organization will reward these achievements. The dotted line between performance and rewards and the feedback loop to motivation are intended to show that motivation is a function of the performance-reward relationship.

It should be noted that the ''ability'' box between ''effort'' and ''performance'' is intended to indicate that performance is a function of ability as much as effort. Ability reflects not just the individual's skills and talents, but also the training and information provided by the organization. Effort thus combines with ability to produce a certain level of performance.

As we have already mentioned, rewards fall into two categories: extrinsic and intrinsic. *Extrinsic rewards* are provided by the organization in the form of money, perquisites, or promotions or from supervisors and co-workers in the form of recognition. *Intrinsic rewards* are those rewards which accrue from the performance of the task itself: satisfaction of accomplishment, sense of influence, sense of competence, or self-congratulation on a job well done. The process of work and the individual's response to it provide the intrinsic reward. But organizations seeking to increase intrinsic rewards must provide a work environment that allows these satisfactions to occur. This is why more organizations are redesigning work and delegating responsibility to enhance employee involvement. (We will discuss ways of enhancing intrinsic rewards and motivation in Chapter 6.)

In the expectancy model, satisfaction is a *result* of performance, not a cause of it as is often thought. Satisfaction does influence motivation indirectly, however, because satisfaction that follows rewards for performance strengthens the employee's belief in the linkage between effort, performance, and rewards. Satisfaction of certain needs can also heighten or reduce those needs. For example, the experience of promotion or achievement may heighten the need for further advancement and achievement. On the other hand, already having a lot of money could lessen the satisfaction derived from yet another incremental increase in pay.

The implications of the expectancy model for the use of pay as a motivator are not simple. The model could lead to the erroneous conclusion that an organization need only relate pay and other valued rewards to achievable levels of performance. First, this is not the only factor an organization needs to control in order to motivate employees. Management-worker relationships, the opportunity to develop, and a sense of contribution to meaningful goals are all very important ingredients in motivation. Second, the linkage between rewards and performance is a difficult one to achieve. It is not easy to develop good measures of performance, to communicate a performance evaluation to subordinates so they will accept it, to identify which rewards are important to employees, or to control the distribution of rewards so that better performers obtain more than poor performers. Yet all of these factors directly affect employee perception concerning the linkage between rewards and performance. Judging by a national survey of randomly selected individuals, a majority of workers fail to see a direct linkage in their organization: only 27.2 percent of those surveyed said they were likely to get a pay increase or bonus if they performed well.[11]

There are numerous reasons for the apparent difficulty organizations have in linking pay to performance. The lack of visibility of pay increases or bonuses makes it difficult for employees to judge if a relationship exists between these rewards and performance. Furthermore, there is the issue of trust and credibility. For individuals to exert effort in anticipation of rewards, they must believe that the rewards will follow. If the organization has not established trust and credibility that belief will be eroded.[12]

Finally, basic questions have been raised about the extent to which pay-for-performance systems reward for effort or reward for ability. If the organization has succeeded in hiring individuals with high need to achieve and contribute (a need that theorists such as Douglas McGregor argue is present in the majority of people), and it has provided a work environment that allows employees to contribute, then pay for performance is pay for ability. All employees are motivated, and the differential in performance is a function of innate ability and/or skill and competence obtained through training and experience. In this instance, pay-for-performance does not motivate; it merely rewards differentially for ability. This is not necessarily bad, but it changes the conception of what pay is doing. It creates an argument for training low performers in skills they need to perform. Such a policy is not likely to be established if the assumption is that motivation is the problem, and that pay for performance will motivate low performers. Therefore, it is important to diagnose correctly whether differential performance is a function of motivation or ability. If it is a function of the former, a pay-for-performance system may be called for if all conditions specified earlier can be met to make it workable. If low performance is a function of inadequate ability, a pay-for-performance system may still be warranted to pay equitably; however, improved selection or training will be needed to obtain better performance.

### Rewards: Equity and Participation

As previously noted, the motivational and satisfactional value of a reward system is a function of the perceived equity of the reward system. Without the perception of equity, trust in the reward system will be low and the contingent linkage between performance and pay will not be accepted. But the motivational and satisfactional value of a reward system is also a function of *who influences* and controls the design and administration of the new reward system. Even though there is considerable evidence that participation in decision making can lead to greater acceptance of decisions,[13] participation in the design and administration of reward systems is rare. Such participation is time consuming and thus costly. But probably a more important road block to participation in the design and administration of a reward system is that pay has been one of the last strongholds of managerial prerogatives. Concerned about the effect of self-interest on compensation system design and compensation costs, corporations do not typically allow employees to participate in pay system design or decisions. Thus, it is not possible to test thoroughly the effects of widespread participation on acceptance of and trust in reward systems.

Experience and research suggest that more participation in pay system design, is desired by employees and that such participation in a limited number of experiments, has generally led to higher satisfaction and acceptance.[14] The desire for participation is especially high when rewards are perceived to be inequitable. Collective bargaining is an outgrowth of dissatisfaction and perceptions of inequity in pay administration. By establishing their influence on pay system design and pay levels, workers feel more assured that they are equitably treated (leaving aside for the moment the problems that occur in large unions where workers are far removed from the bargaining process). Both union and management, particularly those parties directly involved in the negotiation process, are more likely to be committed to some degree to the reward decisions reached when they have participated in the process. Furthermore, survey data suggest that employees want more influence over pay raises than they get, though they do not want as much influence over these decisions as over how to carry out or schedule their work.[15] Finally, a limited number of studies that have examined the effects of participation in decisions about pay system design and pay raises have shown that employees' self-interest does not lead to irresponsible design or pay-level decisions. Later in this chapter we will return to the possible role that participation can play in solving reward system problems.

### Summary of the Theory

The discussion above suggests that pay is generally important to people, that it is related to satisfaction, and that satisfaction or the prospect of satisfaction with pay will influence people to come to work for a company and to stay with it. Pay can also be used to motivate job performance, provided certain conditions are met: employees must believe that acceptable levels of performance can result from their efforts and that important rewards will follow achievement of those performance levels. Both satisfaction and motivation can be eroded by perceptions of inequity in pay system administration. We now turn to a discussion of contemporary compensation practices.

## COMPENSATION SYSTEMS: THE DILEMMAS OF PRACTICE

Companies have developed a wide variety of compensation systems and practices in order to achieve employee pay satisfaction and employee motivation. These systems and practices have tried to take into account, in one way or another, the major factors affecting employee satisfaction and motivation which we discussed in the previous section. Company efforts to keep employees satisfied are reflected in decisions about where to peg the company's compensation with respect to the market; for example, at the fiftieth or seventy-fifth percentile. Those choices have an obvious impact on cost effectiveness. Thus, cost effectiveness and conflict over pay are inversely related. Satisfaction and potential motivation are also reflected in the mix of cash versus fringe benefits. The importance of equity is reflected in a choice of a job evaluation system to identify objectively contribution to the overall organization. Finally, decisions about whether pay should be tied to performance and how that linkage should be accomplished are critical to satisfaction and motivation. Choices such as those inevitably result in consequences for satisfaction, turnover, and motivation.

Experience with compensation systems and practices quickly leads to the conclusion that many of them are flawed in some major way, and generally cannot meet the conditions that research and theory specify are necessary for satisfaction and motivation to occur. One response to flawed compensation systems has been the design of new and presumably better systems. In some cases, this has led to some interesting alternative systems. In this section we will describe the major compensation system choices available to general managers and discuss the problems associated with each. Because many excellent full-length books have been written on the subject, we will not discuss the systems and techniques in depth here. Consistent with our belief that new systems typically hold out more promise in theory than in practice, we will suggest caution in relying primarily on compensation to achieve human resource goals. The traditional emphasis of managers and compensation specialists seems to be that if the right system can be developed, it will solve most problems. We do not think this is a plausible assumption—there is no single right answer or objective solution to what or how someone should be rewarded. What people will accept, be motivated by, or perceive as fair is highly subjective. Rewards are a matter of perceptions and values and it often generates conflict.

If system design is not the ultimate solution, then what is to be done? Communication of pay policies and their intent, participation in pay system design, and trust between management and workers are all key ingredients in making flawed compensation systems more effective. Communication, participation, and trust can have an important effect on people's perceptions of pay, the meaning they attach to a new pay system, and their response to that system. In short, *the process may be as important as the system,* and it should be taken into account when the system is designed and administered.

## *Management's Influence on Attitudes Toward Money*

Many organizations are caught up in a vicious cycle that, in part at least, is of their own making. Firms will often emphasize their compensation levels and their belief in individual pay for performance in recruitment and internal communications. In doing so they are likely to attract people with high needs for money and to heighten that need in those already employed. Money, which is already a symbol of status, power, and esteem in our society, will become even more so. That is because the significance employees attach to money is partly shaped by the manner in which management communicates about it. If merit increases, bonuses, stock options, and perquisites are held out as valued symbols of recognition and success, employees will come to see them in this light even more than they might have at first. Having heightened the importance of money as a reward, management must then be responsive to employees who may demand more money or more elaborate pay-for-performance systems. The development of such systems serves to further underline money as the measure of contribution, success, and worth.

There are understandable forces that push management in this direction. They may indeed believe that money is a very important motivator and yardstick. That belief may come out of their own experience or it may be absorbed from the ideology of the larger society. As we discussed in Chapter 2, that ideology in the United States (as compared with Europe and Japan) has placed great emphasis on individualism and free enterprise in which money plays a very important symbolic role. Furthermore, in some industries compensation plays an especially important role in attracting and keeping employees, thus "forcing" management into an emphasis on money.

Firms must start their thinking about the design and administration of a reward system by considering *a philosophy about rewards* and the role of pay in the mix of rewards. How should money be used? To recognize performance stimulated by other means? To provide direct incentives for performance? What other tools does the organization have at its disposal—tools that might, in fact, be less costly and less troublesome to administer—in order to achieve those outcomes? Unless these issues are addressed up front, the compensation practices which happen to be in place will continue to shape the expectations of employees, and those expectations will sustain the existing practices.

We are not suggesting that money is unimportant, only that its degree of importance and its centrality in the meaning people make out of their work experience is influenced by the type of compensation system and philosophy management adopts. Moreover, we believed that any

given company can differentiate itself somewhat from the prevailing industry pattern with respect to the role of compensation in attracting
and keeping employees. It can do this by attracting employees whose
reward needs are compatible with the philosophy of the company or are
subject to the influence of the company philosophy. Unfortunately,
many general managers have not examined their assumptions about
compensation or have not examined compensation systems for their fit
with those assumptions.

## Fringe Benefits as Part of the Compensation Mix

Though fringe benefits are part of the mix of almost every reward
package, organizations differ in the percentage of total compensation
costs allocated to cash versus fringe benefits. There are wide individual
differences in the preference of people for cash and fringe benefits, depending on age and background. There are also differences in which
fringe benefits individuals prefer. Thus, a standardized benefit package designed for all employees is likely to satisfy few individuals completely, so that overall satisfaction will be relatively low despite the high
costs of such packages. Fringe benefits can be an inducement to motivate employees to join a company, though it is not clear how important
minor differences between companies are. Fringe benefits do not, however, meet the criteria for motivating performance, since there is virtually no linkage between performance and the reward.

While fringe benefits may not be cost-effective, they are offered by
all large companies and most small ones. Thus, they become a competitive tool for attracting prospective employees, making it difficult for
any one company to make radical reductions in these benefits. Perhaps
employees really prefer the security of fringes despite their espoused
desire for higher pay for performance.

A typical fringe benefit package for employees might consist of one
or more of the following items:

1. Extra pay for time worked on holidays, weekends, and shifts.
2. Nonproduction awards and bonuses such as safety awards, and
   Christmas and year-end bonuses.
3. Payments for time not worked such as sick days, vacations, and
   religious holidays.
4. Payment for employee health and security such as insurance,
   pension fund contributions, and payments and supplements to
   workman's compensations.
5. Perquisites for top executive such as bigger offices, reserved
   parking, and expense account arrangements.

As extensive as that list may seem, fringe benefit packages in the United States are far more limited than they are in other countries. Large companies in Japan, for instance, offer benefits that include subsidized food and vacations, company housing, and cost-free loans. (It is this dramatic variance in fringe benefit packages that often makes cross-national compensation comparisons difficult or misleading.)

The cost of fringe benefits in the United States has grown rapidly in recent years. In 1968 the fringe benefit package for an average organization amounted to about 21 percent of the total compensation cost. By the late 1970s, many companies were putting 40 percent of their compensation cost into fringe benefits. There are some estimates that the average organization could be spending 50 percent by 1985,[16] further reducing the compensation dollars available for motivation and forcing companies to find other rewards that will motivate—recognition, work itself, and so on.

A typical aspect of most fringe benefit packages is that the benefits offered differ for different groups of employees. These variations occur, however, not because of differing individual or group preferences, but rather because of hierarchical status within the organization. Thus, hourly workers often receive one benefit package, salaried workers another, and top management personnel still another. Since reward systems can serve as a visible statement about the organization's view of its employees, such differences in fringes reinforce the hierarchical notion of the work force. Companies that are experimenting with new forms of work organization, particularly those attempting to create an atmosphere of cooperation and shared responsibility, have occasionally tried to change this approach. By offering the same fringe benefit package to all their members, they have attempted to eliminate at least one symbol of inequality. At the same time, by eliminating one incentive for climbing the corporate ladder they must find other rewards to motivate employees to take more responsibility.

The possiblity that fringe benefits might be used to motivate employees within a certain organization has been eliminated in some countries by government legislation. In France, fringe benefits such as holidays, sick leave, medical care, retirement, and severance pay are legislated by the national government. The government has also moved to eliminate at least some of the differential in fringe benefit packages between blue-collar and white-collar workers.[17] While such legislation prevents an organization from using fringe benefits to attract people or motivate upward mobility, it does hold some advantages for the organization. Because fringe benefits can differ only slightly from company to company, organizations can turn to other, more flexible and *less* costly rewards to attract and keep employees. Of course with the rise of international competition, national differences in the cost of fringe benefits affect each country's ability to compete, requiring countries that legislate fringes to examine their costs in comparison to other countries.

CAFETERIA-STYLE BENEFIT PACKAGES. Typical fringe benefit packages are aimed toward a working man with a dependent wife and children, but by 1981 such employees constituted less than 15 percent of the work force. In 1974 one American company—the Systems Group of TRW Corporation—experimented with a way of increasing the cost effectiveness of fringe benefits as a satisfier. What they offered their 12,000 employees was a form of cafeteria-style fringe benefit planning. Employees were told how much the company would spend on them individually in fringe benefits. While all employees were required to take a minimum level of certain important benefits (there would be no such requirement under a pure cafeteria-style program), each was allowed to select individually from a list of remaining options until they had spent the total individual package cost. The year the plan was first introduced, over 80 percent of the employees indicated at least some dissatisfaction with their previous fringe benefit packages by asking for changes. Each year thereafter, the requirements became fewer and the options greater. More recently, the American Can Company moved to a cafeteria-style plan with similar results.

Such an approach obviously helps to individualize fringe benefits, thereby increasing congruence. The cafeteria approach, according to the management of TRW, has also increased the company's ability to retain people, an indication of increased *commitment* and resultant increase in *competence*.[18] It would appear that the cafeteria approach to fringe benefits is a more cost-effective approach to spending compensation dollars. It also creates certain problems. It requires additional bookkeeping for the salary administrators. In small companies particularly, it could create problems because the cost of many benefits (like health insurance) depends on participation by a certain number of people. In the two cases cited above, the problem of insurance rates has been dealt with by the requirement of a minimum core of fringe benefits. There are ways to manage the other problems raised by a cafeteria-style plan, and each organization must find appropriate methods to cope with the problems in order to obtain the potential for greater employee satisfaction and commitment.

### Payroll Stratification: A One- or Two-Class Society?

When an organization develops different fringe benefits, pay-for-performance rewards, and administrative procedures for different levels of the organization, it is sending a message to employees beyond the specific behavior these compensation systems are intended to reward. That message is that there are differences between hierarchical levels in their commitment, role, and the degree to which they are full and responsible members of the organization. In many organizations this is the case.

There are several understandable reasons for these differences. To get around the intended effects of progressive tax laws, corporations pay higher management levels in a different form than lower levels. Deferred compensation, stock options, and various perquisites protect executives from taxation that reduces the value of their reward. In the United States, all organizations must make a distinction between *exempt employees* (those who, according to the wage and hour laws, have significant decision-making responsibility—typically managers and professional employees), and *nonexempt employees* (all other regular members of the organization—typically clerical white-collar and hourly blue-collar employees). Nonexempt employees are covered by federal law requiring that they receive overtime pay for a work week that exceeds 40 hours; exempt employees are, as the name implies, exempt from such legislative protections. Because of this legal requirement organizations must maintain records of time worked by nonexempt employees, which often results in the use of time clocks. Different payroll labels are given to these groups: salaried payroll for exempt employees and hourly payroll for production employees, creating a two-class language. It also means that a nonexempt employee cannot demonstrate spontaneous commitment to the organization by offering to stay after regular work hours. This can only be done within the law by negotiating overtime pay with the organization, a process that immediately sets the nonexempt employee apart from the exempt employee. Otherwise, this spontaneous commitment results in collusion between the employee and the company in breaking the law, something that happens quite frequently.

Federal law governing overtime pay for nonexempt employees was created in the 1930s to protect employees from exploitation by management. It can, and often does, have the unintended result of creating or reinforcing certain assumptions made by managers about their employees' commitment to the organization. It might also affect employees' perceptions of their role in the organizations and thereby alter their commitment. In a subtle way, a two-class society is created within the organization.

ALL-SALARIED SYSTEM.    One way that some organizations have attempted to overcome this legislated division of the work force is through an all-salaried compensation system. Workers traditionally by the hour now join management in receiving a weekly or monthly salary (nonexempt employees are still paid on an hourly basis for overtime work). Such a system has been in effect in several large nonunion companies (such as IBM and Gillette) for decades. More recently, the United Auto Workers have encouraged America's Big Three automobile makers to consider it. While an all-salaried system cannot eliminate the legislated distinction between exempt and nonexempt employees, it can at least remove one symbolic, but nonetheless important, difference. Workers then join managers in having more flexibility. Time can be taken off from work with no loss in pay. Workers can be given more responsibility. Such treatment, in turn, can increase their commitment and loyalty to the organization. The fear that such flexibility will lead to greater absenteeism does not seem to have been established. However, there is no solid evidence that such a system in fact increases commitment.[19]

It is not surprising that the all-salaried payroll together with other approaches to standardizing the forms, but not the amount, of compensation cannot of themselves improve commitment. If accompanied by other efforts to create a more egalitarian atmosphere and increase commitment (see Chapter 6), the all-salaried payroll can reinforce these efforts. Just as we have seen overreliance by managers on pay-for-performance systems (which we will discuss later in this chapter), so we have seen a tendency to rely too much on a change to an all-salaried payroll as the means for improving commitment. Though it may be an important symbol needed to sustain changes in the employee influence and work system policy areas, an all-salaried payroll by itself cannot change a two-class company into a one-class company. Nevertheless, as part of an overall shift in corporate philosophy and style, this is a compensation system innovation that can play an important supporting role. Companies such as Hewlett-Packard, IBM, and participative nontraditional plants at Procter and Gamble, Dana, TRW, and Cummins Engine have successfully used the all-salaried payroll in this way.

### Systems for Maintaining Equity

In order to maintain employee satisfaction with pay, corporations have developed systems that are intended to maintain pay equity with internal- and external-comparison persons and groups.

The consequences of inequity in employee pay with respect to external labor markets are potentially severe for a corporation. One result might be an inability to attract and keep the talent required. However, the costs of maintaining pay equity are also high. If a company were to offer to meet all competitive wage offers obtainable by employees—the extreme form of maintaining external equity—employees would search for the highest paying job offers to convince management to increase their pay. This would result in a market system for determining compensation, much like the free agent system in sports, and would be a time-consuming and very expensive proposition for employers which could lead to internal inequities. It would also lead to a self-centered orientation toward career and pay, rather than a primary commitment to the organization and a secondary commitment to pay.

The potential consequences of internal pay inequity are employee dissatisfaction, withholding of effort, and lack of trust in the system. Internal inequity can result in conflict within the organization which consumes the time and energy of managers and personnel people. However, maintaining high internal equity can result in overpaying some people compared to the market—a competitive cost disadvantage to the organization—and underpaying others, thus destroying external equity.

As we shall see, there is continual tension in an organization between concerns for external and internal equity. Line personnel are willing to sacrifice corporate internal equity (never equity within their departments) to attract and keep the talent they want for their own departments. The human resource personnel, who must maintain a corporate view, are placed in the position of opposing such efforts by line managers; they perceive efforts to pay whatever is needed to attract a candidate as a threat to internal equity. They insist on the integrity of the job evaluation and wage survey systems in order to avoid the costly conflicts that they fear will inevitably follow if a large number of exceptions to the job evaluation system are allowed. There is no solution to this dilemma; no new system will eliminate it. The balance must be continually managed to reduce problems and maintain a pay system that yields congruence and cost effectiveness.

JOB EVALUATION. In this country, the most common method of determining pay level is to assess the worth of a job to the organization through a system of job evaluation. About 75 percent of United States firms utilize some form of job evaluation. Simply put, job evaluations begin by *describing* the various jobs within an organization. Then jobs are *evaluated* for their worth to the company by taking into account a number of factors: working conditions, necessary technical knowledge, required managerial skills, and importance to the organization of the results for which the job incumbent is held accountable. A rating for each factor is made on a standard scale, and the total rating points can be used to *rank jobs hierarchically*. Once that is done, a *salary survey* is taken to learn what other organizations are paying for similarly rated jobs. A company must identify comparable jobs in other organizations.

The salary survey, together with considerations such as legislation, job market conditions, and the organization's willingness to pay, lead to the establishment of *pay ranges* for jobs. (The tighter the labor market, the more closely wages will be tied to the going rate. In a loose labor market, the other factors will tend to dominate.) Jobs may then be grouped into a smaller number of classifications, with each assigned a salary range. The level of the individual employee within his or her particular range is determined by some combination of job performance, seniority, experience, or any other combination of factors selected by the organization.

Job evaluation plans in combination with wage surveys have been used in wage and salary administration for more than 50 years. They have proven a useful tool for maintaining internal and external equity. The basic premise of such plans is that the relative value of a job can be established objectively, even scientifically, by formulating a careful description of an individual job and then comparing it with other jobs or assessing the degree to which certain "job worth factors" are present. The assumption is that a system can be worked out for getting managers to describe jobs accurately. A factor rating system can be developed that will allow personnel analysts, presumably objective parties in the process, to rate jobs and rank them. Pay ranges can then be determined accurately by finding comparable jobs in other companies. It is generally assumed that an objective, scientifically determined system will help create employee trust in the ranking and pay range of jobs, thus insuring perceptions of internal equity. Unfortunately, this assumption is not entirely valid.

Fifty years of new and better job evaluation systems have not completely solved the internal and external equity problem. There are always unhappy people in organizations, both workers and managers, who claim inequity in the job evaluation system and attack the personnel department for its inadequacy. Given their current level of sophistication, it would seem that more refined job evaluation systems and better analysis by personnel departments or outside consultants will be able to offer only marginal improvements. "Employee perceptions of the process will ultimately determine its success or failure," Howard Risher has noted. If employees believe that salaries and salary grades are inequitable, the system has failed to achieve the primary objective: increased satisfaction with pay. Management might consider its evaluation system fair and valid, but employees tend to view their jobs somewhat differently from management or personnel specialists."[20] The misperceptions of self and others that we discussed earlier are the root cause.

There are several potential approaches to these problems. First, general management and personnel departments should *reduce their ex-*

*pectations* for solving the problem and claim less inherent validity for their job evaluation systems. This can significantly reduce the expectations of managers and workers. Secondly, *more participation* in the design and administration of job evaluation systems is required. A number of companies have set up job evaluation committees (some with hourly production employees as members) to agree on factors and to be involved in evaluating jobs, at least for "benchmark jobs." Involvement provides more understanding and acceptance of the system by the very managers who may argue for a higher salary for their departmental employees at the expense of internal equity. Broader involvement of employees at all levels, including unions, may help. Thirdly, a company could provide *more information* about pay grades and ranges and about the results of salary surveys, thus reducing misperceptions. Salary survey results are often not shared with employees. Finally, a representative committee of *employees might review* the evaluation system periodically and inform the employee population at large about their findings. These steps will not solve the problem, but they can help manage it.

Even if these steps are taken, no job evaluation system can solve the problem of salary inequities that inevitably occur when new employees are hired or experienced employees are brought in. To recruit successfully in the labor market, firms must offer competitive wages, and this sometimes creates inequities (salary compression) with the salaries of employees who have been with the firm for some time. This occurs because corporations typically do not raise the salaries of incumbents automatically when salary surveys result in an upward movement of the salary range. To do so would be very costly. Not doing so also allows the firms to keep the pay of poorer performers behind the market by denying merit increases. The compression problem is thus created by the desire to reduce costs and to discourage poor performers. It has been argued that companies should solve inequities due to compression by regularly raising wages for everyone when salary surveys so indicate and to manage poor performers through other means. Some companies ask supervisors to position their subordinates within their pay ranges according to performance. Over the years, larger increases are provided for good performers so they will be near the top of their range, while poor performers receive lower increases or no increases to keep them at the bottom of the range. We can see that conflicting objectives—keeping costs down and rewarding good performers—not the job evaluation system itself are the cause of inequity and dissatisfaction. Of these objectives, cost effectiveness is the critical factor that managers must consider, since performance can be rewarded and poor performance discouraged in other monetary and nonmonetary ways. They must decide if the cost of across-the-board increases is worth the benefits of more perceived internal and external equity. To solve the equity problems, general managers must clarify their philosophy and make choices between objectives of cost and equity, a process that is determined more by values and financial constraints than by systems.

Job evaluation systems have created other problems. Salary ranges associated with jobs limit the pay increases an individual can obtain. Thus, significant advancements in status and pay can only come through promotions. This need for promotion can cause technical people to seek promotions to management positions, even though their real skills and interests might be in technical work. If no promotions are available, individuals' needs for advancement and progress are frustrated. Additionally, job evaluation systems cause a certain loss of flexibility in transferring people within an organization. If that transfer is to a job with a lower pay grade, a fear of lower pay and status will reduce the individual's willingness to transfer. While companies usually "red circle" that individual's pay by making an exception and maintaining the individual's salary above the range of the new job, the perception of loss and the reality of actual pay loss over time make transfer difficult.

To solve the problems of job evaluation systems, some companies have come up with an alternative: a person- or skill-based evaluation system. These systems promise to solve the problems of inflexibility and limited growth, but they do not solve all the equity problems discussed above.

SKILL-BASED EVALUATIONS.   Person- or skill-based evaluation systems base a person's salary on his or her abilities. Pay ranges are arranged in a hierarchy of steps from least skilled to most skilled. Employees come into the organization at an entry-level pay grade and move up the skill-based ladder after they have demonstrated competence at the next level. This system encourages the acquisition of new skills and should lead to higher pay for the most skilled individuals. Skill-based systems are generally thought to allow more flexibility in moving people from one job to another and introducing new technology. A skill-based compensation system can also change management's orientation. Instead of limiting assignments to be consistent with job level, the emphasis must shift to utilizing the available skills of people, since they are already being paid for those skills. Moreover, a skill-based evaluation system's greatest benefit is that it communicates to employees a concern for their development. This concern is consistent with the social capital perspective of human resource management discussed in Chapter 1, leading management to develop competence and utilize it, and resulting in greater employee well-being and organizational effectiveness.

Skill-based evaluation systems have been applied to technical personnel in R&D organizations, and are often called technical ladders. They could also be applied to other technical specialists such as lawyers, sales personnel, and accountants. Their use might encourage good specialists to stay in these roles rather than seek management jobs which pay more but for which they may not have talent. The organizations would thus avoid losing good technical specialists and gaining poor managers.

Skill-based pay systems have also been applied to production level employees in the past decade. Companies such as Procter & Gamble, General Motors, and Cummins Engine have introduced plans that pay for the skills that workers possess and utilize rather than for the jobs they hold. The benefits of flexibility and employee growth and satisfaction, which were mentioned earlier, have been experienced in these plants. But it is important to note that many of the plants have adopted skill-based systems to *support*, not *lead*, a change in management philosophy—one that emphasizes employee responsibility and involvement in work. Again, a compensation system is an essential support, but we wonder whether merely changing the compensation system will in fact foster flexibility and employee growth.

There are some problems to be considered in a skill-based approach, however. For one thing, many individual employees may, after several years, reach the top skill level and find themselves with no place to go. If nothing is done by the organization, there will be no pay incentive for employees to continue acquiring new skills. At this point, the organization might consider some type of profit-sharing scheme to encourage these employees to continue to seek ways of improving organizational effectiveness. A skills evaluation program also calls for a large investment by the organization in training, since pay increases depend upon the constant learning of new skills. Furthermore, the matter of external equity is more difficult to manage. Because each organization has its own unique configurations of jobs and skills, it is unlikely that individuals with similar skills can be found elsewhere, particularly in the same community, which is where production workers typically look for comparisons. This is less of a problem for professional employees whose jobs are more similar across companies. Because skill-based systems emphasize learning new tasks, employees may come to feel that their higher skills call for higher pay than the system provides, particularly when they compare their wages to workers in traditional jobs. Without effective comparisons, expectations could rise unchecked by a good reality test.

Since there are incentives for learning new jobs, it is conceivable that employees will want to progress to these jobs before they have mastered their current jobs. If this occurs widely, the organization will have many employees who are barely competent to perform their jobs and will never benefit from full mastery by long-term incumbents. If not managed skillfully, this problem will clearly reduce organizational effectiveness.

By far the most difficult problem facing a skills evaluation plan relates to its administration. In order to make the system work properly, attention must be paid to the skill level of each and every employee. Some method must be devised *first* to determine how many and what new skills must be learned in order to receive a pay boost, and *second* to determine whether or not the individual employee has in fact mastered those new skills. The ease with which the first point is achieved depends on how measurable or quantifiable the necessary skills are. Identification of particular skills is more easily accomplished for lower-level positions than for top-management or professional positions.

Some companies have tried to meet the second point by asking co-workers to pass judgment on their colleagues. But there can be some pressure to award pay increments independent of actual skill acquisition. That pressure may come not only in the form of peer pressure, but also from the fear that an honest evaluation of a co-worker might affect negatively one's own evaluation by that co-worker. If that kind of pressure comes to dominate, then skills evaluation will quickly become a seniority-based system. The success of such an evaluation system depends on a number of factors: an overall organizational culture that encourages cooperation, mutual help as well as openness in peer evaluation, realistic self-appraisal for all members of the organization, and a shared commitment to the well-being of the organization.

Skill-based pay systems hold out some promise of improving competence in a cost-effective way and enhancing both organizational effectiveness and employee well-being. They are not right for all situations, however. Because they depend heavily on solving the problem of measuring and assessing skills or competencies, only an organization with the right climate of trust and an effective process of evaluation is likely to use the system successfully. Without the appropriate culture and process, even a new and innovative compensation system will not work. Moreover, skill-based compensation systems are only right for those organizations in which skill requirements are high and are undergoing constant change. They are also hard to introduce in existing organizations where a traditional job evaluation system already exists.

SENIORITY.    It is also possible to base pay solely on seniority. Seniority has been accepted as a valid criterion for pay in some countries. Japanese companies, for instance, use seniority-based pay along with other factors such as slow promotion to help achieve a desired organizational culture.[21] In the United States, the major proponents of a seniority-based pay system tend to be trade unions. Distrustful of management, unions often feel that any pay-for-performance system will end up increasing paternalism, unfairness, and inequities. For those reasons, unions often prefer a strict seniority system. To many managers in the United States, however, seniority seems to run contrary to the country's individualistic ethos that maintains that individual effort and merit should be rewarded above all else. Therefore, most American companies prefer to make performance a major factor in their pay systems. The notion of pay for performance should be carefully scrutinized both for its advantages and its shortcomings.

*Pay for Performance*

There are many good reasons why organizations should pay their employees for performance:

1. Under the right conditions, pay-for-performance can motivate desired behavior.
2. A pay-for-performance system can help attract and keep achievement-oriented individuals.
3. A pay-for-performance system can help to retain good performers by satisfying their needs and will discourage the poor performers. By not giving poor performers increases or by giving them only small increases, their pay relative to good performers and the labor market will decline.
4. In the United States at least, most employees, both managers and workers, prefer a pay-for-performance system, although white-collar workers are significantly more supportive of the notion than blue-collar workers. Therefore, a pay-for-performance system should lead to higher perceptions of equity and feelings of satisfaction.

For all these reasons, many organizations employ some type of pay-for-performance system for their employees, with unionized and government workers by and large excepted.

Despite the obvious benefits of pay-for-performance systems, there is plenty of evidence that they do not always achieve the motivation and satisfaction they promise. For example, far more management employees express a belief in some sort of pay-for-performance system than believe they are actually operating under a system that does pay for performance.[22] There is a gap, and the evidence indicates a wide gap, between the desire to devise a pay-for-performance system and the ability to make such a system work in practice.

PAY-FOR-PERFORMANCE SYSTEMS. There are numerous forms of pay-for-performance systems, and organizations can select one or more of them. The most important distinction between them is the level of

aggregation at which performance is defined. Are we talking about individual performance, group performance, or organization-wide performance? Under each of these three broad categories, there are a
number of possible options which are summarized in the chart below:

**Pay-for-Performance Systems**

| INDIVIDUAL PERFORMANCE | GROUP PERFORMANCE | ORGANIZATION-WIDE PERFORMANCE |
| --- | --- | --- |
| Merit system | Productivity incentive | Profit sharing |
| Piece rate | Cost effectiveness | Productivity sharing |
| Executive bonus | | (Scanlon plan) |

Historically, pay-for-performance has meant pay for *individual* performance. Piece-rate incentive systems for production employees and
merit salary increases or bonus plans for salaried employees have been
the dominant means of paying for performance. In the last decade,
there has been a dramatic decline in piece-rate incentive as managers
have discovered that such systems result in dysfunctional behavior: low
cooperation, artificial limits on production and resistance to changing
standards. Similarly, more questions are being asked about individual
bonus plans for executives, as top managers discover their dysfunctional effects. At the same time, organization-wide incentive systems
are becoming more popular, particularly as managers are finding that
productivity and innovation suffer due to lack of cooperation. In fact,
one recent survey of large American companies found that nearly one-
third are engaged in some type of organization-wide incentive plan.[23]
However, for these plans to work, certain conditions must also exist. In
this section we intend to review the key considerations when designing
a pay-for-performance plan and the problems which arise when these
considerations are not taken into account.

LEVEL OF AGGREGATION.[24]     At what level should the pay-for-performance plan be aggregated: the individual, group, or organizational
level? Organization-wide plans motivate cooperation, and teamwork
can improve significantly. However, the individual is further removed
from the level of performance being measured and rewarded. Consequently, the perceived connection between pay and performance is diminished. One of the reasons that individual pay-for-performance systems are so popular is that the linkage between individual effort and the
performance being measured and rewarded is tighter. Organization-
wide plans may be introduced to increase the perception of a linkage
between individual effort and organization performance and to increase the incentive for cooperation. If the trade-off between individual

and organization-wide pay-for-performance systems is recognized, managers can take action to minimize the dysfunctional effects of each plan. They can rely on other motivational methods (involvement in work, for example) when using organization-wide plans, or they can urge cooperation in nonmonetary ways when individual bonus plans are used. Alternatively, individual and organization-wide pay plans can be used simultaneously, communicating that both individual performance and cooperation are important. In our experience competition can arise when individual bonus plans are introduced without corresponding communication about cooperation, particularly if the bonuses are substantial. Similarly, organization-wide plans require effective supervision to maintain high individual performance.

NATURE OF THE TASK.   The design of a pay-for-performance system requires an analysis of the task. Does the individual have *control over the performance* (results) that is to be measured? Is there a significant effort-to-performance relationship? For motivational reasons already discussed, such a relationship must exist. Unfortunately, many individual bonus, commission, or piece-rate incentive plans fall short of meeting this requirement. An individual may not have control over a performance result such as sales or profit because that result is affected by economic cycles or competitive forces beyond his or her control. Similarly, an individual may depend on other functions and employees to achieve performance outcomes like sales, cost savings, or profits. Sales volume, for example, may depend more on good products developed by the R&D function, or on advertising by the marketing function, than on individual sales ability. There are few outcomes in complex organizations that are not dependent on other functions or individuals, fewer still that are not subject to external factors.

So long as employees continue to receive bonus payouts, these interdependencies do not become an issue. When performance drops and payouts are reduced, employees begin to point to interdependencies and lack of control over results as flaws in the system. Commitment to the system and trust in it then drops, as does its capacity to motivate and satisfy. Similarly, if individual incentives are offered but cooperation between individuals is required, the seeds for potential conflict are planted. Individuals will blame others for their poor performance and lower pay when these occur.

In our experience, there are few jobs that meet the conditions of individual control and independence; therefore, few individual incentive plans do not fall prey to these problems. Interdependence with other functions or employees and lack of control over aggregate results such as profit lead managers to consider group or organization-wide pay-for-performance plans. These plans communicate to employees their dependence on others in achieving a result; say lower costs or profits. Problems with individual bonus systems also lead managers to introduce subjective judgments into performance ratings. Supervisors are expected to look not just at bottom-line results, but also to make judgments about behavior and to factor out poor results which were beyond the individual's control. This type of system eliminates the problems associated with result-based individual bonus plans, but introduces a new problem: the credibility of the subjective judgment.

MEASURE OF PERFORMANCE.    Choosing an appropriate measure of performance on which to base pay is a related problem incurred by individual bonus plans. For reasons discussed above, effectiveness on a job can include many facets not captured by cost, units produced, or sales revenues. Failure to include all activities that are important for effectiveness can lead to dysfunctional consequences. Because pay is an effective motivator, singling out one measure of performance for financial reward leads employees to give that measure disproportionate attention at the expense of other facets of the job that may also affect short- and long-term performance. For example, sales personnel who receive a bonus for sales volume may push unneeded products, thus damaging long-term customer relations; or they may push an unprofitable mix of products just to increase volume. These same salespersons may also take orders and make commitments that cannot be met by manufacturing. Why not then hold salespeople responsible for profit, a more inclusive measure of performance? It should be clear that the problem with this measure is that sales personnel do not have control over profits.

These dilemmas are constantly encountered and have led to the use of more subjective but inclusive behavioral measures of performance. Why not observe if the salesperson or executive is performing all aspects of the job well? Most merit salary increases are based on subjective judgments, as are some individual bonus plans. Subjective evaluation systems, though they can be all inclusive if based on a thorough analysis of the job, require high levels of trust in management, good manager-subordinate relations, and high levels of interpersonal competence. Unfortunately, these conditions are also not fully met in many situations, though they can be developed if judged to be sufficiently important. Even objective measures of performance require some trust and good relations if a pay-for-performance system is to be perceived as fair and credible. Thus, management is well advised to give considerable attention to how to measure performance, or no pay-for-performance system will work.

A final measurement problem typically encountered with bonus plans is that they are often tied to performance measures that are appropriate for one type of business or economic condition—growth, for instance—but not another. When the business environment changes, managers no longer receive a payout even though their effort has been high. If, as often is the case, they have come to expect and rely upon that bonus, dissatisfaction occurs. Organizations often respond with some modification in their bonus system. The problem, however, results from a more fundamental flaw in the bonus plan: the performance outcomes measured were not a function of effort from the beginning. They were a function of external factors such as growth or decline. The lack of linkage between individual effort and results was not apparent or questioned so long as a payout occurred.

AMOUNT OF PAYOUT. For a pay-for-performance plan to motivate, the amount of the pay increase or bonus tied to good performance needs to be perceived as being *significant*. Significance is obviously a subjective matter that varies from individual to individual. Typically, merit salary increases range from 5 to 15 percent of salary. Since fringe benefits constitute about 40 percent of total compensation, a 5 or 10 percent increase in salary represents a small amount (about 3 to 6 percent) of total compensation, particularly after taxes. It has been argued that these amounts are much too small to have motivational impact,[25] particularly given the potential of pay-for-performance systems for damaging self-esteem. As we mentioned earlier, most people perceive themselves in the eightieth percentile with respect to performance and expect merit raises consistent with their self-perception.[26]

The importance of a large payout makes individual bonus plans based on results more attractive since they typically pay out a higher percentage of base salary. Unlike merit pay, bonuses do not become part of base pay the following year. Thus, unlike salary increases which become annuities, bonuses can result in a decline in the individual's pay. However, the attractiveness of delivering large bonuses based on performance is undercut by the problem of measuring performance.

It is more than likely that the amount of payout is also a function of whether the increase is publicized within the organization. If the payout is public, it affects reputation, status, and pride. Thus, the rewards of recognition and increased prestige are added to the monetary reward. If pay increases are kept private, the dollar amount must carry the motivational message alone. In this case, the monetary amount needs to be large. Most organizations do not publicize payouts for merit or bonus because employees do not want this information known. So the small amounts given in merit increases probably do not motivate. However, organizations might experiment with providing information about the average salary increase or bonus so that individuals can gauge the meaning of their own increase or bonus. Of course, this might lead employees to question their evaluations, putting more pressure on the evaluation system. Because of the necessity of justifying the equity of an open system, managers may hesitate to make discriminatory comparisons about employee performance. For that reason, management often opposes publicizing such information. Nevertheless, more information about the meaning of a pay increase, whether communicated by the supervisor or by general comparison information, is critical to making merit and bonus systems more effective.

Another reason merit salary increases have questionable motivational value is that the amount of the increase is judged by the employee against factors *unrelated* to performance: the rate of inflation, increases negotiated by a union, and the movement of salaries in the market. If salaries in the labor market go up 7 percent during a given year (due to inflation or other supply and demand forces) a 10 percent increase includes only a 3 percent merit increase, a rather small amount. Moreover, individuals often do not know what part of the increase is tied to merit, and organizations are reluctant to communicate this since the sum is insignificant. Without explicit knowledge, feedback is blurred and individuals may actually underestimate the merit component of the increase. It has been argued that organizations should separate salary adjustments from merit increases, providing yearly salary adjustments to everyone but giving merit increases only to a few high performers. Of course, this is more costly and prevents the organization from putting pressure on low performers by actually letting them lose ground relative to inflation.

To deal with the problem of payout amount in merit systems, some organizations have instituted the option of *lump sum salary increases*. Individuals may choose to receive their increase in one or two installments rather than having it buried in their paycheck over a whole year. The advantage is that the salary increase becomes more visible, has more motivational value, and the employee is given some choice.

Organization-wide pay-for-performance plans are not exempt from the problems of payout. Unless the amount received every month is significant, the pay itself has little motivational value (although, as will be discussed below, the *process* of administering such a plan may, in fact, be a motivating factor).

THE PAY-FOR-PERFORMANCE DILEMMA.    The problems of pay-for-performance systems we have discussed have led some observers to suggest that these systems should be discontinued. The costs of dealing with many of the problems cited simply outweigh the limited motivational benefits they offer, according to these observers. Indeed, some organizations have done this. Digital Equipment Corporation, for example, does not use a bonus system to reward its salespeople, a group typically thought to put a high value on pay for performance. European and Japanese organizations use virtually no pay-for-performance systems, so they have to find other ways to motivate. Participation, involvement, and communication are used by the Japanese in place of individual pay for performance to motivate their employees.

Despite many potential problems, pay for performance remains popular in the United States. In order to maintain external equity so as to attract and keep high performance individuals, some organizations feel compelled to offer some sort of bonus or incentive regardless of their potential for motivating dysfunctional behavior. Still others insist that, despite all the potential dangers, it is proper and sensible to pay for performance. To pay on some basis other than performance risks overcompensating poor performers and undercompensating good performers, which in turn could lead to the loss of the very individuals the organization wants most to keep. That fact, plus the benefits of being forced to define what constitutes good performance, providing a realistic individual performance measurement, and encouraging exactly the kind of behavior the organization seeks are all advantages to the organization that are not to be given up lightly. The difficulties of implementing individual pay-for-performance plans are not easily overcome, however. This may account, in part at least, for a growing interest in some sort of organization-wide pay system.

### Group and Organization-Wide Pay Plans

Organizational effectiveness depends on employee cooperation much more frequently than is realized. An organization may elect to tie pay, or at least some portion of pay, only *indirectly* to individual performance. Seeking to foster team work, perhaps, or even organization-wide cooperation and commitment, a company may tie an incentive to some measure of group performance or it may offer some type of profit- or productivity-sharing plan for the whole plant or company. We will discuss only organization-wide pay plans since group plans are relatively rare and are subject to some of the disadvantages of individual plans, such as problems caused by interdependence between groups.

Gains-sharing plans have been used for years and there are many varieties. In many cases, they are simply economic incentive plans and are not part of a broader management philosophy regarding collaboration and participation. In these instances the plan may have some marginal value in encouraging cooperation among people. The real power of a gains-sharing plan comes when it is supported by a climate of participation and when various structures, systems, and processes involve employees in decisions that will improve the organization's performance and result in an organization-wide bonus. The Scanlon plan, for example, involves more than a bonus based on company-wide savings in costs. The plan also calls for the creation of management-labor committees and demands cooperation with workers and unions (if there are unions). The committees seek and review suggestions for reducing costs. Payout is based on improvements in the sales-to-cost ratio of the plant compared to some agreed-upon base period prior to the adoption of the plan. Organization-wide incentive plans that are part of a philosophy of participation require high levels of labor-management cooperation in design and administration (the Scanlon plan requires a direct employee vote with 75 percent approval before implementation). Without that joint participation, commitment to the system will be low, as will its symbolic and motivational value.

There are several critical decisions that influence the effectiveness of any gains-sharing plan.[27]

1. Who should participate in the design and administration of the plan and how much participation will be allowed by management and union?
2. What will be the size of the unit covered? Small units obviously offer easier identity with an organization's performance and the bonuses which result.
3. What standard will be used to judge performance? Employees (union) and management must agree on this for commitment to be high. There are inevitable disagreements.
4. How will the gains be divided? Who shares in the gains? What percentage of the gain goes to the company and what percentage to employees?

When management and employees have gone through a process of discussion and negotiation, allowing a consensus to emerge on these questions, a real change in management-employee and union relations can occur. A top-down process would not yield the same benefits. Gains sharing approached in a participative way can create a fundamental change in the psychological and economic ownership of the firm. Therein lies its primary motivational and satisfactional value. However, only a management that embraces values consistent with participation can make it work.

## IMPLICATIONS FOR THE DESIGN AND ADMINISTRATION OF COMPENSATION SYSTEMS

It should be clear to the reader that the theory of compensation is extremely difficult to translate into practice. A solution to one problem inevitably leads to another problem. What are the implications of these difficulties for the design and administration of compensation systems?

## The Role of Compensation

We do not believe that pay can or should be abandoned as a motivator. It is simply too important to people and has enormous symbolic value beyond its obvious material value. But we do believe that the role of pay in the enterprise needs to be rethought substantially so as to reduce some of its dysfunctional effects. Compensation should be used far *less* frequently as a leading policy area in human resource management, and should be thought of rather as a policy designed to support policies in the other HRM areas: employee influence, human resource flow, and work systems. For example, instead of rushing into the design of a new incentive system for production workers or executives, it might be wise first to discover whether employees are clear about goals, if they received information and feedback, if they have sufficient influence over getting jobs done, if there is adequate collaboration with other functions, and if there is adequate education and coaching to develop needed competencies. Lacking such an analysis, managers often install compensation systems without paying appropriate attention to what *they* must do as leaders to effect changes in employee behavior.

Compensation systems should be designed so that behavior and attitudes which are to follow from policy decisions in the other HRM areas are reinforced rather than contradicted. Money should be used to reward behavior stimulated by other policies, thus becoming primarily a means for recognizing performance and ensuring equity. The approach we are suggesting places much less burden on the compensation system to directly stimulate behavior and attitudes. Thus, pay typically needs to be *less tightly tied* to specific results or behavior, reducing the probability of dysfunctional behavior. Moreover, when compensation is not the leading variable in HRM, managers can be less ambitious in their claims of validity or equity for the system (claims that few systems can meet anyway), resulting in lower, more realistic expectations by employees. More realistic expectations by employees will mean less focus on compensation and less disappointment and dissatisfaction when experience shows these systems to be flawed.

We are arguing for less reliance on elegant compensation systems, particularly pay-for-performance systems, to satisfy and motivate and *more reliance on intrinsic rewards*. Compensation should be used less to initiate behavior and attitudes and more to reinforce behavior and attitudes which are stimulated by other means: involvement in work, identity with the company, and influence over the task. Of course, this approach demands greater management skill and competence. Some of the problems with compensation systems arise because managers do not want or cannot motivate other human beings through leadership and the development of a good work environment. All of this requires that general managers start by defining their *philosophy of rewards*, particularly with regard to the relative role of intrinsic rewards and compensation, but also with regard to where salaries should be pegged and what kind of pay for performance systems will be used.

### Participation in Pay System Design and Administration

Participation in pay system design and administration is a second major way in which the motivational power of compensation can be retained while reducing problems. High levels of participation by employees and unions in the design and administration of the compensation system undoubtedly result in a pay system that fits the needs of employees and the reality of the situation better than the top-down design of compensation systems. Even aside from experience with the Scanlon plan, there is evidence that employees can be involved in designing and administering compensation systems in a responsible manner. Donnelly Mirrors has employee job evaluation committees that rate jobs. Employees in other companies have designed pay-for-performance systems and conducted salary surveys. The result seems to be high satisfaction, effectiveness, and longevity for the compensation system when compared with identical pay-for-performance systems where employees were not involved.

Despite this evidence, pay systems are one of the last vestiges of traditional managerial values regarding authority. Managers protect their prerogatives in this area more closely than any other, believing that employee self-interest precludes participation. This view is understandable, particularly if levels of distrust and hostility are high, or if management, employees, and unions are not willing to take the enormous amounts of time needed to participate in reward system design and administration. We believe that if the conditions and process are right, participation can be a major tool for improving the design of pay systems. It can result in higher commitment of employees to pay systems and a corresponding reduction of dysfunctional behavior, particularly if employees continue to be involved and influence administration of the system. Equity problems can be reduced by such participation, but management must be willing to cede its unilateral power in these areas. One legal caveat is necessary in the case of nonexempt employees: when there is no union, employee influence must be limited to recommendations, since participation could constitute negotiation with nonunion employees, a possible unfair labor practice which could lead to automatic recognition of employees as a collective bargaining unit.

### Communication

Pay systems can be made more effective by more and better communication about their intent. What behaviors and attitudes does management expect employees to exhibit, and how do these behaviors and attitudes support business goals? Too often, employees are left to interpret the meaning of the compensation system on their own. Communication about intent can prevent employees from overfocusing on certain goals or behaviors to the exclusion of others, a frequent by-product of pay-for-performance systems.

Open information about the pay system can also be an important factor in determining its effectiveness. For understandable reasons (employee desires for privacy and management's fear of opening up a Pandora's box of questions and challenges concerning equity), companies are hesitant to provide too much information about compensation systems. Not only are others' salaries, bonuses, and increases kept secret, but so is information about pay ranges and salary survey results. However, the natural tendency of people to misperceive both the pay of others and the value of their own contribution to the organization can actually reduce the power of these systems to satisfy and motivate. A closed system tends to undermine perceptions of equity; and equity, as we discussed earlier, is a critical ingredient if a reward system is to satisfy and motivate.

We do not suggest that all compensation systems should be totally open, or that moves toward openness can or should occur overnight. We do suggest that more openness is possible. Companies should strive to be as open as possible, consistent with their culture. That openness could extend at least to announcing information about the system: for example, pay ranges and the average merit increase or bonus awarded employees in a given year. Organizations that allow some degree of participation in the design and administration of reward systems will be sharing information about that system as a necessary by-product of the participation process. Corporate culture is critical to the development of openness, particularly managers' beliefs about the right of employees to challenge pay decisions.

Manager-subordinate relations and interpersonal competence in handling performance appraisal discussions are key to pay system success, particularly when the pay system is open. Unless these are effective, managers cannot help subordinates understand the meaning of pay decisions, leaving much room for misperception and ambiguity. Pay increases or bonuses under these circumstances simply do not work well and can create unexpected problems.

### Multiple Systems

Since pay systems are limited in the messages they send, and since it is nearly impossible to predict precisely how the message of any single pay system will be interpreted by employees, managers should use multiple systems to avoid narrow, dysfunctional behavior aimed at increasing individual pay rather than at enhancing organizational effectiveness. An organization-wide incentive system may be used to encourage cooperation while an individual pay-for-performance system can be used to stimulate individual motivation. Some organizations accomplish both these objectives by stipulating that bonuses will not be paid until the total corporation's earnings reach a certain level. Similarly, a merit salary system can be anchored to a set of broad, inclusive behaviors thought to contribute to overall organizational effectiveness, while a bonus is paid on top of the salary for achieving certain clearly identifiable and measurable results. In this way, the bonus motivates the short-term performance, while the salary rewards behaviors required for success of the enterprise as a whole. Organizations can then manipulate the richness of the salary component versus the bonus in the total compensation package to avoid overemphasis on short-term performance versus behaviors thought to enhance long-term effectiveness. Another application of multiple systems would be to use a job evaluation plan for one group of employees where jobs can be clearly defined and segmented, while using a skill-based system where greater flexibility and growth is desired. Organizations should weigh the complexities and sometimes contradictions of multiple systems against the potential benefits to the organization of not having to put all their ''eggs'' in one pay system basket.

### Symbolism

Managers should not lose sight of the fact that compensation systems, because of their importance to employees, are powerful symbols. They communicate, beyond their instrumental value, management's philosophy, attitudes and intent. For this reason, managers must examine the implicit meanings employees are likely to derive from a pay system, as well as its implicit messages. For example, what messages are sent to employees when different systems are designed for the top, middle, and bottom of the organization? What messages are sent when top management pays itself a bonus or goes off to a resort for a conference, while lower-level employees do not receive pay increases? A recent example of the symbolic importance of rewards was the announcement of a new executive bonus plan at General Motors on the same day that the United Auto Workers signed a wage concession agreement for their members. The symbolism of that announcement led to a degree of deterioration of trust between workers and top management. It also led to a decision by top management to rescind the executive bonus plan, a powerful reminder that even in the area of executive compensation employees have increasing influence if management requires their commitment. Unfortunately, the belief in the legitimacy of hierarchy in the United States is emphasized clearly in a symbolic way by the wide gap—a much wider gap than in Europe or Japan—between the amount and kind of rewards offered to top executives and to employees at lower levels.[28]

### Loose Coupling

The validity and viability of any given measure of business performance to which pay is tied has a limited lifetime. Business and business environments simply change too frequently. It is probably better, therefore, to tie pay to judgments of performance by others, while specifying clearly what the criteria for judgment are during any given year. Experience suggests that companies spend enormous amounts of time designing and redesigning pay systems because a given measure of performance to which they are tied becomes less relevant over time. Of course such an approach requires a high level of trust and probably a good deal of participation, a condition we have said is important for almost any type of pay system to be effective.

## SUMMARY

We began this chapter by stating that the rewards policy area presents the general manager with one of the more difficult HRM tasks. there are numerous dilemmas and contradictions inherent in the reward system area which make it difficult to design and administer with predictable outcomes. There is the question of how important intrinsic rewards are relative to pay and other extrinsic rewards. What should be the relative emphasis on these rewards, and what effect do policies regarding one set of rewards have on the other? There are questions about what systems are most effective for maintaining internal and external equity with respect to pay, and about how employee perceptions of equity and trust can be enhanced. We also raised numerous questions about-pay-for-performance systems, their efficacy and role in the enterprise. At the same time, we indicated that process may be as important as the design of the system when it comes to compensation. How much participation and communication went into design and administration of the pay systems? How does that amount fit with the culture of the organization? What message has the organization sent about how much influence, involvement and development employees will receive? There is an inevitable need for fit between reward systems and other policy areas. We concluded that reward system policies should, in most instances, follow rather than lead other human resource policies, unless, of course, participation in compensation system design is the guiding philosophy in the rewards area.

# Chapter 6

# Work Systems

WHEN MANAGERS ARE asked what attitudes and behavior they desire to have among the persons they supervise, they ordinarily list the following:

- Initiative, self-starting
- Dependability
- Willingness to take responsibility
- Loyalty to the company and to managers
- Willingness to suggest changes and improvements in the job
- Adaptability, flexibility

To a large degree, this list may be said to envisage a work force strongly committed and involved in the successful performance of work. But when asked if employees exhibit such attributes, managers ordinarily say no, or only to a limited extent.

Instead, employee dissatisfaction, depersonalization, alienation and frustration, physical and psychological stress, low levels of initiative, high turnover and absenteeism, low product quality, and eroding productivity are all too often common at American workplaces.

In the past 20 years we have become increasingly aware of the extent to which negative behavior at work might be tied to the manner in which work is designed and the manner in which people are managed. The relation between work system design and employee productivity and well-being is most obvious at the shop floor level where assembly lines and other applications of so-called rational and efficient production systems have been in evidence since the early days of the Industrial Revolution. However, an examination of work design among office workers, professionals, and managers reveals that many of the same principles of work system design that have been applied to production-level employees may be finding their way to these levels of the organization with some of the same resulting problems. This trend has been heightened by the emergence of increasingly sophisticated office technology and management information systems as well as by the continued adherence to traditional assumptions about people and work.

The productivity crisis now faced by the American economy adds urgency to our needs as managers to understand how work system design affects employee performance and well-being, and how work systems can be designed to achieve desired business and human outcomes. To the necessary concern of businessmen and labor leaders about these issues can be added the concern of government, not only as an interested partner in solving the productivity problem, but as the institution most concerned about the well-being of society as a whole, for there is some evidence to indicate that work system design may have effects on physical health, mental health, and longevity of life itself.

The theme of this chapter is that management choices concerning work system design will have a strong effect on commitment, competence, cost effectiveness, and congruence—the four Cs outlined in Chapter 2. Well-executed changes in work system design can broaden employee responsibilities and result in substantial improvements in all four Cs.

1. *Commitment.* When employees become more psychologically involved in their work, higher levels of motivation, performance, and loyalty will result. There is some evidence that greater involvement in work may increase involvement in the community, thus contributing to the well-being of society.
2. *Competence.* Broader employee involvement increases the attractiveness of the firm to more capable prospective employees. It also develops employee competence and self-esteem.
3. *Cost effectiveness.* Wages and benefits are not lowered by innovation in work system design, and indeed may be increased. However, turnover and absenteeism often decrease; and flexibility, receptivity to change, productivity, and quality often increase.
4. *Congruence.* Management, unions, and employees can achieve a higher perceived coincidence of interest, provided the change itself is achieved by a process all parties regard as legitimate. Fewer grievances and quicker resolution of local contract nego-

tiations are some specific results that have occurred in unionized settings.

How have our assumptions about work system design been shaped
historically? What are the emerging assumptions that are achieving
some of the results just described? What are some of the problems and
considerations in implementing innovations in work system design?
We will turn to these questions after we define what we mean by the
term work system.

## WORK SYSTEM DEFINED

The term work system, as we use it here, refers to a particular combination of job tasks, technology, skills, management style, and personnel policies and practices. These are seen as determining how work is
organized and managed, how employees will experience work, and
how they will perform.

### Job Content

As Figure 6-1 shows, at the core of a work system is the design of
the work itself; that is to say, the job requirements as determined by the
scope and organization of the immediate task. A clerical employee in a
sales order-processing department may perform one task such as book-
ing, then pass the order on to another worker who schedules the order
then passes it to yet another person who handles special problems with

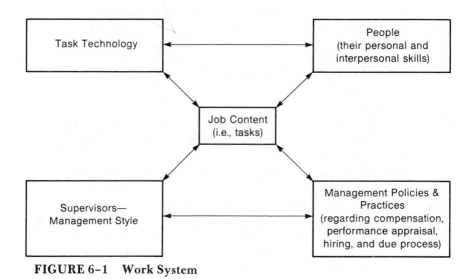

**FIGURE 6-1    Work System**

the customer. Alternatively, these employees can be organized so that each performs all of these order-processing functions for a more limited set of customers. Discretion in their tasks can be very closely circumscribed or it can be broad. Jobs may be highly individualized, or a team may be formally accountable for a whole task. The individual's responsibility may be confined to executing defined tasks or it may include contributing to goal-setting, planning, and problem-solving for the larger organizational unit.

### Task Technology

Job design and other components of an overall system discussed below are influenced by features of the job technology. For example, an assembly line in an automobile plant and a continuous process technology in a paper mill present very different opportunities and constraints on job design and supervisory delegation of planning and problem solving. It is possible for a supervisor to delegate to a face-to-face group responsibility for planning and operating a paper machine that embraces the entire process of converting pulp to rolled paper. In contrast, the magnitude and complexity of the automobile assembly task make it virtually impossible for a small group of individuals to be given comparable responsibility for planning and executing the assembly of an entire car.

### People

Another component of the work system is the set of skills and attitudes that employees bring to the workplace and those which are developed by the work experience. The selection process can place varying emphasis on mechanical skills, mental skills, and interpersonal skills. It can center on the ability of the employee to perform immedately, or take acount of the employee's potential for development. Management can attempt to select either employees who are predisposed to regard the job in strictly economic terms or those who also bring expectations about challenge and involvement. Apart from the predispositions and entering skill levels represented by new employees, management can choose to work toward some preferred profile of developed skills and attitudes. Obviously, this profile must fit the technology and job design, and must anticipate the type of management style and policy choices discussed below.

### Supervision—Management Style

The nature of supervisors, particularly the extent to which a supervisor delegates responsibilities for planning, goal setting, problem solving, and decision making, or allows workers to participate in these activities is a key aspect of a work system. Do supervisors see it as their responsibility to practice their technical skills or to impart them to their subordinates? Do they see their authority simply as delegated authority or do they see it as partly derived from the "consent of the governed?" How much emphasis do they place on developing the capabilities of their subordinates to supervise themselves? These choices about role definitions and management style are critical in conceiving the most appropriate work system.

### Management Policies and Practices

One component of work systems includes certain policies already discussed in the chapters on employee influence, flow, and rewards. The performance appraisal system may or may not require a supervisor to sit down and talk to subordinates about current performance and potential. It can emphasize individually oriented or unit-wide contribution. The employment security policy can determine whether employees must be worried about working themselves—or their fellow workers—out of employment. Finally, if the work force is unionized, then management's labor relations policy will influence whether the union resists or supports the other design choices that make up an internally consistent work system.

## WORK SYSTEMS AT DIFFERENT LEVELS

The work organization of a company encompasses many different, albeit interdependent work systems. There are work systems based on the operational tasks to be performed in a plant and in the office. Our illustrations above have emphasized these. There also are work systems related to engineering and research units. Finally, there is a managerial work system.

Before we examine in detail recent trends which have centered on the plant and office work systems, we will briefly note some of the concepts which have reshaped managerial work systems, modifying both the content of managerial work at various levels and the opportunities for manager involvement. Work systems based on divisonalization and/or the creation of profit centers delegate the responsibility and accountability for decision making. Integration of the functions required to compete in the marketplace also occurs at a lower level. Such changes inevitably orient managers to their competitive environment, determine the content of their work, and affect their motivation for performance.

Management work systems employing matrix organizational

forms are designed to provide for dual focus on function and product or product and geographic area. They require some managers and professionals to report to two bosses—one on each axis of the matrix. Matrix work systems require more communication and create higher levels of ambiguity for managers. These and other managerial innovations such as project management systems and "office of the chairmen" are illustrative of the stream of ideas which have affected the shape of managerial work systems—often in an evolutionary way. They are an important part of American industry's efforts to revitalize itself in the face of international competition.

### Scientific Management

The dominant pattern for organizing work today in the United States has been strongly influenced by the principles established by Frederick Taylor, coincident with the rise of large-scale manufacturing in the period around World War I.

"Each man must learn to give up his particular way of doing things," Frederick Taylor wrote in *Shop Management* (1919), "adopt his methods to the many new standards and grow accustomed to receiving and obeying instructions covering details, large and small, which in the past have been left to individual judgment."

Taylorism, or Scientific Management as it is sometimes called, came into vogue in the 1920s as an attempt to apply scientific principles to the management of workers, particularly the relationship of workers to newly emerging large-scale manufacturing. Work was to be divided into relatively simple and specialized tasks. In order to gain maximum efficiency at desired costs from technology, managers were urged to define precisely the limited tasks of workers, reduce to the fullest extent possible the need to bring human skills to bear on production, and thus minimize the opportunity for human mistakes and human inefficiencies.

Although Taylor's focus was on the job design, all other elements of the work system supported and reinforced these design choices—close supervision, piece-work incentives, minimal training requirements for single jobs, acceptance of turnover as not too costly, and so on. Taylorism relied on what is now characterized as a pessimistic view of an organization's human resources.

## FOCUSED INITIATIVES TO RESTRUCTURE OPERATING WORK

In the past several decades, a number of ideas have been advanced about how to utilize more effectively employees who work in plants and offices. Especially significant are three focuses for work reform, each of which relates to one element of our definitional model of the work system—supervision, job content, and task technology. Each type of work reform grew partly out of a sense of the incompleteness and insufficiency of prior initiatives.

### Participative Style

The idea of employee participation in matters of immediate concern and consequence to them grew steadily through the 1960s. It was a concept of supervision that top management and academics urged individual managers to adopt. Douglas McGregor, in *The Human Side of Enterprise* (1960), argued that, whatever the specific tools that might be employed by managers and theorists, a certain philosophy of management, indeed of human nature itself, underlies those practices. The prevailing theory of human behavior, Theory X, made pessimistic assumptions about human motivation. Taylor's techniques had been based on Theory X. McGregor argued that workers are capable of self-directed effort toward shared managerial goals. He labeled this theory of human nature and motivation Theory Y. The primary challenge of management, as he saw it, was to organize the enterprise in such a way that the potential for self-directed activities, even innovation, could be tapped.

Participative management gained considerably more momentum in the 1970s and early 1980s when the idea became associated with a variety of workplace reforms. In the mid-1970s, U.S. firms began promoting "quality circles," an idea that the Japanese were utilizing to great advantage. Quality circles consist of a number of volunteer employees from a work unit who meet regularly to identify and analyze problems that affect quality, productivity, or cost, and to recommend solutions. These circles frequently do not include a member of supervision. In the United States, the Honeywell Corporation has applied quality circles extensively, particularly in the Defense Group.

Even before quality circles were being discussed in the United States, some managements had begun to experiment with the same idea, referring to the concept then by the more descriptive term, "participative problem-solving groups." In the 1960s Texas Instruments pioneered this idea, reporting significant cost savings and efficiency gains in their manufacturing operations. These experiences led to the publication of *Every Employee A Manager* (1970) by Scott Meyers, who promoted corporate efforts to apply participative management approaches. The book's title reflects the assumption underlying the participative management approach: that employees who are involved in decisions about their immediate work will take responsibility for reducing costs and improving quality in the same way managers are presumed to be able and want to do.

It is not surprising, however, that this idea was found somewhat threatening by unions who saw in these efforts an attempt to reduce employee interest in unions. Indeed many of the firms that applied these ideas in the 1960s and early 1970s were in the electronics industry, which is largely nonunion.

Despite these fears on the part of unions, to which we will return later, it should be noted that participative concepts also were sometimes jointly sponsored by union and management. A prime example is the assembly plant of General Motors in Tarrytown, New York, in which a problem-solving group of workers was successful in finding a remedy for the problem of leaky rear windows. The success of this and similar efforts in the early 1970s led to the spread of such groups throughout the entire plant. The participative problem-solving groups became the main mechanism for improving the quality of work life for workers, a joint objective of plant management and the UAW. It produced benefits for management, union, and workers.[1]

Participative problem-solving groups have also been the primary vehicle for implementing the quality of work life objective of AT&T and the Communications Workers of America. These groups can be initiated without first making other changes in the definition of jobs. Therefore, the barriers to entry appear low. However, the longer-term success of participative problem-solving groups is only possible if management changes other aspects of the work system to encourage the delegation of authority and responsibility, and the improvement of the content of the job themselves. Many programs have foundered because management was not prepared to support fully the spirit of the program and to rethink other aspects of the work system.

### Job Enrichment

While the idea of participative supervision was gaining popularity, some observers were emphasizing a different type of reform—what was needed was to change the core task itself.

Frederick Herzberg has argued that there are two sets of factors involved in work tasks.[2] The first set, called "hygiene factors," have to do with the environment of the job and include such things as company policies, supervisory practices, pay plans, and working conditions. The second set of factors, called "motivators," include recognition, achievement, responsibility, advancement, personal growth, and competence. Employees cannot be motivated by improvement in hygiene factors alone, Herzberg argued. But those factors are considered to be of primary importance by employees. Therefore, any attempts to use job design to motivate employees must first minimize dissatisfaction with the hygiene factors. Only when that is done can motivation be enhanced by providing employees with work that allows them to experience the motivators.

In the 1960s Robert Ford and his associates at AT&T pioneered in the application of Herzberg's theories. Production, service, and office jobs were redesigned to allow workers a greater opportunity for motivator need satisfaction. An early experiment involved clerical workers who answered customer complaint letters. Previously required to answer correspondence by selecting from a set of standard letters signed by their supervisors, employees were now given the opportunity to write and sign their own letters. Some individuals were asked to take added responsibility as experts on certain subjects so that they could be resources to the rest of the department in answering difficult inquiries. The results were higher productivity and satisfaction with achievement, responsibility, and growth in competence.[3]

If jobs are to be designed to increase motivation, it would be helpful to know explicitly what job characteristics might be changed to increase involvement. More recently, a conceptual framework has been developed for analyzing many jobs.[4] Five core dimensions in the framework are:

1. *Skill variety*. The degree to which a job requires a variety of different activities in carrying out the work, involving the use of a number of different skills and talents.

2. *Task identity*. The degree to which the job requires completion of a "whole" and identifiable piece of work; that is, doing a job from beginning to end with a visible outcome.

3. *Task significance*. The degree to which a job has a substantial impact on the lives or work of other people, whether in the organization or the external environment.

4. *Autonomy*. The degree to which the job provides substantial freedom, independence, and discretion to the individual in scheduling work and determining the procedures to be used in carrying it out.

5. *Feedback*. The degree to which carrying out work activities required by the job results in the individual obtaining direct and clear information about the effectiveness of his or her performance.

By redesigning jobs to increase variety, identity, significance, autonomy, and feedback the psychological experience of working is changed. As Figure 6-2 illustrates, individuals experience the work as more meaningful, they feel more responsible for results, and they know more about the results of their efforts. These psychological changes lead to many of the improved work outcomes which have been ob-

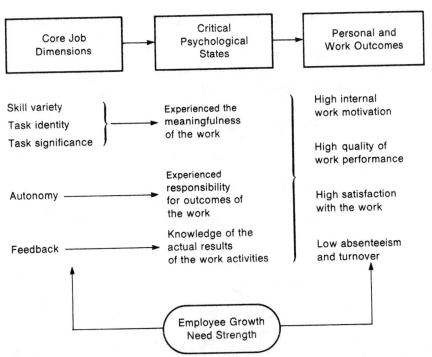

**FIGURE 6-2**   **The Job Characteristic Model of Work Motivation: Work Design**

SOURCE: From J. Richard Hackman, "Job Design," in J. R. Hackman and J. L. Suttle (eds.), *Improving Life at Work: Behavioral Science Approaches to Organizational Change* (Santa Monica, Calif.: Goodyear Publishing, 1977), p. 129. Reprinted with permission of J. Richard Hackman.

served following the redesign of work: higher internal motivation, higher quality work performance, higher satisfaction with the work, and lower absenteeism and turnover.

However, according to theory, only employees who have relatively strong needs for achievement, autonomy, and responsibility are likely to be affected by work redesign in the manner specified by the model (depicted in Figure 6-2 as "Employee Growth Need Strength"). This is not surprising, but it raises important strategic questions about the application of work design concepts. If not all individuals want more responsibility and freedom, are special selection efforts needed in organizations that plan to enrich work? What should be done in older plants about existing employees who do not want more responsibility? Are these employees capable of learning to like and want increased responsibility? Indeed, are their relatively low needs for responsibility a function of the traditional work systems in which they have been working? We will return to these implementation questions later in this chapter.

There are five steps a manager can take if he or she wishes to enrich a job by increasing variety, identity, significance, autonomy, and feedback.

1. *Formulating natural work units.* This means grouping tasks so that, as much as possible, they constitute an identifiable and meaningful whole. Units may be formed according to geography, products, or subassemblies, business, or customers.
2. *Combining tasks.* This means combining what may have been separate and distinct jobs into one.
3. *Establishing client relationships.* This means giving the worker contact with a user of his or her product (another production department, a customer, a sales group, and so on) and giving him or her an understanding of the criteria by which the product will be judged.
4. *Vertical loading.* This means giving the worker as much responsibility as possible in planning, doing, and controlling. Thus the control that management may have exercised through other departments is given to the workers. This often means giving workers responsibility for scheduling work, inventory control, budgeting, and quality control.
5. *Opening feedback channels.* This means giving the worker as much information as possible and as directly as possible about results such as cost, yields, setup, customer complaints, production, and quality.

Figure 6–3 illustrates the task dimensions that are most affected by each of the job design steps. It is thus a guide for redesigning jobs once deficiencies in one or more task dimensions have been diagnosed.

### Technology Policy

A still more recently articulated idea is that it is not enough for management to try to enrich jobs as an afterthought to the already extant technology of the job. The initial design of the new technology should be responsive to social criteria as well as technical and economic criteria.

This idea is particularly apropos in relation to advanced information technology which is still developing. Increasingly, this technology crosses normal departmental boundaries, is on-line, and involves large numbers of clerical, professional, and managerial personnel who directly utilize terminals as part of their normal work routines. A new procurement system in a large multifacility company, for example, may embrace buyers and their clerical support, receiving personnel, and accounts payable personnel. An electronic mail system may place terminals on the desks of all managers and many support personnel. A

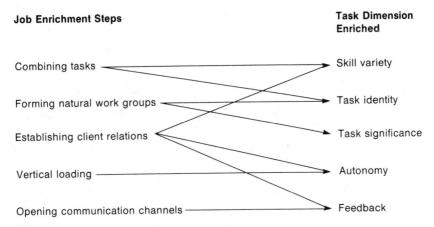

**Job Enrichment Steps**

Combining tasks

Forming natural work groups

Establishing client relations

Vertical loading

Opening communication channels

**Task Dimension Enriched**

Skill variety

Task identity

Task significance

Autonomy

Feedback

**FIGURE 6–3    Effects of Job Enrichment Strategies on Core Job Dimensions**

SOURCE: From J. Richard Hackman, ''Job Design,'' in J. R. Hackman and J. L. Suttle (eds.), *Improving Life at Work: Behavioral Science Approaches to Organizational Change* (Santa Monica, Calif.: Goodyear Publishing, 1977), p. 136. Reprinted with permission of J. Richard Hackman.

centralized word processing system may link those who generate text and who produce it in a very different way, affecting work content and work relationships. The applications—existing and contemplated—are virtually infinite.

The application of this type of information technology can have a profound impact on other elements of the work system, with second-order consequences for employee commitment and developed competencies. The impact can be either positive or negative.[5] Management can increase the positive impact by considering the following implications of design choices:

1. While work systems based on new technology will usually require less skill and knowledge on the part of *some* employees, they will require *more* skill and knowledge from others. System design can influence whether more jobs are being upgraded or downgraded.
2. Work system design can increase or decrease work schedule flexibility to accommodate human preferences.
3. Work system design can contribute to isolation or bring operators in closer touch with each other and with the end product of the work.
4. New technology may render some individual skills obsolete, but it can open career opportunities for learning new skills.
5. Work system design can change—for better or worse—an employee typist into a subcontractor operating a terminal out of his or her own home.

Computer-based technology is becoming less and less deterministic, allowing planners increasing latitude in making design choices that take into account its human impact. Two factors are responsible for this. First, the rapidly declining cost of computing power makes it possible to consider more technical options, including those that are relatively inefficient in the use of that power. Second, the new technology is less hardware-dependent, more software-intensive. It is, therefore, increasingly flexible, permitting the same basic information-processing task to be accomplished by an ever greater variety of technical configurations, each of which may have a different set of human implications. For example, one system configuration may decentralize decision-making; another may centralize it. Yet both will be able to accomplish the same *task* objectives.

Not many corporations or vendors of the new information technology are incorporating human consideration in the design or installation of new technology. Technical people in the client or vendor organization are simply not attuned to the long-term human implication of the technology. Workers who are affected by the technology and managers who will inherit the long-term human and management problems that will result are generally not given a voice in designing and installation decisions. It has been suggested that organizations develop a social impact statement before introducing any new technology.[6] That statement must account for the human and organizational consequences of the new technology and for how the champions of the technology have chosen to deal with them. Another approach to the problem would require a broadly constituted committee of technical people, managers, and human resource specialists, each with their own perspective on the benefits and costs of the technology, to manage the introduction of any new technology. A consensus of what technology is to be introduced and how it is to be introduced would be required before implementation could proceed. Finally, employees who are to be affected by the technology can be directly involved in the design or choice of equipment and in implementation. Presumably their needs would be taken into account through this process. For example, in a recent introduction of word processing equipment, clerical workers who were affected suggested that the equipment be placed in small centers distributed throughout the office building instead of being consolidated in one large word processing center. They said this would result in closer identity with client managers and greater responsiveness to their needs, a principle of job design we described earlier.

## COMPREHENSIVE REDESIGN OF WORK SYSTEMS

Both in the United States and abroad there have been many years of experimentation with alternative arrangements between employees and employers that embrace all of the above initiatives and others as well. The intellectual and practical pioneering of this comprehensive approach was done by Eric Trist and his colleagues at the Tavistock Institute in London. Their initial project in the British coal mining industry after World War II spawned a theory, a method, and a skilled cadre of advocates of this school of thought. The new paradigm of work they advocated included the following principles:

1. The *work system*, which comprised a set of activities that made up a functioning whole, now became the basic unit rather than the single jobs.
2. Correspondingly, the *work group* became central rather than the individual job holder.
3. *Internal regulation* of the system by the group was thus rendered possible rather than the external regulation of individuals by supervisors.
4. A design principle based on the *redundancy of functions* rather than the redundancy of parts characterized the underlying organizational philosophy. Redundancy of functions means developing multiple skills in the individual and thereby immensely increasing the capability of the group to respond to a variety of task demands.
5. This principle valued the *discretionary* rather than the prescribed part of work roles. Individuals would have more freedom to decide what to do and when to do it.
6. It treated the individual as complementary to the machine rather than as an extension of it.
7. It was *variety-increasing* for both the individual and the organization rather than variety-decreasing in the bureaucratic mode.[7]

Over the two decades after World War II, socio-technical concepts were employed in projects that covered a wide variety of industries in a number of different countries, including a textile company in India, a hospital in Australia, and telecommunications in Holland. An especially important set of projects was initiated under the direction of the Norwegian Industrial Democracy Project in the 1960s. However, in none of these countries, including Norway, did the new paradigm of work become a significant trend before the 1970s.

A few new plants in the United States in the late 1960s and early 1970s were designed according to socio-technical theory, although they did not necessarily follow the design methodology or employ socio-technical language. A Procter & Gamble soap plant in Lima, Ohio and especially a General Foods dog food plant in Topeka, Kansas became visible prototypes that influenced the design of an important fraction of new plants started up in the 1970s. In the United States, the socio-technical approach to work system design was subsumed by and was promoted by the quality of work life (QWL) movement which became a national phenomenon in the 1970s.

The term "quality of work life" was coined in an international conference held at Arden House in 1972 and gained institutional status when the UAW and General Motors used it as the umbrella concept for the work reforms they would sponsor jointly.

When the work system experiments began in American manufacturing in the late 1960s, there were both successes and failures. Most of these early experiments took place in new nonunion facilities. In these situations supervisors and employees could be selected to fit the new work system concept. The restrictive work practices and traditions of union-management conflict often found in older plants did not inhibit implementation. In several instances work system innovations proved to be quite fragile with the passage of time. As new management and/or workers flowed into the experimental plants, regression in innovative practices and their effects took place. In other instances conflict between managers of innovative plants and corporate headquarters began to develop over the number of exceptions from traditional corporate policies these innovative work systems were to be granted. Instead of being seen as pioneers, managers of the innovative facilities felt they were being restricted, perhaps even stymied in their careers. Some innovations began to unravel; a few disappeared completely.

As the years have passed experiments have continued and a great deal has been learned, particularly about implementation. An increasing number of work restructuring projects have been jointly sponsored by management and union in older plants.

What was the nature of these experimental work systems? It is simplest to contrast two alternative work system models. The first model is an attempt to capture the traditional work system, the one that developed with Taylor's principles as its cornerstone. It is the model generally prevailing today. Employees perform jobs which are narrowly defined in content. They stay in jobs and specialize unless they are promoted or transferred. Pay is according to the specific job, and sometimes according to individual performance. The employee works under close supervision, and employee performance is evaluated by direct supervisors. Persons are assigned overtime or are transferred temporarily under elaborate rules, especially in unionized organizations. The employee's career is one of specialization, with little opportunity to grow in competence beyond that specialization. (As a practical matter, ordinarily American business has no concept of a career for any employees other than professional and managerial personnel.)

The experimental model, which we believe signals an emerging pattern, departs in almost every detail from the one just cited. It elaborates upon the socio-technical approach. In the experimental model jobs are broadly defined, teams of employees are assigned to perform a group of jobs, and employees are rotated through the various jobs. In effect, the team is given a business to conduct. The team is responsible for inventory, materials scheduling, personnel scheduling, production goals, cost targets, and product quality. Employees are paid according to the number of tasks which they have mastered. Ordinarily employees are assigned a particular task for six months or more, so that there is a built-in length of service element in the pay system. There is little direct supervision. Employees are supervised and evaluated by the team, and respond to the requests of peers rather than the orders of a supervisor. The assumption is that peer pressure is more compelling than a supervisor's orders. In place of rules about overtime and transfers there are a few general practices (such as six months' job rotation periods) and informal arrangements stressing shared burdens among the team members. An employee may now be said to have more of a career because progression occurs as the employee masters the assorted skills required in the teams. Because the breadth of tasks is large, an employee with an aptitude for technical or administrative advancement is able to demonstrate it. Furthermore, the company considers that it employs a broad-gauge person with various capacities, rather than one with a specialized and limited-usage input to the production process. Thus, the personality, intelligence, flexibility, and general effectiveness of the person become more important in determining effectiveness

## TABLE 6–1   Alternate Work Systems

| Model A—Traditional Work System | Model B—High-Commitment Work System |
|---|---|
| Narrowly defined jobs | Broadly defined jobs |
| Specialization of employees | Rotation of employees through jobs |
| Pay by specific job content | Pay by skills mastered |
| Evaluation by direct supervision | Evaluation by peers |
| Work is under close supervision | Self- or peer-supervision |
| Assignment of overtime or transfer by rule book | Team assigns members to cover vacancies in flexible fashion |
| No career development | Concern for learning and growth |
| Employees as individuals | Employees in a team |
| Employee is ignorant about business | Team runs a business; business data shared widely |
| Status symbols used to reinforce hierarchy | Status differences minimized |
| Employees have input on few matters | Broad employee participation |

on the job. Finally, because of broad skills and because of the flexibility that the team approach brings to production (often resulting in better productivity), employees' jobs may be somewhat more secure. Recognizing employees as a greater asset, employers will try harder to keep them even in difficult economic periods.

The contrasts between the two models just discussed are summarized in Table 6–1. The theme of the first model (A), which is still the prevailing one used in blue-collar and clerical work, is a direct focus on efficiency and control. In contrast, the theme of the emerging model (B), is to build human commitment by direct attention to the integration of individual needs and organizational requirements, and to achieve control and efficiency as a second-order consequence. Therefore, we will sometimes refer to the emerging models as a "high-commitment work system."[8]

## MANAGEMENT ASSUMPTIONS AND VALUES

As we stated earlier, managerial behavior reflects fundamental assumptions, often implicit, about the motivation and competence of human beings and their capacity to become involved in work. It is not surprising, therefore, that the basic assumptions that underlie the design of "emerging" work systems are considerably more optimistic than those underlying "traditional" work systems. The assumptions most often explicitly articulated by the managers who have designed and started up these high-commitment work systems are:

- People *want* to work hard, perform well, learn new skills, and be involved in decision making that affects their jobs.
- Creative talents are widely distributed at all levels of a work organization.
- Participation can lead to quality decisions and commitment.

It is not uncommon for the founding management team of these new plant work systems to spend up to a week discussing assumptions which should guide the new plant. This is usually done with the help of a consultant, through education on human motivation and management theory, and by examining their own managerial assumptions, beliefs, and behavior. This process finally shapes a philosophy of management that guides all their design decisions.

The design phase itself often takes from several months to a year prior to plant start-up. During this period, team members begin to hire the next level of management and make decisions about job design, compensation systems, mechanism for employee voice, work rules, promotion and employment security policies, and so on. In each of the four policy areas policies are typically articulated and tested for consistency with the basic assumptions and philosophy set forth at the beginning. The design phase and later implementation sometimes cause reexamination of assumptions and values and occasionally changes in them. By and large, however, the three basic assumptions listed above are reflected in all of the high-commitment systems of which we know. And the articulation of a philosophy of management is critical in enabling management to break with the past, examine their own managerial behavior, and design highly internally consistent policies in the employee influence, flow, rewards, and work systems areas. It is the internally consistent nature of these policies that makes it possible for employees to understand management's expectations for performance, involvement, and responsibility.

While the clarification of assumptions may have been useful to management in designing and managing these new work systems, it also contributed to the conflict between management and corporate headquarters to which we referred earlier. The clearer these managers became about the assumptions that guided their innovative plants, the more apparent the differences became between their own assumptions and those of corporate management. When those differences were not managed well by either side, problems arose that ultimately led to the departure of key managers in the innovative plant. These types of problems are associated with many innovations, not only those in human resource management. They will be less in evidence the more the assumptions underlying the new work systems become the assumptions of American management, a transformation that we believe is well underway. The tensions that have arisen from differences in assumption and values underscore that corporate transformations in human resource management cannot occur without a transformation in the assumptions and values of management at all levels.

## SOME CONSISTENT POLICIES AND PRACTICES

It is not surprising, given common assumptions about human motivation and competence, that many new innovative plants have similar human resource policies to support the development of a high-commitment work system.[9]

In the *employee influence* policy area many of the plants have developed mechanisms for giving employees a voice in the governance of the plant. For example, open-door policies, small group meetings of employees at all levels with the plant manager, committees and task forces to study various problems and make recommendations, and permanent boards of employee representatives are not uncommon. Participation of employees is sought in many decisions beyond their immediate work, including layout of machinery, equipment, and the plant itself.

A flat organization structure, with the plant manager only several steps above production workers (sometimes as few as three or four), makes it easier for employees at the bottom to talk to management at the top. Finally, egalitarianism is established by eliminating unnecessary distinctions between employee groups in dress codes, office space, parking, and eating facilities. Egalitarianism is also fostered by an all-salaried work force (see Chapter 5), which eliminates the distinction between hourly and salaried workers (except of course for the legal requirements governing overtime pay for nonexempt employees).

In the *human resource flow* policy area, high-commitment plants depart from the traditional approaches to selection, promotion, and training, often allowing more employee influence in these decisions. For example, the traditional approach to selection (the personnel department carefully screens, tests and selects among applicants) is often replaced with work teams being allowed to select their own members. Extensive front-end training and orientation emphasize not just specific content skills, but interpersonal skills; they help acclimate new employees to the climate of high involvement and high commitment.

In the *reward systems* policy area, new innovative plants incorporate several similar pay policies and again allow more employee influence on these policies. To encourage growth in competence and to allow the flexibility in job assignments required by the team approach, a skill-based pay system (as opposed to the traditional job-based system—see Chapter 5) is typically installed. Employee pay levels are determined by the number of skills they have acquired. Typically, a five- or six-level ladder is established. Teams are expected to evaluate their members and decide when they are eligible for a raise, although not all plants incorporate this feature because it is the most difficult to implement, requiring considerable skill and maturity on the part of the team. Employees help design and administer these pay systems, reevaluating their efficacy from time to time or assessing whether pay levels are equitable compared to other plants in the company or region. Sometimes a profit-sharing or cost-savings bonus is used to encourage cooperative behavior in the plant, reinforcing commitment to the whole rather than the individual or group.

Finally, these high-commitment systems redefine the duties of first-line supervisors. They become facilitators and consultants to work teams and are not supposed to take on the usual directive role of traditional supervisors. Since most teams in a new plant do not have the experience or maturity to work autonomously early in the life of the plant, supervisors must be more directive at first and slowly work themselves out of that role and into one of facilitation. The unique demands of this role make it hard to find people who fit it well or to keep people in it, a special problem of high-commitment job systems that needs continual attention.

As noted earlier, in the United States these experimental systems initially were developed in new production facilities without unions. They are now being introduced into unionized facilities, both newly constructed and old.

It is in the area of attitude changes that the new systems make their greatest demands on management, union, and employees. There is great flexibility in the experimental systems. As a result considerable trust is required between management and labor to make them work successfully. Employees must not be concerned that management will utilize flexibility to exploit workers, and managers must not be concerned that employees will use flexibility to impose inefficient practices on the company. The new systems can build trust between labor and management, but they also depend upon its prior existence.

The life of an employee is different under the new system. Rather than carrying out orders in a repetitive fashion and leaving all problems at the workplace each evening, the employee assumes much more far-reaching obligations. The stress of meeting production targets now falls directly on the team and its members. Employees must learn to accept criticism from other members of the team, and to react in a constructive fashion. Employees must be able to communicate effectively with one another, including the transmission of technical information and production requirements in a clear and understandable fashion. Employees must continue to learn on the job as new skills are mastered and new processes, new technology, and new products are introduced. Employees in effect assume what are now managerial functions, and they experience as well the stress which accompanies administrative jobs. The employee takes the job home at night, and family relationships may be disrupted unless the employee is able to cope with stress successfully. The new systems require a much higher degree of commitment from the employee to the workplace then do the old systems. Their apparent advantage in productivity arises from this higher commitment and the flexibility in production which accompanies high commitment.

## THE CHOICE BETWEEN MODEL A AND MODEL B

Many managers will acknowledge that there are advantages in the Model B approach, including greater employee commitment to their jobs and improved performance. However, managers often are either skeptical that the approach is realistic or fear the apparent loss of control when they relinquish decision-making authority (either formally or in practice) to subordinates. How is a manager to decide when it is appropriate to try to design or develop a Model B type work system?

Some managers and behavioral scientists have suggested that Model A is better fitted to some technologies than Model B and vice versa. Specifically, it has been asserted that in machine-paced processes, such as automobile assembly, there is no room for employee initiative of the type envisioned by Model B. However, some of the most effective experiments with Model B have occurred in the assembly-line environment. By and large it now appears that technology does not dictate the form of work organization, though it is an important influence in detailed work design, as we have mentioned previously.

## UNIONS, MANAGERS, AND QUALITY OF WORK LIFE

Though traditionally not the subject of collective bargaining, the design of work and the involvement of employees in decision making is becoming a matter of joint union-management concern as evidenced by quality of work life (QWL) programs at General Motors and AT&T and the Employee Involvement program at Ford. Such programs are not so much concerned with job design as with ways of seeking, implementing, and institutionalizing participation in and influence over the working lives of employees and the operation of the organization.

Not all union leaders agree on the efficacy of involvement with management on QWL or innovative work system programs. There are two main views. Some union leaders see joint QWL programs as a further step (after collective bargaining) toward industrial democracy. Irving Bluestone of the UAW is the best example of a union leader who had this view when he began the process of building a cooperative relationship with the management of General Motors. But others dismiss the efforts. For example, in 1973 William Winpifinger of the Machinists Union dismissed job enrichment experiments as "a stopwatch in sheep's clothing. . . . The better the wage, the greater the job satisfaction. There is no better cure for the 'blue collar blues'."[10]

The majority of unions have not endorsed QWL, while the AFL-CIO's top leadership has expressed, at best, guarded optimism. Those who do favor QWL programs insist that they should be established only with union presence and involvement. QWL in a nonunion setting becomes, in their view, a paternalistic "gift" that can easily be taken back. Says Glenn Watts of the CWA, without a union "bosses will never give up the idea of being a boss.'' Still, some union leaders see cooperation as a sellout, ''getting in bed with management.'' Others feel that their role as sole protector of the rights of workers is threatened. Still others find old adversarial patterns and ways of thinking and behaving hard to break. But QWL does raise an important question, even a challenge, to union leaders in the upcoming decade. Traditionally, unions have shied away from questions of participation of job design, concentrating almost exclusively on tangible matters like pay and hours. The shrinking economic pie that seems to be the country's lot in the near future, however, will likely make monetary victories hard to come by. Unions that can no longer promise members ever-increasing wages might find participation and job enrichment promising avenues to consider. An increasingly well-educated work force might, in fact, demand that union leaders break their old habits and move in the QWL direction, or members may seek new leaders. Such innovative union leaders could begin making demands for jointly administered employee surveys or the right to review the performance and effectiveness of supervisors. They might make demands to become involved in decisions about technology as the Communication Workers of America have or to review all job assignments and training plans as Japanese unions regularly do. This approach would require a union leadership educated in human resource innovations, something that—with few exceptions—they are not. It would put management that is lagging in these innovations on the defensive and would be a major force for change in American industry, if not also a source of revitalization for unions.[11]

The National Labor Relations Act raises another set of questions concerning quality of work life activities—those having to do with the legal ramifications of QWL in both union and nonunion settings. The NLRA makes it unfair labor practice for employers to dominate or interfere with *any* labor organization, whether that organization be a union or some sort of employee committee. It is likely that under current labor law and judicial interpretations most QWL programs in nonunion settings are either totally or in part illegal. Does the NLRA allow for *any* formal cooperation? The matter is yet to be decided by the Supreme Court, but scattered circuit court rulings have suggested that a primary consideration should be *intent*. The labor organization must truly represent the wishes of employees, and the employer must not intend to dominate the group in any way. In other words, the more freedom of participation an employer grants under some type of QWL mechanism in a nonunion setting, the more likely is that QWL program to be found legal. The more an employer attempts to restrict, interfere, or control an employee committee, the more likely is that employer to be found in violation of the NLRA. It should be noted, however, that very few legal challenges have been raised to QWL programs in either union or nonunion settings.[12]

## CHALLENGING QUESTIONS ABOUT HIGH-COMMITMENT WORK SYSTEMS

Accepting that there will be individual differences, do most workers want to work under such a high-participation, high-commitment work system? Should prescreening before hiring be used to identify those who do? Can most managers manage effectively under such systems?

Do new measures of success under altered work systems need to be developed? Does managerial competence need to be defined and measured differently? Within an organization, how can different work systems be measured to determine relative success? Should they be compared? Will organizations adopt and continue to support these types of work systems when they don't have hard financial evidence that they are superior?

First-line supervisors are the immediate contact between management and nonmanagement employees, but are often most resistant to changing work systems, to giving up "authority" and control. Do they have the necessary interpersonal skills to manage high-participation systems? What about union stewards, whose role may be similarly affected?

There are many other questions that become salient *after* those high-commitment work systems have enjoyed a period of success.[13]

Will they gravitate toward the conventional patterns they seek to replace? Will the rules and structures developed to solve a particular problem take on a life of their own? Will individuals and groups tire of the flexibility and uncertainty inherent in Model B and instinctively attempt to define and protect their own turf—whether it be differentiated roles or special privileges? Will the initially egalitarian society become stratified to accord more status to those who have accepted more responsibility? If not, why not? How does one repeal or avoid the "iron law of bureaucracy"?

Do these high-commitment work systems, which require careful development and nurturance during their formative periods, remain in a "fragile, handle-with-care" state? Or do they, because they are aligned with both individual and organizational needs, become robust and difficult to destroy?

Will the greater involvement of workers in decision making lead to ever-rising expectations for influence? Does having some voice regarding "managerial agenda" such as machine layout lead to expectation of voice in other areas—subcontracting, plant location, product design, and inventory policy? If so, can these expectations be accommodated? How should expectations be managed, or should they?

These questions are among many that must still be answered in order for the assumptions and concepts underlying innovative high-commitment work systems to become more widely applied, for high commitment work systems to become the norm rather than the exception. We believe, however, that the experience and evidence to date is sufficiently encouraging for effort to be made by American industry to innovate in work system design on a broad front—in traditional and new plants, in union and nonunion settings, at the shop floor and in the office, and at the operating and management levels. Indeed, as we saw earlier, these ideas can be applied to the introduction of new information technology, the area in which rapid change provides potential for innovation but in which traditional thinking can recreate in the office the problems we are now trying to solve in the plant. The experience of innovation is required to grapple with the problems suggested by the questions above. With sufficient commitment to innovation, to the transformation of the relationship between manager and managed: solutions will be found to the new set of problems created by innovation. This after all is the nature of organizational and social change, solutions created to solve old problems are accompanied by a new set of problems which themselves require solution for the innovations to survive. Competitive pressures and changes in work values will demand that management undertake the commitment required to manage major organizational transformations. As we mentioned earlier, several large companies such as General Motors, Ford Motors, Cummins Engine, Goodyear Tire & Rubber, AT&T, and Bethlehem Steel, among others, are making innovations in work systems a major part of their strategy for competing in the 1980s and beyond.

## SUMMARY AND CONCLUSIONS

The productivity crisis and changing values in the work force have stimulated a stream of innovations in work system design that transform traditional relationships between the task, workers, managers, technology, and personnel policies. These innovations have started at the shop-floor level but are applicable to the office and management levels, particularly as new information technology is introduced. Instead of narrowly defined jobs, specialization of employees, pay for specific job content, close supervision, employees assigned to individual tasks, status differentials which reinforce hierarchy and little employee influence (what we have called Model A), innovations in work systems have tended to define jobs broadly, rotate employees through many jobs, pay for skills mastered, emphasize self or peer supervision, assign whole tasks to teams, remove status differentials and emphasize egalitarianism, and allow substantial employee influence and participation. We have called such systems Model B or high-commitment work systems. These systems are based on the assumption that employees want to work hard, that creative talents are widely distributed, and that participation can lead to quality decisions and commitment. High-commitment work systems, therefore, require substantially different managerial values and skills than are found in most organizations, including a willingness to delegate and give employees information and influence. High-commitment work systems have threatened some union leaders and have been embraced by others.

This chapter concludes where it began—with a recitation of the "stakes" associated with work system design. When the Model B-type work systems have been implemented effectively, managements report the following types of benefits of high commitment: higher in-plant quality, lower warranty costs, lower waste, higher machine utilization, fewer operating and support personnel, lower turnover and absenteeism, and faster start-up of new equipment. However, to achieve these gains, managers have had to invest extra effort, develop new skills and relationships, cope with higher levels of ambiguity and uncertainty, and experience the pain and discomfort associated with changing habits and skills.

Union officials who have entered into joint sponsorshop of QWL reforms of traditional work systems report a number of benefits: improved product quality, reduced absenteeism and turnover, reduction in discharge, disciplinary layoffs, and grievance load; re-election of union officials who are proponents of QWL; and enhanced financial rewards.[14] They also expect greater job security to derive from improved competitiveness. Like management, they must make a heavy investment of time, and experience the frustrations associated with change. They also have to be wary of the political risk of becoming too closely associated with management.

The stakes for the worker include the following: higher influence and more autonomy in exchange for accepting more responsibility; more social support from peers in exchange for operating in a more interdependent mode; and more opportunity for development and self-esteem in return for accepting more ambiguity and uncertainty. Apparently for most participants in the emerging work system, but not for all, that is a good bargain.

*Chapter 7*

# The Integration
# of Human Resource
# Management Policies

THIS FINAL CHAPTER concerns the difficult task all managers face in integrating their organization's many human resource policies and practices into a coherent whole that meshes with the other aspects of the firm's operations. In all too many firms today HRM policies and practices are not well coordinated, the right hand actively blocking the work of the left hand. For example, a firm can be redesigning its plants to increase the challenge of the work at the same time it is introducing new office technology in a way that diminishes the work challenge. The reasons why the coordination of HRM efforts ought to be a central concern of senior line managers as well as human resource managers are not hard to find. When, as is so frequently the case, HRM policies and practices are treated as a long list of isolated tasks, they get farmed out to specialists whose concerns are limited to avoiding obvious problems and assuring technical consistency and accuracy within their particular practice areas. For instance, the expert in pension benefits generally consults only with other pension specialists and is consequently focused on the logic of devising what he sees as the ideal pension system for the company. All too often the impact of such planning on other HRM practices and especially on the firm's overall business strategy is a neglected issue.

In considering the integration of HRM policies, it is important first of all to review the conceptual overview we presented in Chapter 2. The map of the HRM territory (Figure 2–1) has obvious utility in working out an integrated set of HRM policies in any given firm. It helps to clarify the multiple factors that must be considered in shaping HRM policy. It also highlights the relevant constraints, the multiple stakeholders, and the types of outcomes that are directly relevant to management's choices in the four policy areas. In this chapter we propose to supplement this basic analytical tool with the consideration of four additional topics: integrating approaches, the choice of one or two cultures, management values, and the HRM change process.

## INTEGRATING HRM POLICIES: BUREAUCRATIC, MARKET, AND CLAN APPROACHES[1]

In the interest of integrating HRM policies, the first question we must answer is to what end or purpose integration is sought? Clearly, from the *organizational* standpoint, any HRM system should be integrated so as to attract and hold the right mix of people and to establish the type of working relationship between these people that will carry out the organization's strategic plan, once that plan has taken into account any relevant human resource constraints and opportunities. In other words, HRM policies need to *fit* the business strategy. Later in this chapter we will elaborate and expand on this definition of the purpose of an integrated HRM system, but for now it serves as a useful starting place for our discussion by immediately suggesting a second question: How should one define a good fit between a given strategic plan and the design of an HRM system? Toward this end earlier chapters in this book have sorted all HRM practices into the four major policy areas: employee influence, flow, rewards, and work systems. Further toward this purpose, we will now propose three generalized approaches to integrating across the four policy areas of any HRM system: the bureaucratic approach, the market approach, and the clan approach. To see how these methods of analysis can help managers integrate their human resource policies and practice, we will first discuss the distinction between the three approaches.

The *bureaucratic way* of unifying HRM policies is based on the assumption that employees are subordinate and responsive to traditional authority. Its use in industry has grown with the expansion of large industrial organizations in this century, this industrial application having been anticipated by its earlier development in church and military organizations. Over the years it has been successful in coordinating the work efforts of a great many people, but in recent years it has faltered as the primary way to achieve employee involvement and adaptation to changing environments.

The strength of the bureaucratic way of unifying an HRM system lies in its contribution to achieving control and efficiency. Not surprisingly, the chief symbols of this approach are the chain of command (traditional lines and boxes of the organizational chart) and the rule book (standard operating policies). From the employee's standpoint the approach appeals to a desire for order, building as it does upon legitimated authority and property rights, and on a desire for equity in terms of due process. From the organizational standpoint, this approach is based on the necessity for an organization's being able to coordinate its methods of collecting relevant information, making commitments based on such information, and, in turn, giving directions for actions necessary to fulfilling the commitments. Implicit in any such information/decision/command network is the necessity of clearly establishing a division of labor for both operational acts and coordinating acts.

A number of specific HRM practices have evolved which support and implement the consistent use of the bureaucratic way of establishing employment relationships. For convenience these bureaucratic practices can be grouped into the four policy areas of flows, rewards, work systems, and employee influence. In terms of flows, the usual career track begins with lower-level positions that can lead to promotion within each specialized chain of command. Superiors evaluate the employee with criteria for advancement focused on technical qualifications, compliance with the direction of superiors, willingness to pass all relevant information upward, and willingness to supervise in detail the work of all subordinates. In terms of rewards, the bureaucratic method relies on the development of detailed job descriptions that are then rated for their relative economic value to the firm (the job evaluation system described in Chapter 5). This approach generates a pay-for-the-job system of wages and salaries.

In terms of work systems, the bureaucratic way of handling HRM relies on making jobs as simple and unskilled as possible at the bottom of the organization with the supervisory structure entirely responsible for coordinating these jobs (in keeping with the principles of Frederick Taylor). The chain of command is thought of as the way for workers to express their opinions and influence their work life. In this familiar "open-door" policy, management expects that all workers will take problems to the boss for resolution within an accepted procedural framework. In sum, when a consistent set of bureaucratic HRM policies and practices, including competitive pay rate, are carefully and fairly executed, they work to provide a competent, compliant, predictable work force—as long as the technology remains stable and the level of employment does not decline. If either changes dramatically, however, and employees are considered expendable as a way of cutting costs or are required to adjust to new technologies, this method is almost certain to run into serious trouble.

The *market approach* to integrating an HRM system is based on the principle of explicit and immediate exchanges between the organization and its members. Because exchange, in its broadest sense, is probably the most basic principle governing human relations, it is also relevant to bureaucratic and clan approaches. Although in prosperous times the underlying dynamics of market exchanges can become somewhat obscured, they come back into focus in times of adverse economic conditions. The market approach to HRM draws upon the universal norm that there should be reciprocity in exchanges between people and also draws upon the tendency of individuals to repeat behavior that is given positive reinforcement. Market mechanisms appeal to the calculative self-interests of employees and are designed to achieve a congruence between these self-interests and the interests of the organization. The symbol of market HRM practices, the paycheck, represents the exchange of work for money. The rewards policy area, discussed in Chapter 5, is the means by which the organization defines this exchange. As we shall see, however, the paycheck is only the first step in an elaboration of HRM practices that are market-like in character.

The market approach to designing and selecting HRM systems can be described in still other ways: in the language of contributions and inducements and the language of the psychological contract.[2] Employment relationships in organizations where the market approach is dominant are characterized by the high turnover and the bidding for talent associated, for example, with the high-fashion merchandiser, the advertising account executive, the newsbroadcaster, the professional baseball player, the actor or actress, and the stockbroker.

HRM practices that have market-like qualities can best be understood by examining the market flows system that can be summarized as "in-and-out." At its extreme, the employee is virtually a subcontractor in a deal struck with the employer to perform a specified amount of work for an agreed-upon price. When this transaction is completed the relationship is ended until another contract is made. There is no single entry point; employees come into the system at any level, depending upon the needs of the organization and the availability of required talent. Neither is there an established promotion ladder. The market for jobs is not only external but also internal, witness the practice of job posting. In a market-oriented HRM system, employee evaluation is clearly a two-way process; employees as well as employers are constantly evaluating the quality of exchanges, with each party prepared to seek a better deal elsewhere. In terms of rewards, the epitome of the market HRM system is piece-rate payment. There are other variations on this theme of paying for individual performance: executive performance bonuses, sales commissions, merit increases. Other reward practices built upon the exchange principle are cash awards for suggestions, prizes for sales performance, special recognition for technical achievements, and the like.

The way employees influence a market-oriented firm is through negotiation and bargaining. This can take the form of individual bargaining for a formal, or more frequently an informal, employment contract, or the form of collective bargaining carried out by unions on behalf of employees. The work system that is consistent with the market approach involves breaking work into discrete, individualized tasks that are filled by a bidding process. The market-oriented HRM system is particularly effective when flexibility in the employment relationship and responsiveness to sudden environmental changes are important. The price tag for the employer is uncertainty when needed talent is scarce, and uncertainty for the employee when jobs are scarce. Contracts are used to help reduce the uncertainties. A logical, consistent, and integrated set of HRM practices built around the market approach can work in those special instances when it truly fits the nature of the business.

The *clan approach* to integrating HRM policies and practices has not been clearly identified as one aspect of customary practice but is still important. As the name suggests, this ancient form of employment relationship derives from early kinship systems. The clan approach also has thoroughly modern relevance, however, as industry realizes its potential for increasing employees' involvement more than is possible with only bureaucratic and market mechanisms. Based on shared values, shared risks, and shared rewards, and oriented to a joint or collective achievement, the clan approach appeals to employees' desire to identify with and contribute to a social entity and to goals beyond immediate self-interest. For the clan approach to work there must be a gradual evolution within an organization of a shared set of beliefs that are regularly backed by supporting policy and action. An emphasis on this approach is associated with such consistently well-managed firms as IBM, Texas Instruments, and Kodak, as well as some of the outstanding Japanese firms.

HRM practices can be gathered into a unified clan system beginning with a flow policy of assuming long-term employment of all employees. People are chosen not for their immediately available specialized skills but for their anticipated long-term adaptability to the organization. Once employed, they go through an extensive learning and indoctrination process, both to acquire basic skills and knowledge of the industry and to learn how to be effective to the organizational culture. As in the bureaucratic approach, the point of entry is usually at the lower job level, but mobility is as often lateral as upward as employees broaden and deepen their skills. The employee evaluation process relies on the judgments of peers as well as superiors. With the clan approach rewards are linked to group and total organizational performance. This linkage most often takes the form of profit sharing or other means of gain sharing. As we indicated in Chapter 5, interest in organization-wide incentives is growing as companies seek to develop the clan approach. People who are promoted have demonstrated not only their competence but their fit with the company culture; misfits are either discharged or given more peripheral roles. Thus, using terminology we introduced in Chapter 4, these firms tend to define effectiveness in terms of behavior as much as results.

The work systems in a clan-oriented firm make extensive use of teams—of semiautonomous work groups at the operating level, and of special task forces at the managerial level. The hallmark of these teams is cross-training and task-sharing with the goal of creating a climate of interchangeability, enrichment, and group independence. Symbols of status are understandably minimized. In Chapter 6 we described a high-commitment work system—Model B—that highlights these features of clan-oriented firms. With this approach, worker input affecting procedure and policy is voiced through discussion and consensus. Involving all employees in relevant aspects of the decision process not only takes advantage of their experience and ideas but reinforces their commitment to the decisions that are finally put into effect. A significant part of HRM in a clan-oriented company is the time and attention given to wide circulation of facts concerning the business environment: trends in products, sales, competition, regulations, and technology. This provides all organizational members with a broad understanding of the problems to whose solution everyone is expected to contribute. The clan approach to integrating an HRM system aims at building the high level of mutual commitment between an organization and its employees that is necessary if the organization's success depends on quality and especially on innovation.

Table 7–1 is a diagrammatic summary of HRM policies that we have discussed as characteristic of the bureaucratic, market, and clan approaches. Now that we have described in general the differences between these three approaches to integrating human resource management, a host of practical questions present themselves. Are the three systems either/or options, or are combinations of these approaches viable? How does one match a firm's product/market strategy with the appropriate HRM approach or combination of approaches? Must a single approach be taken for all categories of employees or can different approaches be used with different groups within the same organization? This last question can be further sharpened by asking if compa-

**TABLE 7-1  Matrix of HRM Policies**

| | NATURE OF EMPLOYMENT RELATIONSHIP | | |
|---|---|---|---|
| HRM POLICY AREAS | *Bureaucratic (employee involved as subordinate)* | *Market (employee involved as contractor)* | *Clan (employee involved as member)* |
| Employee influence | Up through chain of command | Negotiated contracts | Consultation and consensus (e.g., quality circles) |
| Flow | Bottom entry—rise to level of competence within functions | In-and-out employment (i.e., job posting) | Long-term employment with lateral as well as vertical movement |
| Rewards | Pay based on job evaluation | Pay based on performance (i.e., piece rates or executive bonuses) | Pay based on seniority, skills, and gains-sharing |
| Work systems | Fine division of labor coordinated by chain of command | Group or individual contracting | Whole task with internal coordination; peer pressure as motivator |

nies are to have one set of HRM practices for exempt managers and professionals and a different set of HRM practices for nonexempt employees. Is there to be one overall corporate work culture or are there to be two, one for managers and one for the managed, as has been typical in American industry?

On reflection, it should be clear that every organization of any appreciable size makes at least some use of all three approaches regardless of which is emphasized. The U.S. Postal Service, for instance, is known for its heavy use of bureaucratic HRM methods but still makes a limited use of such market mechanisms as merit raises and such clan mechanisms as sponsored athletic teams. The question, then, is not whether some mix is possible, but which approach can most suitably be emphasized under given conditions. The choice must take into consideration the importance of establishing a dynamic three-way fit between situational constraints, the firm's strategy regarding products, markets, and financial requirements, and the chosen HRM approach (see Figure 7-1).

Calculating the merits of the various possible fits between strategy, situational factors, and combinations of bureaucratic, market, and clan HRM systems is clearly a complex procedure. It helps to simplify the choice when we realize that certain paired combinations of approach have special merit. The combination of bureaucratic and market approaches is particularly relevant to situations where economies of scale are possible, where markets and technology are stable, and where prices are highly competitive. In such circumstances emphasis needs to be placed on efficiency, and the bureaucratic/market combination does just that. If a firm is competing in a highly complex and uncertain environment, and innovation and flexibility are the key success factors, the combination of clan and market approaches would be most likely to fit the need. Under business circumstances in which the essential resource

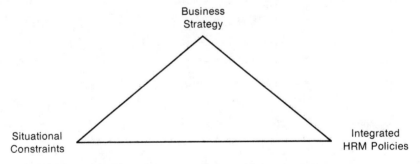

**FIGURE 7-1   An Integrated Approach to HRM**

is a steady and reliable work force, the combination of clan and bureaucratic methods would be most likely to create the needed quality of work life. Finally, if the firm's strategy and environment call for the simultaneous achievement of high efficiency, innovation, and quality of work life, some creative blend and overlap of all three approaches would be indicated.

The suggestion that all three approaches be given equal emphasis may seem like an impossibility, but analysis of the way rewards are sometimes determined will show how practical the simultaneous use of the three approaches can be. The construction of a reward system can begin with the customary base of job descriptions that are evaluated relative to one another to determine basic pay levels (a bureaucratic method). These basic pay levels can then be supplemented by merit increases determined in terms of sustained levels of individual performance (a market method). Finally, an overall profit sharing or another type of gain-sharing bonus based on total organizational performance can be added (a clan method). Combining all three approaches is not always so easy, of course; in fact, in some instances the respective methods are clearly incompatible so that a choice must be made. For example, a firm cannot possibly reconcile the long-term employment practices of a clan system with the in-and-out employment practices of a fully developed market system for the same employees. Making a choice is inevitable.

The interest in seeking ways to emphasize all three HRM approaches is no accident. In today's competitive world more and more firms are finding it essential to be leaders in efficiency, innovation, and quality of work life. Being leaders in one or two areas is often not quite enough. For instance, if United States Steel wants to compete with its Japanese counterparts, can they neglect any of these three areas of performance? A company is also motivated to find ways to combine all three approaches by the different attractions these approaches have to employees. If the HRM strategy calls for getting employees as involved as possible in the affairs of the business, why not use all the ways of doing it? From the employee's standpoint the biggest appeal of the bureaucratic approach is the promise of equitable treatment. For the clan approach it is the appeal of membership and personal caring. For the market approach it is the appeal of being rewarded in a realistic, supply-and-demand manner for one's own contributions. This combination of organizational and individual payoffs is shown in Figure 7–2.

It must also be acknowledged that each of the three approaches is prone to certain abuses. In fact, the possible abuses inherent to each approach and the capacity of the other approaches to counteract them add a final reason for the attractiveness of the threefold combination.

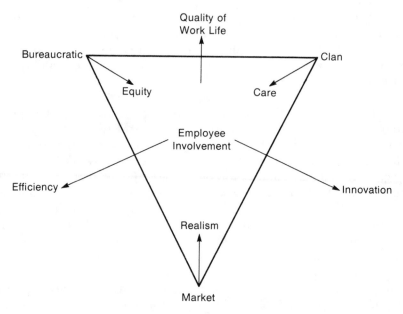

**FIGURE 7-2   Organizational and Individual Payoffs of HRM Strategies**

The clan approach, for instance, carries the hazard of becoming paternalistic; market realism can help correct this tendency. It is almost certainly a mistake for any company to promise explicitly or even infer that it can deliver lifetime job security. Since business uncertainties will almost certainly force some degree of employment fluctuation, HRM policies should provide for these contingencies. Companies cannot and should not try to shield people entirely from economic realities. Clan practices also carry the hazard of breeding favoritism; the due process provided by bureaucratic procedures can counteract this tendency. Market mechanisms, while they promise needed realism, can by themselves be harsh and also unfair to employees. The addition of the caring associated with the clan method can take into account hardship cases— for instance, during a layoff period—even as the due process associated with bureaucratic procedures can assure fair use of rules such as seniority. An exclusive use of bureaucratic methods is prone to the simultaneous hazards of being totally impersonal and being overly expensive. The former problem can be softened by the caring spirit of the clan, while the excessive red tape characterizing the latter problem can be disciplined by the pressure of market mechanisms. Getting the best from all three approaches is by no means automatic, however; it will always take skillful management to achieve these multiple outcomes.

## ONE CULTURE OR TWO CULTURES

An important question which is becoming increasingly critical in U.S. industry remains: can one set of HRM practices serve all types of employees or should different systems be used for different groups, especially for the exempt and nonexempt? Ever since the industrial revolution became well established, the split between the organizational worlds of the managers and the managed has been pointed out by political commentators, social scientists, novelists, and even the writers of folk songs. The distinction has been expressed in many ways: thinkers and doers, capitalists and proletarian workers, skilled and unskilled employees, master and servant. In many large organizations this division of labor has evolved into two ways of life, two different work cultures, which are typically adversarial. We submit that it is no exaggeration to refer to both sides of this split as being work cultures. Local culture has often evolved in the sense of embodying beliefs and rituals that reinforce complex friendship networks. A richness of association has grown out of shared adversities and pleasures that are reinforced by language and custom. The terms and symbols of the crafts or trades of those who work with their hands are rich in meaning; as are also the terms of the professional manager. But in many organizations these cultures have been polarized. Although many say that this split is unavoidable in large organizations of any kind and in any known political system, firms like Hewlett-Packard come close to being a one-culture work system characterized by a mutuality of interests and association throughout the work force. Many of these one-culture firms are not only economically viable but outstandingly successful and—whether American, Japanese, or whatever—are making life very difficult for their competitors. This new well-documented phenomenon of the successful competitive pressure generated by one-culture organizations is receiving more and more attention throughout the business world.

While the competitive pressure from one-culture, high-commitment firms is the primary stimulus to questioning traditional adversarial systems, several other important developments push in the same direction. Low-cost, high-performance microprocessors are now making the long-awaited automated factory at least a partial reality; in fact, industry's entire tool box is rapidly changing as this technology plays out its present potential. The impact on jobs is usually to minimize the importance of motor dexterity and to increase cognitive requirements, so that operators' jobs can frequently be redesigned to include certain managerial responsibilities. These increased mental requirements may combine with the generally higher educational achievements of the new work force to break down the sharp distinction between manager and managed. Meanwhile, as has been widely noted in the press, the traditional distinction between owner and wage earners is eroding as the latter group, through their pension funds, own an ever-larger share of the total industrial equity. The reduced birth rate in the United States also signals that before too long we will need to run industry with a relatively smaller work force or else delay retirement significantly. Finally, the evidence compiled by those who analyze our value systems indicates that Americans at all levels increasingly expect to influence their workplace in some meaningful way. Although all of these factors are converging to break down the time-honored distinction between manager and worker, counterforces to such basic change are equally in evidence.

Federal legislation is a pervasive, although unintentional, reinforcement to the adversarial, two-culture system. For instance, federal wage and hour legislation, which was passed to protect working people from being pressured into working long unpaid hours, establishes the distinction between exempt and nonexempt employees (note the puzzling, double-negative term). Although this law had no part in the original rise of the adversarial work system, it has inadvertently become an unnecessary and stubborn force perpetuating the two-culture system. Business firms are virtually required to keep two sets of records on their employees and to have two sets of ground rules governing employment; often they wind up having two separate personnel departments. The law started a causal chain that has, in a multitude of subtle and not-so-subtle ways, strengthened the wall that divides the two cultures. The federal labor laws legitimating collective bargaining have had a similar unintended consequence. Although the intent was to outlaw phony "company" unions, the laws have sometimes been interpreted to preclude management's being able to encourage workers to participate in the organizational decision process. We suggest that such unintentional side effects might suitably be addressed by fresh legislation.

Many historical reasons have also contributed to the prevalence of the adversarial or two-culture system. Americans, while priding themselves on a relatively classless society, have, in fact, perpetuated a diminished version of the class system they inherited from their European ancestors. To the extent that this class system persists, it is likely to be reflected in industrial hierarchies. Although the beginning of the industrial revolution has aptly been described as a replacement of muscle energy with hydrocarbon energy, human hand and motor skills were still essential for manipulating physical objects. Such work first appeared in quantity in the early textile mills and is seen today in all forms of assembly work. Until these jobs can be automated, industry needs employees who are virtually willing to check their brains at the door; clearly technologies based on this need both create and perpetuate two-culture systems. Industry's response to the growth of higher education also perpetuates and strengthens the two-culture system. When college education was for the few, industries invented special points of entry and special promotion ladders for their college-trained recruits. As the number of college graduates going into industrial organizations grew, the gap between the two cultures grew correspondingly. Educational differences have tended severely to limit the chances of promotion for the noncollege worker, giving college-trained middle managers a vested interest in maintaining the status quo. Middle managers, in fact, not only defended but even invented distinctions and perquisites to separate them further from the nonexempts. Support for the growth of unions was built on the backlog of workers' repressed anger and resentment. Collective bargaining with its periodic and often bitter strikes has institutionalized the adversarial relationship between management and labor. Although the collective contract started out as a market-like mechanism, as it accumulated more and more work-rule clauses it evolved into a strongly bureaucratic mechanism and a frequent bulwark of the two-culture work system. Finally, the rather recent growth of large investment institutions backed by high-speed information systems has pushed industrial managers toward a focus on short-term profits and the related view of seeing employees as variable costs. The consequent tendency for managers to turn quickly to the layoff of nonexempt workers in response to a dip in the economy is also a compelling reinforcement of the two-culture system.

In its extreme form, the two-culture work system consists of a management group governed by HRM practices that emphasize clan methods, facing off against a separate population of nonexempts governed by a heavily bureaucratic set of HRM policies. Because many firms that have followed this course are now in serious competitive trouble, some have begun searching for ways to move toward a one-culture work system and a mutality of interests in order to involve all employees with the company's competitive problems.

By way of contrast, Hewlett-Packard represents a company that was founded upon an explicit set of HRM beliefs, which have successfully guided corporate strategy and policies toward the goal of creating a one-culture company. It is hard to say whether the founders' desire to live by certain HRM beliefs, including the expectation of long-term employment, dictated their choice of product/market/financial strategy or whether the chosen strategy dictated their choice of HRM policies; probably influence flowed both ways. In any case, the two elements clearly dovetail advantageously. Certainly the founders knew what kind of employment relationship they wanted, visualizing their employees as involved, enthusiastic, and creative. Their HRM practices accordingly emphasized clan methods fully supported by an extensive use of compatible market and bureaucratic methods. As a result, Hewlett-Packard has a strong record of continually reconciling the seeming opposites of innovation and efficiency and providing a quality of work life that is highly valued by most of its employees. An analysis of Hewlett-Packard suggests that HRM practices must be initiated and nurtured by open expression of appropriate beliefs and values by top management. The success of an integrated HRM system at Hewlett-Packard (a success confirmed in a recent *Fortune* poll which placed Hewlett-Packard together with IBM at the very top of the list of best-managed companies in the United States) simply does not make sense without acknowledging the importance of the two founders' values regarding their employees.

## TOP MANAGEMENT VALUES AND HRM

The values held by top-level management must, in fact, be considered a key factor in determining whether or not HRM policies and practices can and will be unified. No discussion of integrating an HRM system can be complete without considering these values and the way they are transmitted. The values of senior management, as expressed in words and deeds, either do or do not give employees a sense of confidence about the many different HRM practices. The degree to which management's respect for individual employees infuses HRM practices is especially crucial. Employees will not continue to be emotionally involved in the affairs of the business if their contributions are not respected by their managers. Similarly, employees cannot be expected to be actively committed to the organization if the organization does not show its commitment to them. The institutional commitment must be rooted in the sincerity and durability of the values of top management; managers who adopt expedient solutions at the expense of employees cannot expect employee commitment in return. Various contractual and institutional guarantees of due process are helpful, but they are by no means a substitute for senior management's belief in the importance of equity.

The values managers hold are revealed in many ways besides direct verbal expression. In fact, the old adage that actions speak louder than words applies incontrovertibly to the transmission of values. Earlier in this book we enumerated the three levels of analysis we proposed to use in examining our cases: organizational, individual, and societal; the predicted impact of proposed action was to be tested at all three levels. Managers who regularly analyze their options at all three levels are manifesting their concern and respect for every level even though trade-offs among all three levels will have to be made. Management values also come through in the style by which a manager acts on day-to-day problems. Does the manager listen to subordinates and involve them in decisions? Does the manager delegate responsibility or control subordinates closely? We are not suggesting that only one personality type can be effective. Instead, a variety of people with quite different personalities can adopt a management style compatible with building mutuality.

We have discussed the major variables that influence the development of a consistent and integrated HRM system; we have considered the need for fitting HRM policies to both business strategy and situational constraints, we have indicated how a knowledge of the distinctions between bureaucratic, market, and clan approaches can help make HRM practice coherent in all four policy areas, and, finally, we have examined the critical role of management values. We would like now to consider how this all bears on the pressing issue many companies face in today's competitive environment of finding ways to work out of a traditional adversarial relationship between managers and the managed.

HRM policies are central to the question of whether adversarial two-culture relations are to be superseded by mutuality and a one-culture system. In Figure 7–2, which diagrams these elements, employee involvement is shown to be the critical linkage between HRM policies and the successful achievement of efficiency, innovation, and quality of work life. Although evidence supporting this hypothesis concerning the role of employee involvement is not yet conclusive, management in many companies is still sufficiently impressed by rapidly accumulating evidence to undertake serious and multifaceted steps to move from an adversarial relationship with the work force to a relationship of mutuality. Companies where this change is being effected find that the transition is difficult, but see it as essential all the same.

## CHANGING HRM POLICIES AND PRACTICES

A brief consideration of how companies change HRM practices in general and of how, in particular, they can bring about a change toward a one-culture system concludes our discussion of the integration of HRM policies. Most corporations change HRM policies and practices in response to crisis. When turnover among senior professionals in a professional service firm is high, for instance, it is easy enough to respond quickly by raising salaries and increasing bonuses. But such a move may increase cost without solving the problem, or may create problems of equity with another group of employees. It is still rare for a corporation to examine its human resource management policies and practices as a whole and to chart a course consistent with its long-term situational factors and business strategy, yet this is exactly what we are proposing.

Charting a new course is never easy, but the conceptual framework based on the four policy areas and the bureaucratic/market/clan approaches should make it possible for managers to think systematically about human resource management. The framework is a guide for the necessary analysis, conceptualization, and planning. There are two approaches to the problem of deliberately changing HRM practices: one we call the situational approach, the other the normative approach. Both should be used in parallel.

The *situational approach* (sometimes called environmental scanning) charts future trends. Companies such as Exxon and General Electric typically start their HRM planning by asking a number of questions: What is our long-range strategy and what are its implications for our human resource needs? When we recruit, what skills and what values will we find among prospective employees? How will demographic and educational trends affect labor markets? What changes in ideology, culture, and society's expectations can we anticipate and how might they affect government legislation and the expectations of individual employees as well as of the community? What changes in the role and attitudes of the unions can we expect?

Having grappled, however imperfectly, with these general questions, these firms next address questions centering on HRM policies: How might these possible environmental trends affect us in each of the four major policy areas? If we were to retain our current policies, what would happen to HRM outcomes as perceived by management, employees, and society? If we are dissatisfied with these predicted outcomes, what policies do we need to reformulate? Should we put more emphasis on one or another of the bureaucratic, market, and clan approaches?

The situational approach to HRM planning goes from the outside in; it analyzes given and projected situational factors and fits HRM policies and practices to them. The *normative approach* asks different questions; it works from the inside out. What are our values and beliefs about people at work? What needs and expectations do they share in common? What do we know about the conditions under which people become committed, develop competence, and show a coincidence of interest with the organization? What do our answers to these questions imply for our choice of particular HRM practices in each of the four policy areas?

The importance of top management values in shaping a one-culture company, in communicating to all employees the principles that should shape day-to-day decisions and interventions, has led a number of companies who have not had one-culture values or have not articulated them clearly to do so. Such a process, sometimes aided by outside consultants, typically begins with the chief executive officer examining his or her own values. He or she might then involve other top executives in this process by asking them to define their own management values and inviting them to attend a series of meetings where similarities and differences in these values are discussed. When a consensus emerges, a statement of values is communicated widely throughout the organization by means of the company newspaper, speeches, and perhaps videotaped statements. Moreover, examples of plants and managers that are developing organizations which reflect these values can also be widely publicized and held up as examples of the values management wishes others to adopt.

Such a formal process of value definition and communications will have to be undertaken by companies that do not have one culture and whose top management has not previously articulated these values. Of course, the process itself informs the top managers of the company about their own values and how well they will fit with one-culture values, a necessary step for adapting or exiting from the firm to take place over time. Such a value definition process requires a CEO who believes in the one-culture idea and is willing to lead. As Chester Barnard has said, the task of leadership is essentially one of shaping values.

The situational and normative approaches to HRM policy formulation each have advantages and disadvantages. The normative approach has the advantage of assuring greater internal consistency between HRM policies over a long period (20 to 30 years). As the situation changes, efforts to adapt HRM policies to new realities are usually made in a way that is consistent with the existing philosophy. The disadvantages of the normative approach, as with any general belief, are that it may not fit all employee groups or all situations. A normative approach can be too rigid, generating policies which are outdated by changes in the environment. Depending on its philosophical foundation, the normative approach can be either overly optimistic and naive or overly pessimistic and cynical. If the philosophy is optimistic, it tends to raise employee expectations beyond the organization's capacity to fulfill them. If it is overly pessimistic, it tends to dampen employee motivation and capacity to develop.

The disadvantages of the normative approach are the advantages of the situational approach: reality-based, pragmatic policies can be fit to each group and to any situation. However, the very flexibility of the situational approach makes it more difficult for employees to develop a stable, long-lasting identification with the organization. Likewise, the approach is significantly dependent on an accurate reading by managers of just what the situational reality is. A reading that fails to correspond in some important way to the reading of various stakeholders can seriously undermine the trust of managers, erode the commitment to organizational goals, and replace congruence with costly conflict.

Clearly, it is wise for managers to apply both situational and normative thinking to HRM policy formulation if the interests of both pragmatism and idealism are to be served. The tensions that often exist between the two are actually likely to strengthen the resulting HRM policies and practices. The situational approach to planning is, of course, keyed to the environmental constraints discussed above even as the normative approach is tied to top management values. Both approaches are needed for the creation of a model for future integrated HRM policies, and such a model is one of three requisites for effective implementation of HRM change.

The second factor in successful change is a negative one—discontent with the status quo. Without dissatisfaction with things as they are, it is unlikely that members of an organization will rally the energy needed to effect significant change. Important change always requires time and resources, and it will not happen if people are content with the current situation. Dissatisfaction with an organization's HRM policies can be caused by any number of factors: a costly, crippling strike; a changing marketplace that raises questions about the firm's ability to adapt or places special pressures on labor costs, quality, and productivity; inability to secure the proper mix of personnel to allow rapid expansion in a fast-growth market; to name just a few. Whatever the source, dissatisfaction seems always to be a necessary element in any meaningful change in HRM policies.

To be successful, any change must, moreover, move through a sequence of events and employ a variety of change mechanisms; these are the process factors of change. Different organizations select different policy areas as the initial locus of change. For instance, a decision to adopt the Scanlon plan (see Chapter 5) uses the organization's reward system (participation in profits that come from cost improvements) as the first step toward a more complete change in the employment relationship. In industries such as autos and steel, a number of U.S. companies have initiated programs—variously called Quality of Work Life, Employee Involvement, and Labor-Management Participation Teams—that place employee influence mechanisms (participation in problem solving and policy formulation) at the leading edge of their HRM changes, while some innovative nonunionized companies have changed the employment relationship by concentrating more on work system design (participation in day-to-day management of the task by semiautonomous work teams). Each of these very different starting places is often part of a comprehensive process of change.

In most instances where significant HRM changes are occurring, skillful leaders from the company and/or the union make use of potentially powerful models and symbols of change. Innovative but somewhat isolated (and protected) plants within the corporate structure are used as tangible symbols of new possibilities for others within the organization. Key leaders themselves—a CEO, a union leader, a plant manager—can symbolize the change, articulating the desirable future and giving people faith in its realization. Belief in the future always involves a subtle attention to the level of expectations. Expectations that are too high bring disillusionment; expectations that are set too low fail to inspire the necessary energy. In other words, for leaders to be successful in effecting change, they must paint a realistic picture of the considerable time, resources, and commitment involved but they must also describe an exciting picture of the possible future.

The process of change also requires the right mix of skills and competencies. Education often plays a crucial role in the acquisition of necessary skills. At times people must also be replaced to get the right skills into key organizational positions. In addition to having appropriate skills, key leaders need both the consistent values and the courage that must underlie every significant change.

In conclusion we would like to say that as we review the current scene in human resource management, we are struck by the many opportunities for significantly improving existing conditions. Existing HRM practice is all too frequently a hodge-podge of policies based on little more than outmoded habits, current fads, patched-up responses to former crises, and pet ideas of specialists. HRM practice urgently needs to be reformed from the perspective of general management. HRM issues are much too important to be left largely to specialists. A company's policies and practices in this area (whether, for example, they are pursuing the traditional adversarial employment relationship or attempting to move toward greater mutuality), can make the difference between success and bankruptcy.

We believe that fundamental forces are moving organizations toward the increasing involvement of all employees in the important affairs of the enterprise. We cannot be sure about the immediate future of this trend: near-term changes in the economy, in popular ideas, and in the political climate could speed up or even reverse it. In the long run, however, we believe this movement is the best hope for achieving a better reconciliation of the needs of the organization with the needs of the individual and of the broader society.

# Notes

## Chapter 2. A CONCEPTUAL OVERVIEW OF HRM

1. Charles P. McCormick, *The Power of People* (New York: Penguin Books, 1949).
2. This compliance framework has been suggested by A. Etzioni, "Compliance Structures," in A. Etzioni and E. W. Lehman (eds.), *A Sociological Reader on Complex Organizations*, 3rd ed. (New York: Holt, Rinehart & Winston, 1980), pp. 82–100.
3. The discussion which follows is based on George Lodge, *Context Ideology*, Harvard Business School Case Services No. 9-380-071 (1979). In the original, he uses the term *community* instead of *society* to indicate that any collection of people with a common need and purpose (factory, corporation, town, or union) develop an ideology.

## Chapter 3. EMPLOYEE INFLUENCE

1. George Lodge, *The New American Ideology* (New York: Knopf, 1975), pp. 9–11.
2. Stephen Marsland and Michael Beer, "Note on Japanese Management and Employment Systems," in Michael Beer and Bert Spector (eds.), *Readings in Human Resource Management* (New York: Free Press, 1985).
3. Cris Argyris, *Personality and Organization* (New York: Harper, 1957).
4. *New York Times*, 9 December 1983, p. 1.
5. *Buy Out: Hyatt-Clark Industries, Inc.*, Harvard Business School Case Services No. 9-383-122 (1983).
6. Joseph R. Blasi, Perry Wehrling, and William Foote Whyte, "The Politics of Worker Ownership in the United States," in Frank Heller et al. (eds.), *The International Yearbook of Organizational Democracy for the Study of Participation, Cooperation, and Power* (Sussex, England: John Wiley and Sons, 1981); and William Foote Whyte, *In Support of Voluntary Job Preservation and Community Stabilization Act* (Ithaca, N.Y.: Cornell University Press, 1978).

7. Quoted in D. Quinn Mills, *Labor-Management Relations*, 2d ed. (New York: McGraw-Hill, 1982), p. 195.

8. Writes Jeanne M. Brett, "Fear appeals are notoriously ineffective in changing firmly held attitudes and opinions. Employees who are basically fearful of retaliatory moves against them by an employer are not likely to have signed authorization cards in the first place. And in all probability, those who do sign authorization cards have already come to terms with their realization of the employer's hostility toward the union and his ability, albeit illegal, to use economic power against them. . . . In fact, pro-union employees may view threatening employer behavior simply as confirmation of their poor opinion of him and as support for their previous decision that they need a union to deal with him." Brett, "Why Employees Want Unions," *Organizational Dynamics* (Spring 1980), pp. 53–54.

9. If, in furtherance of its actions against one company, a union were to take actions against a second company—say a customer or supplier of the first—in order to bring increased pressure against the first company, they would be engaging in a secondary boycott.

10. Benjamin M. Selekman, in fact, suggested eight varieties of bargaining relationships: containment-aggression, conflict, power, deal, collusion, accommodation, cooperation, and ideological. Selekman, "Variety of Labor Relations," *Harvard Business Review* (March 1949), pp. 177–185.

11. Marsland and Beer, "Note on Japanese Management and Employment Systems."

## Chapter 4. MANAGING HUMAN RESOURCE FLOWS

1. This section draws on the work of John Van Mannen and Edgar H. Schein, "Career Development," in J. R. Hackman and L. J. Suttle (eds.), *Improving Life at Work: A Behavioral Science Approach to Organizational Change* (Santa Monica, Calif.: Goodyear Publishing, 1977), pp. 30–95.

2. Van Mannen and Schein, "Career Development," p. 31.

3. Ramsey Liem and Raymar Ponla, "Health and Social Costs of Unemployment," *American Psychologist* 37 (October 1982), pp. 1116–1123.

4. "Bosses on the Barricades," *U.S. News and World Report*, December 20, 1982.

5. A. Kornhauser, *Mental Health of the Industrial Worker* (New York: Wiley, 1965).

6. James Walker, *Human Resource Planning* (New York: McGraw-Hill, 1980).

7. Ralph Katz, "Job Longevity as a Situational Factor in Job Satisfaction," *Administrative Science Quarterly* 23 (1978), pp. 204–223.

8. Conference Board Report on performance appraisal cited in R. Landsbury, *Performance Appraisal* (South Melbourne: Macmillan of Australia), 1981.

9. Walker, *Human Resource Planning.*

10. Edgar Schein, "Increasing Organizational Effectiveness Through Better Human Resource Planning and Development," *Sloan Management Review* 19 (Fall 1977), pp. 1–20.

11. Noel M. Tichy, Charles J. Fombrun, and Mary Anne Devanna, "Strategic Human Resource Management," *Sloan Management Review* 23 (Winter 1982), pp. 47–62.

12. Paul R. Lawrence and Davis Dyer, *Renewing American Industry* (New York: Free Press, 1983).

13. "Bosses on the Barricades."

14. Leonard Greenlaugh, "Maintaining Organizational Effectiveness During Organizational Retrenchment," *Journal of Applied Behavioral Science* 18 (1982), pp. 155–170.

15. Greenlaugh, "Maintaining Organizational Effectiveness."

16. Lawrence J. Styble, "Matching Those Pink-Slip Blues," *Industry*, January 1983.

17. This conclusion is based on an internal company study conducted at Corning Glass Works during the 1974–75 recession.

18. M. R. Cooper, B. S. Morgan, P. M. Foley, and L. B. Kaplan, "Changing Employee Values: Deepening Discontent?" *Harvard Business Review*, January-February 1979.

19. David W. Ewing, *"Do It My Way or You're Fired!": Employee Rights and the Changing Role of Management Prerogatives* (New York: John Wiley and Sons, 1983).

20. Marsland and Beer, "Note on Japanese Management and Employment Systems."

21. See Lincoln Electric, Harvard Business School Case Services #9-376-028.

22. Parts of this next section are based on "Personnel Planning," in Herbert G. Heneman, Donald A. Schwab, John A. Fossman, and Lee A. Dyer, *Personnel/Human Resource Management* (Homewood, Ill.: Richard D. Irwin, 1980).

23. The Exxon and GM examples are taken from Tichy, Fombrun, and Devanna, "Strategic Human Resource Management."

## Chapter 5. REWARD SYSTEMS

1. E. L. Deci, "Paying People Doesn't Always Work the Way You Expect It To," *Human Resource Management* 12 (Summer 1973), pp. 28–32.

2. R. Quinn and G. Staines, *The 1977 Quality of Employment Survey* (Ann Arbor, Mich.: Institute for Social Research, 1979); Edward E. Lawler, *Pay and Organization Development* (Reading, Mass.: Addison-Wesley, 1981).

3. William A. Schiemann, ''Major Trends in Employee Attitudes Toward Compensation,'' in Schiemann (ed.), *Managing Human Resources: 1983 and Beyond* (Princeton, N.J.: Opinion Research Corporation, 1983).

4. Edward E. Lawler, *Pay and Organizational Effectiveness: A Psychological View* (New York: McGraw-Hill, 1971).

5. William J. Kearney, ''Pay for Performance? Not Always,'' *Compensation Review* (1979), pp. 47–53.

6. *Fortune*, July 12, 1982, pp. 42–52.

7. The discussion in this section is based on the work of Edward Lawler, a leading theorist in the rewards area, particularly Lawler, ''Reward Systems'' in J. R. Hackman and J. L. Suttle (eds.), *Improving Life at Work: Behavioral Science Approaches to Organizational Change* (Santa Monica, Calif.: Goodyear Publishing, 1977), pp. 163–226 and Lawler, *Pay and Organization Development*.

8. Edward E. Lawler, ''Managers' Attitudes Toward How Their Pay Is and Should Be Determined,'' *Journal of Applied Psychology* 50 (1966), pp. 273–279.

9. H. H. Meyer, ''The Pay-for-Performance Dilemma,'' *Organizational Dynamics* 3 (1975), pp. 39–50.

10. L. W. Porter and Edward E. Lawler, *Attitudes and Performance* (Homewood, Ill.: Richard D. Irwin, 1968).

11. Quinn and Staines, *The 1977 Quality of Employment Survey*.

12. Meyer, ''The Pay-for-Performance Dilemma.''

13. V. H. Vroom and P. W. Yetton, *Leadership and Decision Making* (Pittsburgh: University of Pittsburgh Press, 1973).

14. Lawler, ''Reward Systems.''

15. P. A. Renwick and Edward E. Lawler, ''What You Really Want from Your Job,'' *Psychology Today* 12 (1978), pp. 53–66.

16. Some of the technical data in this chapter comes from D. W. Belcher, *Compensation Administration* (Englewood Cliffs, N.J.: Prentice-Hall, 1974).

17. Thomas Kennedy, *European Labor Relations* (Lexington, Mass.: Lexington Books, 1980), pp. 52–57.

18. Lawler, *Pay and Organization Development*.

19. See R. D. Hume and R. V. Bevan, ''The Blue Collar Worker Goes on Salary,'' *Harvard Business Review* 53 (1975), pp. 104–112; Lawler, *Pay and Organization Development*, pp. 62–64; and J. H. Sheridan, ''Should Your Production Workers Be Salaried?'' *Industry Week* 184 (1975), pp. 28–37.

20. Howard Risher, ''Job Evaluation: Mystical or Statistical?'' *Personnel* (Sept.–Oct. 1978), pp. 23–36.

21. Marsland and Beer, ''Note on Japanese Management and Employment Systems.''

22. Lawler, ''Managers' Attitudes Toward How Their Pay Is and Should Be Determined.''

23. *People and Productivity: A Challenge to Corporate America* (New York: New York Stock Exchange Office of Economic Research, 1982).

24. This discussion is based on Lawler, *Pay and Organization Development.*

25. Meyer, "The Pay for Performance Dilemma."

26. Meyer, "The Pay for Performance Dilemma."

27. Adapted from Lawler, *Pay and Organization Development*, pp. 134–140.

28. David Kraus, "Executive Pay: Ripe for Reform?" *Harvard Business Review*, September–October 1980, pp. 36–48.

29. Marsland and Beer, "Note on Japanese Management and Employment Systems."

## Chapter 6. WORK SYSTEMS

1. Robert H. Guest, "Quality of Work Life—Learning from Tarrytown," *Harvard Business Review*, July–August 1979, pp. 76–89.

2. Frederick Herzberg, B. Mausner, and B. Snyderman. *The Motivation to Work* (New York: Wiley, 1959).

3. Robert N. Ford, *Motivation Through the Work Itself* (New York: American Management Association, 1969).

4. Ricky W. Griffin, *Task Design: An Integrative Approach* (Glenview, Ill.: Scott, Foresman, 1982), pp. 17–51; J. Richard Hackman, "Work Design" in J. R. Hackman and J. L. Suttle (eds.), *Improving Life at Work: Behavioral Science Approaches to Organizational Change* (Santa Barbara, Calif.: Goodyear Publishing, 1977), pp. 96–162.

5. Richard E. Walton, "Social Choices in the Development of Advanced Information Technology," *Human Relations* 35 (1978), pp. 1973–1983.

6. Walton, "Social Choices."

7. Eric Trist, "The Evolution of Socio-Technical Systems," *Issues in the Quality of Work Life. A series of occasional papers*, No. 2, June 1981, p. 9.

8. Richard E. Walton, "Establishing and Maintaining High Commitment Work Systems," in J. Kimberly and R. Miles (eds.), *Organizational Life Cycle* (San Francisco: Jossey Bass, 1980).

9. Edward E. Lawler, "The New Plant Revolution," *Organizational Dynamics* (Winter 1978), pp. 3–12.

10. William Wimspisinger, "Job Satisfaction: A Union Response," *AFL-CIO American Federationist*, February 1973.

11. Michael Beer and James W. Driscoll, "Strategies for Change," in Hackman and Suttle, *Improving Life at Work: Behavioral Science Approaches to Organizational Change* (Santa Monica, Calif.: Goodyear, 1977), pp. 409–11.

12. Thomas J. Schneider, "Quality of Work Life and the Law." A speech given at the Kennedy School of Government and Public Policy, 19 November 1981.

13. Richard E. Walton, "Topeka Work Systems: Optimistic Visions, Pessimistic Hypotheses, and Reality," in R. Zager and M. Rosow (eds.), *The Innovative Organization* (New York: Pergamon Press/Work in America Series, 1982).

14. Irving Bluestone, "Labor's Stake in Improving the Quality of Working Life," in Harvey Kolodny and Hans van Beinum (eds.), *The Quality of Working Life and the 1980s* (New York: Praeger, 1983).

## Chapter 7. THE INTEGRATION OF HUMAN RESOURCE MANAGEMENT POLICIES

1. This approach is based on a framework suggested by William G. Ouchi, "Markets, Bureaucracies, and Clans," *Administrative Science Quarterly* 25 (March 1980), pp. 129–141.

2. C. I. Barnard, *The Functions of the Executive* (Cambridge, Mass.: Harvard University Press, 1938); H. A. Simon, *Administrative Behavior*, 2d ed. (New York: Free Press, 1957); Harry Levinson et al., *Men, Management, and Mental Health* (Cambridge, Mass.: Harvard University Press, 1966).

# Index